REINVENTING THE AMERICAN PEOPLE

ROBERT ROYAL is vice president of the Ethics and Public Policy Center. He is the author of *1492 and All That: Political Manipulations of History* (Ethics and Public Policy Center, 1992).

REINVENTING THE AMERICAN PEOPLE

Unity and Diversity Today

Edited by

Robert Royal

Essays by ■ Michael Barone ■ Stanley Crouch ■ Mark Helprin
Gertrude Himmelfarb ■ Glenn C. Loury ■ Harvey C. Mansfield
John O'Sullivan ■ Frederick Turner ■ *and sixteen others*

ETHICS AND PUBLIC POLICY CENTER
WASHINGTON, D.C.

WILLIAM B. EERDMANS PUBLISHING COMPANY
GRAND RAPIDS, MICHIGAN / CAMBRIDGE, U.K.

Published jointly 1995 by the Ethics and Public Policy Center and
Wm. B. Eerdmans Publishing Co.
255 Jefferson Ave. S.E., Grand Rapids, Mich. 49503 /
P. O. Box 163, Cambridge CB3 9PU U.K.

Library of Congress Cataloging-in-Publication Data

Reinventing the American people: unity and diversity today /
edited by Robert Royal.
p.   cm.
Includes index.
ISBN 0-8028-0878-6 (pbk.: alk. paper)
1. United States — Civilization — 1970-   2. Pluralism (Social sciences) — United States.
3. United States — Ethnic relations. 4. United States — Race relations.
I. Royal, Robert, 1949-   .
E169.12.R44   1995
973.92 — dc20   95-39734
                                                          CIP

Contents

PART TWO:
POLITICS, CONSTITUTION, LAW, INSTITUTIONS

PART THREE:
RELIGION AND THE CIVIC ORDER

INTRODUCTION

Restoring Self-Governing Community

Robert Royal

What unites the people of the United States in the 1990s? In many ways, this is an odd question. America is the most powerful nation on earth, one of the wealthiest, and—failures notwithstanding—the most successful democracy in human history. Millions of people around the world still emigrate to America, or hope to, not only because this country promises prosperity, but because it provides basically decent treatment and a sturdy defense against foreign enemies to those within its borders. We are a far from perfect nation. But judged by world-historical standards, as Hegel and his late unlamented Marxist followers used to put it, we are not doing so badly either.

Yet the question of what unites us has no little contemporary resonance. The end of the Cold War removed a long-standing external threat, but also a nationally unifying purpose. While we were occupied with stopping the spread of Marxism, some large tears opened in our social fabric. In addition, cultural questions have arisen that threaten our old understanding of ourselves as a people made *e pluribus unum*. The old American ideal, while acknowledging pluralism and variety, definitely saw movement from the Many to the One. But in the last few years a new notion has been gathering force, one that may, for convenience, be simply called multiculturalism. The spirit behind multiculturalism is quite different from the old notion of pluralism and denies the very idea of Americans as a single people. It was doubtless that spirit, more than a mere slip in construing the Latin,

1

that in 1994 led Harvard-educated vice president Al Gore to translate publicly *e pluribus unum* as meaning "out of one, many."

Today, however, we have begun to recognize the dangers of making many out of one—or at least some of us have awakened to the problem. Instead of overemphasizing diversity and difference, we are seeking a new form of national purpose in response to some pressing and potentially divisive internal challenges. It is quite easy to list developments within American society that have made us uncertain about our national identity. Americans trust the federal government less now than at any time in recent decades. During the past thirty years, we have experienced unprecedented increases in crime, illegitimacy, divorce and family breakdown, suicide, and drug abuse, as well as spectacular ethical lapses by politicians, artists, educators, and businessmen. Racial and ethnic tensions continue. Most American cities are in an advanced state of decay, our suburbs are increasingly isolated in an attempt to keep out crime and drugs, and our few remaining farm communities stand on the brink of extinction. The widespread sense of the need to restore community reflects a palpable uneasiness about how we live now. We want to take charge of our destiny as a people again, which means rediscovering the old American understanding of ourselves as a free and self-governing community.

The Quest for Community

"Community" has some bad overtones in the waning years of the twentieth century. Any casual grouping of Americans, however distant from one another in concrete ways, may invoke this once venerable term: thus we have the medical community, the gay community, the Hollywood community. After the 1995 bombing of a federal building in Oklahoma City, the director of an explosives-research center told the *New York Times* that the terrorist act had horrified "the entire explosives community." The promiscuous use of the term, however amusing at times, attests to the wish to feel ourselves connected with one another. But the restoration of real communities in the 1990s will involve some significant and far-ranging changes.

Historically, Americans have found community and opportunities for self-governance within the immediate relationships of neighborhoods, schools, churches, and workplaces. Participation in the activities of those institutions entailed participation in local politics. *Pace* the old saw, not all politics is local—just nearly all. When American political institutions are functioning properly, local communities and local politics constitute the point of entry for most people into the less direct and more limited relationships of national life. But as Harvard political scientist Robert D. Putnam has shown in a much discussed article called "Bowling Alone," since the 1960s there has been a significant drop in participation in church groups, unions, parent-teacher associations, political organizations, fraternal societies, volunteer activities (such as the Red Cross and Boy Scouts), and even bowling leagues.[1] And this has significantly damaged the social capital and political participation we once relied on to meet the inevitable challenges of democracy.

Americans have joined other private associations, but these tend to be of different kinds than in the past. Self-help and twelve-step programs are common everywhere, but do not have the same civic dimensions as the traditional small groups.[2] Putnam also points out that survey data on group membership have been skewed upward because of the growth of large national movements like the Sierra Club, the National Organization for Women, and the American Association of Retired Persons. These large associations have their place in modern America, but they do not serve the same sociological function as the older groups. The newer groups are organized around rather abstract interests, and the members may not know any other members. The older-style smaller groupings gave people a chance to develop personal ties and discuss concrete issues informally. As the late Christopher Lasch argued in The Revolt of the Elites and the Betrayal of American Democracy, the older groups also performed the crucial democratic function of promoting conversations across class, racial, and ethnic lines.[3]

Civic Amity and the Good Life

While these forms of community were alive and well, we took them for granted. We cannot afford to do so any longer. In fact, the fate of American democracy may hinge on the renewal of such associations or something like them. The suburbanite who feels isolated or the city-dweller who wonders what happened to the old neighborhood is not merely suffering from neurosis or nostalgia. We need to rediscover the ancient insight that the purpose of political communities is to enable us not just to live, but to live well. And just now we desperately need the rich and civically fruitful social ties that formerly contributed to public decency and social amity. Professor Putnam's humble but graphic example is that while more Americans are bowling than ever before (more than vote in presidential elections, in fact), fewer bowl in leagues. Activities that once were both personal and communal are becoming more restricted to individuals and their immediate families.

American life is conspicuously less social in a variety of other simple but significant ways. With the decline in neighborhoods and the rooted private institutions that make them vital, traditionally informal meeting places such as taverns, coffee shops, and local markets have disappeared in many areas.[4] At first sight, these places may seem to have little to do with our civic culture. But it has been precisely in such settings that the give and take crucial to the development of common public opinion and general standards of decency has taken place. In some urban areas now, the introduction of a coffee bar by a national chain like Starbucks fills a gap by providing a humane place for neighborhood gathering. But the social location is the key: the same coffee bar in a mall would have little of this sort of civic value.

Perhaps the largest shift in American identity over recent decades has been the absence of life lived in these smaller settings, formal or informal, and the relatively large emphasis that has been placed on the federal government, and government in general, as a guarantor of national unity. It is not necessary to idealize the old town meeting or the virtues of a simpler life to recognize that, whatever else has occurred in recent decades, most Americans' sense of participating in a self-governing community—or in a community of any kind at all—has waned. When most people think of government now, they think of cumbersome and contested national politics, which has intruded on and often usurped the functions of the multi-layered jurisdictions that once fostered the various levels and degrees of citizen participation foreseen in our Constitution.

A chicken-and-egg question presents itself: Did the well-intentioned growth in federal activity throughout this century, but especially since the 1960s, lead to the demise of self-governance in communities? Or did the decay of older communities force the federal government to step in? As with most either-or questions, the answer is, both. The two processes have been going on simultaneously. However we parse out American social development in the last few decades, though, we are now faced with a set of challenges that are both political and cultural.

The Politics of Social Fragmentation

It is by now an old and often repeated tale how the federal government in the name of urban renewal cleaned up many inner cities in the 1950s and 1960s, but also disrupted long-standing urban social networks that have never recovered. In addition, other well-intended attempts to get mental patients, drug addicts, and alcoholics out of sometimes inhumane hospitalization put thousands of homeless people, many of them dangerous to others as well as to themselves, out on city streets.[5] The sexual revolution and breakdown of the family, aided and abetted by the welfare culture, sent the number of fatherless young men in cities soaring—young men who account for a good deal of the drug dealing, crime, and general sense of danger that have come to characterize city streets.

But just as no man is an island, the urban problem does not exist independent from the suburban one. The rapid suburbanization of America with its standard litany of woes like anomie, materialism, mall culture, and social insulation is the flip side of the breakdown of America's cities and the departure of many of urban America's most stable and productive citizens. For many Americans in the 1990s, suburban life is clearly preferable to life in the cities. Yet suburban families, too, face serious challenges to community.

The suburbs in the United States since World War II were, by and large, not planned with an eye to fostering community, even the simple community of families clustered around a public school. Suburban communities often lack basic conveniences like sidewalks where children and adults can gather informally in a common space. Suburban children often grow up now, not walking or riding bicycles to playgrounds, but being driven by mom and dad from soccer to lacrosse to gymnastics to ballet to church group. These activities are all fine in themselves, but it may not be an exaggeration to think that the frenzied after-school life of children is a substitute for a more authentic form of community.

Some large-scale social changes have also contributed to the suburban problem. Suburban neighborhoods are almost deserted during the day because large numbers of women now hold jobs. This has been a mixed blessing. Women of particular talents and ambition have been given greater opportunity. In some cases, families simply need the extra income (though this is not nearly so common as is usually assumed). But more and more families in America are deciding that the cost children pay for this may not be worth the return in mere money. One of the saddest sights in modern America is to see babies and very young children being dropped off early in the morning to spend a long day among strangers at a daycare center.

Decisions by individuals and families to give children a more traditional and nurturing early experience of home and neighborhood are the leading edge of a movement toward restoring community for both children and adults today. In inner cities, fatherhood initiatives and programs designed to prevent illegitimacy are the *sine qua non* for saving many neighborhoods. So are welfare reforms that will restore families and efforts to socialize young men to resist sex, drugs, gangs, and crime. As Gertrude Himmelfarb has demonstrated in her book *The De-moralization of Society,* historical precedents give us reason to be optimistic about efforts at social reconstruction.[6] The suburbs need similar efforts to make them something more than housing tracts. Most suburbs suffer from poor physical layout. (Architects and planners seem to have understood this problem, and sanity is returning to community design.[7])

Both city and suburb dwellers, however, also need more face-to-face contacts outside the family. Television, in addition to the moral and cultural damage it has inflicted on American society, has divided as much as united us. We all now watch the same programs, political speeches, and sports, and catch glimpses of distant communities— each in the privacy of his own home. The information superhighway promises more—much more—of the same. Communicating on the Internet may be better than not communicating at all, but the faceless, rather distant connections that occur there cannot take the place of face-to-face encounters. Only when we put aside the keyboard and the channel-changer and actually meet together to decide about matters of common interest can anything remotely resembling self-governing community emerge again.

Return to Civil Society

Seen from the inside of American society, these challenges evoke nostalgia for a better time and sometimes a rage against the seemingly irresistible forces that make community regeneration difficult. Seen from outside our immediate circumstances, however, the problem of community is part of a larger global recognition—stimulated by the experience of Eastern and Central Europe under Communism—of the importance of civil society to democracy. America and the West have been spared the horrors of totalitarian government. But we have experienced in our own fashion the world-wide drive, over the past century and more, toward relying more and more on national government for a host of things once provided by smaller government bodies or private institutions.

That era is now coming to an end. It is not only that the collapse of Marxism and crises within welfare states have revealed ambitious government to be ineffective. For many Americans the concentrated power of the state has become a source of hatred and fear. In the spring of 1995, just after the horrifying deaths of more than 160 people in the terrorist bombing of a federal building in Oklahoma City, the *Washington Post* asked in a survey whether the federal government threatens liberties. The results were surprising: somewhere between 40 and 50 per cent of Americans believe that the federal government as currently constituted poses a threat (one poll question said "an immediate threat") to their rights and freedoms. This sentiment was not simply a "right-wing" phenomenon confined to extremists who imagine malevolent conspiracies in high places to impose a New World Order on America. Other polls at the time discovered that large minorities—in one survey a slight majority—of both liberals and conservatives had the same fear, with liberals showing a slight edge.

The media initially viewed Oklahoma City as a part of the "angry white male" reaction they thought had given Republicans a majority in Congress in the November 1994 elections. In this view, the right-wing militias and bombers were merely an extreme, paranoid form of angry white male resentment. In fact, as the surveys showed, if suspicions of the federal government represent "paranoia," then slightly more liberals than conservatives are "paranoid" about government.[8]

Fear of the federal government, however, is only one sign of the political and psychological disengagement of Americans from national politics. Since the 1960s, voter turnout has declined by a quarter. In the past twenty years, people who say they have "attended a public meeting on town or school affairs" in the past year have dropped from 22 to 13 per cent, while those saying they trust Washington only "some of the time" or "never" have risen from 30 per cent thirty years ago to 75 per cent.[9]

Under the circumstances, attempts to restore faith in government by engaging in more of the old-style national politics seem doomed to failure. Federal programs, even if well designed, cannot overcome popular skepticism and fear about government. Some intelligent liberals such as Arthur Schlesinger, Jr., see the new moment, entailing as it does rethinking welfare, affirmative action, and the relationship of national to state and local jurisdictions, as a crusade to destroy national government. Schlesinger described the Supreme Court's 1995 decision in *Lopez*—that federal authorities do not have constitutional authority to ban guns in schools—as a sign that "a near majority of the Supreme Court even seems to want to replace the Constitution by the [much looser] Articles of Confederation."[10]

Decentralization and Devolution

Viewed from the standpoint of what many American liberals assumed would be the continuing role of federal power, such developments are shocking. But however unexpected it may be, at the end of the twentieth century some recalibration of local and national powers is emerging. The decision in the *Lopez* case, it is worth noting, does not mean that communities such as states and municipalities cannot individually exercise jurisdiction over guns in schools. On the contrary, for the first time since the New Deal, the Court refused to invoke the commerce clause or some other vague constitutional warrant to trump local authority. Instead, it underscored a constitutional restriction on federal powers in such matters, and emphasized the rights and responsibilities of local bodies.

Lopez is also significant for other reasons. It may spell the beginning of the end of Procrustean national legislation for problems that are quite different in different settings. It does not take much imagination, for example, to see that a law on guns in schools that would be applied uniformly in the south Bronx and west Texas may lack something even in terms of legal prudence. Parents, citizens, and local authorities in the south Bronx will doubtless agree to ban guns from schools, and have every right, as self-governing Americans, to do so. Parents, citizens, and local authorities in some rural west Texas district where rattlesnakes are common may or may not arrive at the same conclusion.

In a similar vein, local solutions are being applied to other problems. Both Washington, D.C., and Dallas have instituted curfews for adolescents to try to get some control over violent inner-city crime. Strangely, many of the same people who think federal gun legislation is warranted to control violence argue that such curfews are a violation of civil liberties. In the current political and social climate, such arguments will ring increasingly hollow. If local jurisdictions can show that curfews significantly reduce teen crime (such measures have been highly effective wherever they have been tried), far from curtailing civil liberties they will actually be restoring the constitutional rights of law-abiding citizens to be secure in their persons and property in their own neighborhoods.

Can such local authority be misused? Of course. Just as a state may drive people across borders by imposing punitive state income taxes, communities that become overly strict will meet with resistance and opposition. But when citizens feel the bite of a local law they have far less distance to travel to make their grievances heard than when federal rules are imposed. Some communities may be foolish, some may be lax, but some may return to something like authentic and effective self-governance. Such differences and risks are what self-government is all about.

In the long run, the rebirth of self-governing communities will be good for federal government as well. It will free us from the vexing habit of trying to decide every question at a national level and will return respect to the federal authorities in the matters for which they truly have constitutional warrant. As the post-Communist experience has shown, we can reinvigorate civil society by simultaneously opening up new space for independent action and decentralizing state power so that civic forces can take responsibility for local and state action again. National politics in our time can, paradoxically, do more to restore national solidarity by doing less.

MULTICULTURAL CULTURE WARS

Every one of the steps that local, state, and federal government will have to take in restoring self-governing communities will be contested. However inefficient and tumultuous it may appear, that process is essential to real democracy. The unity of a people does not mean unanimity, but merely agreement on the procedures by which differences shall be discussed and resolved. If power becomes more decentralized in America in coming years, that process will lead to richer discussion and, perhaps, more disagreements, but also to greater engagement in civic life. One large factor threatens this whole enterprise, however, because it denies the very theoretical and institutional forms of American democracy. That threat is the movement known as multiculturalism.

To ask what unites us in the 1990s is both an empirical and a normative question. It asks about what is happening today, but more importantly it asks what *should* happen. Most of us agree that institutions of American governance at their best provide both sound civic practice and civic ideals such as impartiality, the rule of law, limited government, checks and balances, and various other achievements of American—and more broadly speaking, Western—civilization. The multicultural challenge is radical. It not only claims unjust practices in America, but disputes the very Western notions on which our institutions rest.

Marginalized but Central?

The multiculturalist view finds itself within a sort of double bind. Gary B. Nash, the primary author of a highly controversial set of national history standards, is a fairly typical exponent of this kind of multiculturalism. On the one hand, he maintains that "Anglochauvinists"[11] invented a hegemonic national story that marginalized or excluded various groups. On the other, he tries to show that those who were marginalized were actually central to the development of American society. In fact, the multicultural myth can survive only by exaggerating the monolithic nature of the dominant Anglo-European culture, and by exaggerating the contributions of subcultures. Its claims to contemporary relevance flip back and forth between asserting victim status for certain groups and touting their great achievements.

At the same time, multiculturalism in its commonest form demands that institutions—schools, museums, and government programs—be recast to avoid a "Eurocentric perspective." The charge here is broad and, in the form in which it is presented, inherently irrefutable. Existing institutions are based on European thought and practice. That thought and practice was responsible for slavery, racism, and other evils in America's past. Therefore, "European" culture *per se* cannot provide a standard of fairness in the 1990s. Some multicultural, non-Eurocentric perspective exists that will lead to better thought and institutions.

The fact that only Western societies would even pay attention to supposed outside critiques such as this is lost on most multiculturalists. Nash's views are fairly representative of how American history is construed by many in the universities today and also by no small number of political actors. Like many other commentators, Nash does not even notice that the earlier figures he cites in support of his argument contradict the myth of a monolithic American triumphalism. Thus we find Dead White Males who are part of the American canon inexplicably expressing opinions now thought to have been unheard of until the present, when unprejudiced and far-seeing scholars have managed to dispel age-old bias and ignorance. The untutored Herman Melville was able to write over a century ago: "You can not spill a drop of American blood without spilling the blood of the whole world. On this Western Hemisphere all tribes and people are forming into one federated whole." Nash can only say that of course most white Americans had no intention of federating in that way.

Ralph Waldo Emerson, who labored under the disadvantage of having taken no required courses in multiculturalism at Harvard, was still able to see that "the energy of Irish, Germans, Swedes, Poles, & Cossacks, & all the European tribes—of the Africans and of the Polynesians, will construct a new race . . . as vigorous as the new Europe which came out of the smelting pot of the Dark Ages." And Frederick Jackson Turner, in an address upon the four hundredth anniversary of Columbus's voyage to the New World, remarked, "In the crucible of the frontier the immigrants were Americanized, liberated, and fused into a mixed race, English in neither nationality nor characteristics."

These men may not have been representative of the masses. They certainly were not representative of the far less distinguished advocates of a pure European racial and cultural purity. But something characteristically American shines through that it did not take the advent of multiculturalism or postmodernism or historical revisionism to explain to us. It would be difficult to construct a simply marginalizing

American culture from the main cultural tradition. America is, more than any other nation in history, a culturally integrating place. Huck Finn and "Nigger Jim," Hawkeye and Chingachgook—the American cultural canon presents many instances of racial and cultural relationships that do not fit into easy stereotypes.

A nation's high culture is by definition something different from its popular practices. Mark Twain and James Fenimore Cooper were not simply reflecting society; they were trying to see through to a better life. Both confront ignorant busybodies, old and young, with limited perspectives. But both also express something that presumably millions of American readers throughout the years have resonated to.

To deny that abiding American openness is quite troubling, because we are a people uniquely dependent on finding ways for the many to become one. History matters in a different way to Americans than it does to most other peoples. We are all immigrants, of earlier or later vintage. Even Native Americans, we now know, migrated to this continent probably around 12,000 years ago. And subsequent tribal expansions, contractions, conquests, defeats, genocides, slavery, and migrations—current myths notwithstanding—show patterns that changed in scale but not in their basic human features long before Europeans arrived here.[12] Unlike recent European history, American history is less a matter of groups that had long been settled in a certain area than it is of a conscious decision to become a nation.

An Idea or a People?

Earlier in this century, the English writer G. K. Chesterton remarked that America is a "nation with the soul of a church."[13] By this he meant that an American is anyone who professes belief in the principles embodied in the Constitution and submits to living out those principles within the country's institutional framework. Chesterton also noted that for Americans there are ethnic groups at the other end of the street who for Englishmen are at the other end of the earth. These remarks anticipated a debate that has currently arisen with new force: Is America an idea or a people?

Americans are not a people in the way that, say, the French are a people. The French Revolution and the consolidation of the French Republic were later than their American counterparts. Yet behind the sense of French identity lie centuries more of common life and language than Americans possess, reinforced also for centuries now by far more centralized state institutions. All French children receive the same education in French history, a uniformity that "Anglo-chauvinists" (Chauvin, be it noted, was one of Napoleon's minions) in America, lacking a national curriculum and facing the jigsaw puzzle of state and local jurisdictions, could only dream of. We find our unity less in centralized indoctrination than in a willing and conscious participation in a historical process that is simultaneously both one and multiple.

That circumstance makes accurate history all the more crucial. Contrary to the multicultural myth about American education, earlier periods were not entirely unappreciative of difference, or uniformly kind to "Europeans." The Dutch influence in New York and the Germans in Pennsylvania were part of the story. Scandinavian presence in the upper Midwest, Spanish influence on the Southwest and West (reflected in California's easier lifestyles), regional differences in the South, New England, and Northwest—all these persist. Nor were these European groups a monolithic privileged class. There has been prejudice against Europeans as well as others. Jews were long discriminated against, Eastern and Southern Europeans disliked. Out of anti-German sentiment, during World War I, Wisconsin—a state with many German-Americans—even outlawed the teaching of German. These are less than glorious episodes in American history, but their gradual resolution may teach us an important lesson for our time. Any group, even those now considered privileged, may have suffered handicaps in the past. American history is a story of growing inclusiveness, and gives reason to believe that current prejudices may be temporary as well.

Black history presents special problems, of course, because Americans of African background are by and large the only group who did not willingly choose to come here (West Indian blacks and recent African arrivals are an exception). Recovering that history in both its pre- and post-slavery dimensions is a matter of mere justice and truth. And we must make sure that prejudice finds no place in modern American institutions. But using the historical record to suggest that American institutions are by nature unjust, and thereby advocating, as do the extreme multiculturalists, Afrocentric, separate, or privileged arrangements, can only portend the end of a noble experiment in self-governing community.

Ethnic conflicts in America today, it is worth noting, are sharper and more frequent between "minorities" than between mainstream and minority groups. Recent clashes between blacks and Asians in inner-city areas, for instance, or competition between Hispanics, Asians, and African-Americans for affirmative-action preferences are a sign that the multicultural story of center and margins may not be a good guide to current social reality. In fact, the current decline in affirmative action reflects a growing recognition throughout society that attempts to remedy past injustices by current prefer-ences are not working, and may actually be exacerbating social tensions. In the 1995 *Adarand Constructors* v. *Peña* case, Supreme Court Justice Sandra Day O'Connor, writing for the majority, re-minded us that the Constitution guarantees equal protection to *individuals,* not groups, and that *individuals* must demonstrate unfair treatment under our common rules of evidence before compensa-tion is justified.

The Multicultural Vulgate

African, Asian, Native American, and Hispanic societies are often used as foils to highlight the alleged materialism, individualism, en-vironmental damage, and spiritual aridity of modern America. There is a kernel of truth in these comparisons: pre-modern societies do tend to be more communal, closer to nature, and more religious than their modern counterparts. But the kernel of truth should not be allowed to obscure some much larger truths. We may admire the tight-knit bonds of African or Native American tribes, for example, but we would not want to imitate tribal attitudes toward outsiders in a place like America. It is precisely the achievement of equality before the law, however imperfectly applied to specific groups in the past, that maintains peace and fairness among social sectors without resort to traditional tribal warfare. Disruption of our legal system would harm minorities as much as anyone.

In fact, the genius of American society has always been to find protection of persons, property, and liberty in the very factionalism that tears other societies apart. James Madison wrote in *Federalist* No. 10 that competing factions, in a system like ours, would actually lead to greater liberty as each group sought fair treatment. And that is largely how it has worked. Religious groups agree on separation of church and state because, despite their conflicts and competition, it best preserves religious liberty for each and all. Groups like the National Rifle Association and the American Civil Liberties Union often clash over liberal/conservative questions. Yet in 1994 they joined together with many other associations to petition the federal government to undertake a comprehensive examination of the activities of federal agents against U.S. citizens.

Confidence in American institutions, however, is a prerequisite to that result. Liberals and conservatives still think fairness may emerge from the political system. Other groups are not so sure. Immigrants, for example, were once encouraged to become part of this American ethos, and most of them continue to want to do so. Unfortunately, because of several cultural currents within America itself, a mistaken notion of preserving foreign cultures has entered even institutions like the public school and the Immigration and Naturalization Service (INS).[14] All immigrant groups have striven to retain links with their countries and cultures of origin. But it was understood in the past that such links were no business of the U.S. government. Today, a mistaken notion of "diversity" has led many to believe that the U.S. government, which has the responsibility of preparing immigrants to participate as U.S. citizens, also has some obligation to preserve other cultures. The weakened drive toward becoming part of a common Americanness means that people not only will participate less fully in American social life but will be isolated and limited in political expression as well.

This may have consequences exactly opposite to what the multiculturalists intend. As Arthur M. Schlesinger, Jr., has argued:

> The militants of ethnicity now contend that the main objective of public education should be the protection, strengthening, celebration, and perpetuation of ethnic origins and identities. Separatism, however, nourishes prejudices, magnifies differences, and stirs antagonisms.[15]

And this is not, says Schlesinger, merely a matter of social disharmony. It may have graver consequences: "Other countries break up because they fail to give ethnically diverse peoples compelling reasons to see themselves as part of the same nation."[16] Until recently, America was one of the world's masters in providing that common vision.

Educating for Self-Governing Society

It may be that the American ethos will wear down this sort of multiculturalism into just one more voice within American pluralism. That is a consummation devoutly to be wished. But in the meantime, multiculturalism of a virulent and uncompromising kind has established itself in universities. Signs of a strict authoritarianism accompanying this development do not bode well. If one of the institutions most dedicated to free discussion in our society now finds itself held virtual hostage to partisan positions, the immediate prospect is not bright.

We might ignore multiculturalism as a rarefied intellectual or social movement were it not that the institutions of civil society are in such a sad state of disrepair. Strong multiracial, multiethnic communities would, absent multiculturalism, negotiate most of the social conflicts that crop up. But in the current absence of such communities, multiculturalism has tended to issue ultimatums and to send everyone back into competing enclaves that manipulate state institutions, even as they denounce them, for particular interests.

The crisis is particularly grave in the public schools. The public school is the one place where the combination of community and civic institution still has a chance to bring people together. To do so today, however, would require more than bringing together different groups physically. It requires instilling some common understanding and respect for our institutions and history. That process need not be a merely pious whitewash of the past nor a denial of conflict. It does have to transmit to a new generation a sense of confidence that American institutions and American ideals may serve us well, if we learn about them and use them properly. For the moment, however, the schools are mired in the same multiculturalism as the universities.

It is the sad experience of most nations, "Eurocentric" and not, that difference leads to civil conflict, and conflict to bloodshed. For no little time now, America has managed to avoid such all-too-human ways of dealing with difference, even in the difficult struggles over civil rights thirty years ago. The civil-rights movement succeeded precisely because it appealed to long-standing American notions of fairness and respect toward individuals of all backgrounds. We need to return to that vision and renew its embodiment in politics and communities all over this country. If we do not, we may be multicultural, we may be open, we may be tolerant, but we will not long remain a free and united people.

About This Book

The essays included this volume grapple, in their various ways, with the double problem of multiculturalism and American institutions. They look at the plight of American institutions designed for creating self-governing community at a historical moment when many people distrust not only those institutions but the very cultural foundations on which they rest. Consequently, they explore the tensions between freedom and community, the individual and the state, or, simply put, the notion of *e pluribus unum* in the 1990s. They also examine political philosophy, law, schools, police, religion, race, ethnicity, immigration, universities, culture, the family, art, and many more subjects. And they do all this for a very good reason: the way back to self-governing communities will require a broad redefinition and recasting of our current national beliefs and practices on several simultaneous fronts.

Other books have looked at the individual strands of the problem; this one tries to deal with the question of Americanness in the 1990s as a fabric woven from those fraying strands. The authors collected here do not agree with one another on specific solutions. At times, they even clash in the way they formulate the problems we face. They are united, however, in their belief that something serious must be done to preserve the old *e pluribus unum* ideal in our day. The interchange in these pages is an example of an attempt at public discussion that will, we may hope, in turn lead to the reinvigoration of self-governing community.

One of the great pleasures in carrying out a project like this is precisely the chance to participate in a stimulating community of democratic discussion. I am deeply grateful to James Capua and the William H. Donner Foundation as well as William Boxx and the Philip M. McKenna Foundation for their financial and moral support of this project. I thank all the authors included here for their written contributions and for their personal exchanges with me during the preparation of this book. At an early phase, Gretchen Baudhuin (now Tombes) helped organize the project. Carol Griffith and Mary Hittinger, two highly talented editors, made widely differing thinkers fit harmoniously between the covers of the book. Christopher

Ditzenberger and Marianne Geers turned manuscripts in various states of disarray into presentable texts. I am grateful to them and to my other colleagues at the Ethics and Public Policy Center, who have contributed more than they know to my own sense of what constitutes the good community.

PART ONE

The Multicultural Question

1

Whose America Is It?

Michael Barone

The story is told that the morning after the 1930 election, when it was still unclear which party would win control of the House, Speaker Nicholas Longworth, who was accustomed to giving Minority Leader John Nance Garner a ride to work in his official limousine, sent a telegram to Garner reading, "Whose car is it?" In 1994, just weeks after the victory of the Republican party (which no insider thought would ever again win control of the House), the question being asked widely around the country, not quite in so many words but in tones that unmistakably betray feelings from foreboding to exultation, was, "Whose country is it?"

The answer, from wherever you stand waiting for your ride, is not obvious. The politics of the post–Cold War, post–Gulf War era has been marked by wild oscillations in public-opinion polls and election results. For example, George Bush's job approval rating fell from a peak of 91 per cent after the Gulf War to 37 per cent on election day some twenty months later. Ross Perot, with no institutional base, led the two major-party candidates in polls for two months and won 19 per cent of the vote after telling voters he left the race for a time because George Bush was sending in the Air Force to strafe his

Michael Barone is a senior writer for *U.S. News & World Report*. He is co-author of *The Almanac of American Politics* and the author of *Our Country: The Shaping of America from Roosevelt to Reagan*.

daughter's wedding. Bill Clinton, hailed by a sympathetic press during his inaugural festivities as the Baby Boom liberal who would set the tone of politics for the next generation, was repudiated in the 1994 off-year elections as soundly as was Herbert Hoover in the Great Depression year of 1930.

And if we step back from our focus on the small part of the total number of waking hours that is taken up by politics, and look at the broader society—at what the Eastern Europeans and George Weigel have trained us to call civil society—we see a milleflorescence of cultural variety, a thousand flowers blooming. We see a nation largely made up of religious believers, of all different kinds—and an articulate media whose members are almost exclusively secular in their religion and in their cultural attitudes. We see a nation where, despite a deep commitment to civil rights, people of African descent live in large part away from others; they not only reside in different neighborhoods but, as polls tell us, they take a quite different view of the nation. Today we are a nation of apparently greater ethnic variety, and certainly a much higher proportion of first- and second-generation immigrant stock, than the nation in which all but the oldest and youngest of us grew up. We see a nation in which most of us live in cultural enclaves, watching different cable channels, listening to different music, attending different churches, or therapy groups, or New Age sessions, and we know very little about the cultural enclaves of others, even of our neighbors down the street or the people moving past us in the shopping mall.

The Ties That Bind

This cultural variety leaves us uncomfortable. We wonder what we have in common. The diversity is especially unnerving because most of us grew up in a country that seemed to have a unified culture— the America of the years around World War II and the long post-war generation afterward. That America, for all its ethnic differences and economic divisions, seemed to have a unitary cultural style: the jauntiness, friendliness, and buoyant optimism captured by the movies of the 1930s and 1940s, and by television situation comedies of the 1950s, a spirit that permeated the political styles of Franklin D. Roosevelt and Ronald Reagan. Americans then prided themselves on being average or (in the case of those exposed to Freud) normal. Our worry was not that we were too different from one another, but that we were too much the same, that we were, as David Riesman said, too often "other-directed," or that too many of us were, as sociologist William Whyte put it, "organization men." (It was assumed that women were at home ironing shirts and preparing dinner, prisoners of what Betty Friedan would call "the feminine mystique.")

It is against this background that we must understand a mistake made by our current vice president, which, if made by his immediate predecessor, would have been the subject of immense media ridicule. Al Gore, with even less aptitude for Latin than Dan Quayle showed for spelling, explained last year that our national motto, *"E Pluribus Unum,"* means "From one, many." Gore apparently thinks that America was once a uniform, culturally non-diverse, white-bread country, which only now is becoming multiracial, multiethnic, and multicultural. Where exactly we are going, or what will be the result of all this diversity, he did not say.

It is my argument that this misconception of the past, which comes easily to most of us, misconstrues almost all of American history. More importantly, it misses what America is all about—whose country it has been, is, and will be. For the apparent cultural uniformity of the long generation during and after World War II is the exception in our American history, not the rule. During these years, to outward appearances at least, we were a far less diverse and segmented society than we have been in almost all the years before and since. The aberration is not the culturally diverse America we live in now, but the culturally uniform America we grew up in.

If we stretch and look back to the America that we and our parents never saw with our own eyes, we will find there some tantalizing resemblances to our own country and discover important clues about how America works today and where it is going. If we look back from 1994 to the America of 1894, or even 1794 (I might add 1694 if I were more confident of my grounding in colonial history), we will see what historian Robert Wiebe has called "the segmented society"—a country whose citizens differ widely in race, ethnic stock, regional origin, and cultural values.[1]

Yet this country of various and strong identities stayed together despite the terrible trauma of the Civil War, and grew stronger, and became what it is now—a beacon of hope to the world. Something held these diverse Americans together and made them stronger than the sum of their parts. Part of that something is tolerance, a tolerance made easier by the vast geographic expanse and economic affluence of our nation. As Wiebe puts it, "what has held Americans together is their capacity for living apart." Part of that something is also the web of ideas emanating from our Declaration of Independence and Constitution, from Thomas Jefferson, the Founders, and Abraham Lincoln: the truth we hold as a people that human beings are endowed by their Creator with inalienable rights and that we have a government of the people, by the people, and for the people. Another something that binds Americans together is the active desire to be an American, and the opposite—or at least the absence—of the antagonism toward the *unum* articulated by the Confederates of the early 1860s or by the counterculturalists of the late 1960s. What binds us together is our willingness to affirm our belief in the goodness of the American enterprise, to endorse enthusiastically the American idea. It is the refusal to make this endorsement, and the persistence of an adversarial frame of mind, that has characterized so much of the university, media, and public-policy elite over the last quarter century; and this is what has disqualified them, in the opinion of most American voters, from leading the country, despite their credentials, skills, and pretensions.

One Common Culture?

Does this something that holds us together also include, as John O'Sullivan has argued in the *National Review,* a "common British culture"? Well, yes and no. Certainly the English language in its American form and political institutions and habits whose roots come almost entirely from the British are part of the essence of what it means to be American. But has the "common British culture" ever constituted an *unum?* Henry Adams, when he described the America of 1801, devoted a chapter to each of the three separate cultures of the nation: New England, the Middle States, and the South.[2] David Hackett Fischer's *Albion's Seed* shows how the political attitudes and the civil societies of Virginia, New England, the Delaware River Valley, and the Appalachian chain came from four distinct regional cultures of the British Isles. And he adds that there are other regional cultures as well—for instance, Black America, with some significant origins in Africa; and New York City, with some characteristics that can be traced back to the numerically almost insignificant Dutch.3 While these regional cultures have important things in common, they are in important ways different. Our country has held together not by asserting the primacy of one culture—as France is held together by Paris —but by allowing each culture to flourish. We stick together because we allow each other mostly to stay apart.

It is widely proclaimed, by cultural liberationists as well as cultural traditionalists, that things are getting worse, that America is flying apart, that the center will not hold. Certainly that seems true when we compare the culturally diverse America of today with the much more culturally unified America of half a century ago. But if we compare ourselves to where we were in 1894, I think we will find that our prospects of holding together—of getting a satisfactory *unum* out of our *pluribus*—are arguably better than they seemed a century or two ago. Then our country's unifying forces—tolerance of diversity, acceptance of fundamental ideas, and the active desire to be an American—were weaker than they are today. In that regard, I believe that today's "multiculturalists" will ultimately be unable to fracture the American *unum*. They have no good prospect of solidifying the divisions between us and making us, as they would like to, a society of apartheid, quotas, and suppression of speech. For they have one very severe handicap: their hostility to the American project is out of line with the feelings of the very large majority of the American people.

Race and Ethnicity

The most vexing challenge to American society and the *unum* is race. A century ago, America was using the force of law to require and enforce racial segregation. Legal segregation, as C. Vann Woodward showed a long generation ago, was not instituted immediately after the Civil War; it began hesitantly in the 1870s and 1880s, with segregation laws still being written and debated in the 1890s. Segregation became most effective in the first forty years of this century. And it was exceedingly—chillingly—effective. Blacks in the South lived mostly in rural areas, disciplined by the terror of frequent lynchings. Black migration from South to North was barely a trickle in these years. From the Civil War to World War II, when some 27 million immigrants crossed the ocean and moved to northern cities and farmlands, only about one million blacks crossed the invisible boundary from the South to the North, despite higher wages and better working conditions up north. A century ago, blacks and whites were in every way moving further apart. Today, though blacks tend to live more separate lives than anyone is comfortable with, the movement is by no means all toward separatism, and the preponderance— though it goes so slowly—may well be in the other direction.

Indeed, blacks today in many ways resemble the Irish of one hundred years ago—and so here let us pass from race to compare ethnic groups of the 1890s and 1990s. Blacks, like the Irish, are concentrated in big cities, with high rates of crime, family breakup, and substance abuse; but many become police officers, and they preserve a strong church tradition. Blacks, like the Irish, have not moved easily up the economic ladder, but they have performed well in public-sector and bureaucratic hierarchies. Both have histories that have given them reason to question the legitimacy of the rules of the larger society. Today's Hispanics, by contrast, are more like the Italians of one hundred years ago. They come from societies with traditions of non-democratic centralism, in which ordinary people trust no institutions but their own families. Both groups have tended to leave school early, to work at hard physical labor, and to marry early and stay married—family being more important than education or economic advancement. Today's Asians, like the Jews of the 1890s, are different still. The children of diaspora, always in danger of persecution and physical destruction, they perform spectacularly well in schools and in the highest-skilled jobs, but are discriminated against by elites.

Many of the elites of one hundred years ago—Theodore Roosevelt is the most vivid and one of the most articulate examples—worried that these hyphenated Americans would stay separate and apart from the dominant English language and the British-descended political culture. The elites had plenty to worry about, at least in numbers. Immigration in the peak year of 1907 was 1.7 million to a country of 86 million—about twice the number of immigrants we receive today with three times the population. The concentration of the immigrants, the strangeness of their languages, their lack of exposure to American culture—all warned of future division. Yet they became Americans in every sense of the word, even while changing a bit in each case the definition of what it is to be American.

Patterns of Integration

The high substance-abuse and crime rates of Irish-Americans per-sisted, as Daniel Patrick Moynihan has noted, for about three genera-tions. But around 1950—at about the same time that their utter dominance of the city politics of New York and Chicago ended—they began to perform better than most Americans on just about every scale. They lost their doubts about the legitimacy of the larger society and came to see that, despite some lingering discrimination, there was a clear connection between effort and reward. Millions of American blacks have already done the same thing and risen free from the underclass; we must hope, and there is some reason to believe, that millions more in time will do the same.

More quietly and with almost no chronicling apart from gangster movies and TV shows, Italian-Americans have also worked their way up to national levels of education and income in the 1950s, and well beyond that today. Their habits of family loyalty served them well in a society whose institutions they eventually came to trust, understand, and use. One can see the same progress among Hispanics today. (The Hispanic label, of course, includes several different groups, from the prosperous and well-educated but still Spanish-speaking Cubans to the too frequently welfare-dependent Puerto Ricans.) But anyone who travels to California or Texas, where most American Hispanics live, will find that they have been moving rapidly out of the central-city ghettos (where newspaper reporters usually look for them), via the freeways, toward every quadrant except the very highest-income and most chic—just as Italian-Americans have long since moved out of the nation's Little Italies. The taco has followed the pizza in becoming a food as American as the hamburger and apple pie.

The story of the Ashkenazic Jewish immigrants to America is another success unparalleled in human history: second-caste people from third-rate backwaters became, in one generation, the top-ranked people in the number-one society. And all this in spite of their suspi-cion of American culture, as well as other majority cultures—evi-denced by a greatly disproportionate interest in socialism and even Communism; by trenchant cultural criticism; and by hostility to the elite (and mostly Republican) universities, law firms, and clubs that imposed quotas on them or altogether barred them from their ranks. Today's Asian immigrants are different from the Jewish immigrants of the 1890s in important ways. Many have arrived here with a highly positive attitude toward America. (Koreans are happy we intervened militarily in Korea; Vietnamese are unhappy not that we intervened in Vietnam but that we left.) They see as their current adversaries the (mostly liberal) universities with their racial quotas, or the black boycotters and rioters who are treated gently by the liberal establishment. The Asians of the 1990s seem at least as determined as Jews a century ago to assimilate into American society, and they are likely to do so very quickly.

A High-Tech Tocquevillean Nation

With the reminder of the attraction to socialism among Jewish immigrants, let us move from ethnic divides to economics, and consider the America of one hundred years ago. America in 1894 was already more industrial than agricultural (William McKinley beat the agrarian William Jennings Bryan); it had already established itself as the most productive and prosperous nation in the world; and it was being linked together by giant economic enterprises, whose power frightened many citizens, and by technological inventions—electricity, the telephone, the automobile—that were a universal source of wonder. But amid all this progress, the socialist idea was gaining strength. Progressives like Theodore Roosevelt and Woodrow Wilson believed that if they were to prevent socialism from spreading among American factory workers as it already had among the workers of Germany, Britain, and France, they would have to expand government's hold over the economy by breaking up some great aggregations of capital and by regulating others. It seemed then, as it has for most of the twentieth century, that history was moving relentlessly to the left, toward larger and stronger government, away from markets and toward bureaucracy.

Today we live in a different world. The collapse of the Communist empire has been accomplished by the less noisy but just as consequential collapse of the idea of socialism. Other countries have moved as I would argue America is about to move—toward a ratcheting down of government, regardless of the motives of elected officials. At the same time, the impulses toward centralization, standardization, and bureaucratization, which, aided by new technologies, prevailed just a little less than one hundred years ago in the Progressive Era, seem likely now to be overwhelmed by impulses toward decentralization, customization, and marketization, assisted by technologies that have proved not to be forces for enslavement—as George Orwell feared in *1984*—but forces of empowerment.

The result is, I would argue, an America closer to its long-term rule than to its mid-twentieth-century exception, a new-old, high-tech Tocquevillean America. This is an America where our ability to live in our own segments and enclaves, connected electronically with like-minded fellow citizens, makes us more inclined to live at peace with our neighbors in other segments and enclaves, more willing to share a common national bond because we can live apart.

The Elites v. the Ordinary

Let me conclude by going back to where I began. Speaker Longworth's question, "Whose car is it?" did not receive a definitive answer for a year, for in those days Congress did not begin its regular sessions until thirteen months after it was elected, and only after several special elections did it become clear that Garner's party was in the driver's seat. The question "Whose country is it?" will be argued for about as long as there is an America, and the fact that it can be argued is perhaps one of the things that holds us together. But I think that the 1994 election goes some distance toward providing an answer, at least until some major disorder—something on the scale of the economic disorder of the early 1930s or the cultural disorder of the late 1960s— erupts. For the Republican victory in the 1994 off-year congressional elections goes a very long way toward proving that the presidential elections of 1980, 1984, and 1988 were the rule, and that the 1992 election was the exception. The forces that elected Republican presidents are now operating in House races. And the institutional advantages Democrats enjoyed through the 1980s—superior candidate skills, redistricting, the perquisites of office and the pork-barrel projects—for different reasons no longer obtain.

At some time in the 1970s, two different factors, one economic and one cultural, turned Americans against ever-increasing government. The economic factor was the huge increase in the tax burden on ordinary citizens—the result of inflation and of bracket creep that pushed working people into tax brackets originally intended for the affluent. The cultural factor was the increasing dominance of the liberation-minded cultures of care-giving professionals—of educators who think students should not be required to learn much or believe much that is good about their society, of social workers who think welfare recipients should not be required to work or honor conventional moral standards, of penologists who think that prisoners should not be required to serve much time in jail or be morally condemned for their criminal acts. These liberation cultures are fundamentally adversarial to the American project, but they have been widely embraced by university and media elites as well as by the care-giving professionals. These politically adept classes have been able to use the political system not just to secure and dominate their own enclaves in America but to invade the space of others. They seek not just to keep churches out of the schools but to install a militant secularism, not just to protect private lives but to promote sexual liberation, not just to allow gay men to live as they please but to require that their mores be imposed on a largely hostile military.

Ordinary voters, disconnected from one another, relatively inarticulate, and regarded with a certain contempt by the mainline media, have struggled clumsily, with varying success, to scale back an expensive, inefficient, and intrusive government. The victories of Ronald Reagan have been balanced, until now, by the continuing Democratic hold on the House. And conservative local governments have been frustrated by adept liberal politicians from Mario Cuomo to Willie Brown. But the atomized opponents of big liberation-minded government have stumbled onto new tactics and media—from the term-limits movement to talk radio—and have won a victory with the potential to set in motion political forces that will reduce the size and scope of government, instead of, as in the fifty years after the New Deal, inflating it.

The media write this movement off as the wrath of angry white men eager to take out their frustrations on the poor. I see it as an attempt to get government and politics to catch up with the people, to make us again a Tocquevillean nation in which we can live harmoniously together because we leave one another free to live as we want. I expect there will be much angry resistance to the forces that won a famous victory in 1994, but I am hopeful that in time we will be willing to live peaceably together, tolerating our differences and upholding the ideas of our Founders—and celebrating the America that, more than any other nation, allows such a disparate people to do so.

2

Individualism Before Multiculturalism

Glenn C. Loury

Since the Founding, America has struggled to incorporate the descendants of African slaves into an estate of full and equal citizenship. One hundred thirty-two years after the Emancipation Proclamation, this process, though well advanced, remains incomplete, and we must now consider whether, and how, further progress can be made. But we must first determine who "we" are.

Who we are depends on who's talking and to whom. In our society, public race-talk is part of the larger political conversation concerning national affairs. But there is private race-talk too—that conversation among segregated confidants who speak with a candor not possible in public. Civil rights, affirmative action, multicultural education, and voting-rights policy are discussed publicly in explicitly racial terms while the implicit racial themes of crime and welfare simmer beneath the surface of public conversation. Race-talk has always dominated communal deliberations among blacks as we have sought, through heated internal dialogue, to come to terms with the inherited disability of second-class citizenship. I am sure that whites too engage in lively, if guarded, private deliberation on race-related matters.

These two levels of race-talk—public within the national polity,

---

Glenn C. Loury is a University Professor of Economics at Boston University and the author of *One by One from the Inside Out: Essays and Reviews on Race and Responsibility in America* (Free Press, 1995).

and private among blacks and among whites—interact in important and complex ways. What is acceptable and effective to argue in either forum depends on the nature of the discourse in the other. Prudent discussion of racial matters must always attend to these interrelated contexts. So I am engaged here in two connected but distinct conversations, practicing a kind of "doublespeak" if you will. On the one hand, I speak as a public man, an American, to the whole nation, offering advice on how "we"—that is, all of us—should approach questions of race. But I also speak as a black, addressing "my people" about how "we" should endeavor to make progress.

This dual role limits what I can say without risk of misunderstanding by one or another audience. Both audiences may extend to me a certain license because of race but, for the same reason, may also demand a certain fealty: each listener will search for evidence of disloyalty to cherished values and for confirmation of strongly held convictions. Inevitably, some of you must be disappointed.

As a veteran of the academic culture wars during a period of growing racial conflict in our society, I have often had to balance my desire to fulfill the expectations of others—both whites and blacks, but more especially blacks—with my conviction that one should live with integrity. Sometimes this has led me to act against my initial inclination in ways that would elicit approval from my racial peers. After many years, however, I came to understand that unless I risked the derision of the crowd, I would not have the chance to discover the most important truths about myself or about life—to know and accept my "calling," to define and pursue what I most value, to contribute to my family and community that which God has uniquely endowed me to do. (The stakes are now too high for any of us to do otherwise.)

This small private truth points toward larger social truths: that the seductive call of the tribe can be the siren's call; that no group goals or purposes exist prior to, or independent of, the life plans and the ideals of individual persons; that unless individualism is truly exalted, multiculturalism descends into crass ethnic cheerleading; that, after all is said and done, race is an epiphenomenon, even here in America —even for the descendants of slaves.

Race-talk like this is a heresy to those I call racialists. Racialists hold the doctrine that "authentic" blacks must view themselves as objects of mistreatment by whites and share with other blacks in a collective consciousness of that mistreatment. For decades, true believers in this creed have effectively shaped the public discussion of racial affairs in America; they have also policed and thereby stifled black communal discourse. They have argued, in effect, that the fellow feeling amongst blacks engendered by our common experience of racism should serve as the basis for our personal identities. Only if whites acknowledge their racist culpability, they insist, can the black condition improve. In this they have been monumentally and tragically wrong. They have sacrificed, on an altar of racial protest, the unlimited potential of countless black lives. These are strong statements, but I regard them as commensurate with the crime.

The ineluctable truth of the matter is that the most important challenges and opportunities confronting any person arise not from his racial condition but from our common human condition. Group membership alone tells us nothing about how we should live. The social contingencies of race, gender, class, and sexual orientation are the building blocks, the raw materials, from which an individual constructs a life. The life project is what brings about the development and expression of the individual's personality. Whatever our race, class, or ethnic identity, we all must devise and fulfill a life plan. By facing and solving this problem, we grow as human beings and give meaning and substance to our lives.

Because we share this problem—identical in essentials, different only in details—we can transcend racial differences, gain a genuine mutual understanding of our respective experiences and travails, and empathize with each other. As Sartre might have said, because we all confront the existential challenge of discovering how to live in "good faith," we are able to share love across tribal boundaries.

From the Inside Out

Ironically, to the extent that we individual blacks see ourselves primarily through a racial lens, we sacrifice several possibilities for the kind of personal development that would ultimately further our collective racial interests. For if we continue to labor under a self-definition derived from the outlook of our putative oppressor, confined to the contingent facts of our oppression, we shall never be truly free men and women.

The greatest literature of ethnic writers begins from this truth. In *A Portrait of the Artist as a Young Man,* James Joyce says of Irish nationalism: "When the soul of a man is born in this country there are nets flung at it to hold it back from flight. You talk to me of nationality, language, religion. I shall try to fly by these nets. . . . Do you know what Ireland is? . . . Ireland is the old sow that eats her farrow." Just as Irish nationalism stultified Stephen Daedalus in *A Portrait,* so too has the racialist emphasis on a mythic, authentic blackness worked to hold back the souls of young blacks from flight into the open skies of American society.

Toward the end of chapter sixteen of *The Invisible Man* Ralph Ellison makes a similar point. His hero recalls a lecture on Joyce that he heard while in college at Tuskegee, Alabama, in which the teacher argues:

> [Joyce's] problem, like ours, was not actually one of creating the uncreated conscience of his race, but of creating the uncreated features of his face. Our task is that of making ourselves individuals. The conscience of a race is the gift of its individuals who see, evaluate, record. . . . We create the race by creating ourselves and then to our great astonishment we will have created a culture. Why waste time creating a conscience for something which doesn't exist? For you see, blood and skin do not think![1]

This is precisely the point. Ellison understood it. A later generation of black writers has refused to see it. Skin and blood do not think. The "conscience of the race" must be constructed from the inside out, one person at a time. If this is a social truth, it has important consequences for political life and discourse in contemporary America.

My colleague Charles Griswold has nicely captured the impossibility of discourse in a society that is dominated by mutually insulated groups—those who define themselves by race, from the outside in. In a recent essay he writes:

> One frequently hears people declare, with passion: "Speaking as an (X) I can inform you that (Y)," where 'X' is the name of the relevant group and 'Y' stands for some description or evaluation of the condition or beliefs of X. An auditor not in group X cannot speak with any authority about that group; one must and usually does defer immediately. The moral authority embodied in statements preceded by "Speaking as an (X)" stems in part from an epistemic thesis to the effect that the point of view shared by all members of X is not accessible, or at least not sufficiently accessible, to non-X persons.[2]

Griswold is interested in the paradox of these mutually insulated groups, neither capable of understanding the other, that nevertheless insist upon equal group recognition. This is an apt description of the current state of American pluralism. But we must ask whether recognition can be demanded when understanding is denied to the outsider. How can genuine respect arise from mutual ignorance? How can the white, who "has no idea what black people have endured in this country," really honor the accomplishment of blacks who have transcended the barriers of racial constraint? How can a black, who could "never see things the way a white man does," ever hope to persuade that "white man" to meet him half-way on a matter of mutual importance?

It would appear that empathy and persuasion across racial lines are impossible unless an understanding obtains that the conditions and feelings of particular human beings are universally shared. Such an understanding can be had, but only if we look past race to our common humanity. This implies that the problems facing poor, black Americans should not be presented as narrow racial claims, but should be conveyed to the rest of the polity in essential human terms. From this perspective, the racialist assertion of epistemic privilege is more than a philosophic stance. In our pluralistic democracy it leads, as Griswold notes, "to the destruction of any notion of community except as the arena within which war is waged for recognition, and for the political and economic benefits which follow from recognition."[3]

A Politics of Despair

Black-white relations are actually far worse than Charles Griswold's assessment. Racialists have waged a "war for recognition" under the banner of black victimization for the last twenty-some years. This war has ended with a plaintive demand to be patronized. In a stunning attempt at political jujitsu, the voices of black authenticity insist that the proof of white culpability is the very helplessness of their group —to which the only fitting response is the recognition of their claims. This is a politics of despair. Especially since the 1994 elections, we can see that other white responses are possible. The racialist strategy has proved disastrous.

The backlash against race-conscious politics and policies continues to grow. Survey researchers Paul Sniderman and Thomas Piazza found in their recent study that "merely [mentioning] the issue of affirmative action [to whites] increases significantly the likelihood that they will perceive blacks as irresponsible and lazy."[4] In the 1994 elections, white men voted in favor of Republican congressional candidates over Democrats by a margin of 63 to 37 per cent. This fact has many explanations, among which resentment of race- and gender-based preferences figures prominently. Claims of "reverse discrimination" by white men have long been treated by liberals as a mere annoyance, or as reactionary expressions of distaste for the noble goal of "civil rights." These resentments can now be seen for what they really are—manifestations of the costs to the American polity of the reification of race. Ignored for a quarter-century by those who make and administer our laws, the unpredictable consequences of race-based politics have now found their way into our political life. For instance, a ballot initiative in California outlawing affirmative action may become the Proposition 187 of the 1996 campaign. Can anyone doubt that it will attract considerable electoral support?

One consequence of all this is that the black poor are especially vulnerable politically. Democrats all, the racialist black leaders of inner-city communities have cast their lot with those who seek to expand the welfare state, increase taxes, and promulgate more regulations. Blacks reliably provide one-fourth of the Democratic votes in presidential contests. Black congressional representation depends significantly on gerrymandered districts that elect ultra-liberal black candidates without the inconvenience of dealing with white voters. This political dependence on the left has persisted despite the rightward political drift of the nation over the last generation, and notwithstanding the cultural conservatism of a deeply religious black American population. These leaders have struck alliances with feminists, gay activists, and civil libertarians while building few bridges to right-of-center political organizations. It is now obvious that a conservative political majority can be constructed in this country, and that it can govern—without the support of urban minority voters.

Poisoning Democracy

The paradigm of racial accountancy has, of course, spread beyond politics, with deleterious effects. In *The Bell Curve* (1994), Richard

Herrnstein and Charles Murray point to a large gap between the average IQ scores of blacks and whites, suggesting that much of this difference is fixed by genetic factors.[5] The authors have received perhaps unwarranted criticism for simply stating the fact that, on average, blacks lag behind whites in cognitive functioning. They certainly deserve criticism for implying, as they do, that we should accommodate ourselves to this difference in mental performance between the races, and to the consequent social inequality. Yet Herrnstein and Murray can claim, with cause, that they are merely responding to the zeitgeist: their psychometricians' brew is expressed in the terms of racial grouping previously anointed by the advocates of social equity. They are saying, in effect, Counting by race wasn't our idea; but since you've mentioned it, let's look at all the numbers!

Black American economic and educational achievement in the post–civil-rights era has certainly been ambiguous—great success mixed with shocking failure. The loudest black activists have tried to bluff past this ambiguous record by cajoling and chastising anyone who expresses disappointment or dismay. (For instance, on the UMass, Amherst, campus these days, it is considered a racist act to observe publicly that black basketball players are flunking their academic courses.) These activists treat low black achievement as an automatic indictment of the American social order. Racialists, however, are hoist on their own petard by the arguments of *The Bell Curve*. Having insisted on the primacy of the racial lens, they now confront the specter of a racial intelligence accountancy that offers a rather different explanation for the ambiguous achievements of blacks of the last generation.

So the question now, for blacks as well as whites, is whether given equal opportunity blacks are capable of gaining equal status. It is a peculiar mind that fails, in light of American history, to fathom how poisonous this question is for our democracy. Let me state my unequivocal belief that blacks are, indeed, so capable. Still, any such assertion is a hypothesis, or an axiom—not a fact. The fact is that we blacks have something to prove, to ourselves and to what W. E. B. DuBois once called "a world that looks on in amused contempt and pity." That is not fair; it is not right; but it is the way things are.

Some conservatives have signaled their belief that blacks can never pass this test. Some black radicals agree. More increasingly and openly, they argue that blacks cannot make it in "white America" and so should stop trying, that we should go our own way and burn a few things down in the process. At bottom these parties share the view that blacks cannot meet the challenge.

Yet the challenge that confronts blacks today is not racial at all. It is primarily the human condition, not our race, that we must all learn to cope with. What Paul wrote to the Corinthians many centuries ago remains true: "No temptation has seized you except what is common to man. And God is faithful; he will not let you be tempted beyond what you can bear. But when you are tempted, he will also provide a way out so that you can stand up under it."[6] The Greek word for "temptation" can also be translated "trial" or "test." If, indeed, blacks must now bear up under the weight of a great trial, still God remains faithful. We can either confront and dispel our difficulties, or deny and avoid them. That we can and must meet this challenge makes the core of Herrnstein and Murray's race-talk spectacularly unhelpful. What they are actually saying is that success is unlikely given blacks' average mental equipment, but never mind, because cognitive ability is not the only currency for measuring human worth. This is racialism at its worst.

Whatever the merits and demerits of IQ tests, the scores need not be bandied about in aggregate terms of race. If low intelligence is a problem, then changing the racial identities of those at the top and bottom of the IQ scale doesn't solve it. Similarly, crime has nothing to do with the skin color of the perpetrators or victims. It is a great —if common—moral and political error to advance the view that a person's race is his most important characteristic. To make victims of a handful of vicious criminals—who happen to be black and who prey disproportionately upon other blacks—is an egregious act of racialist propaganda. The failure to elicit white sympathy fosters contempt for and fear of the communities from which these criminals come. Racism-mongers, smugly confident of their moral superiority in pursuit of "racial justice" for death-row inmates, are unable to see how shrill and hysterical their claims sound to the average American.

Toward the Unum

How can we begin to overcome the fragmentation of the *unum* that is the result of racialist politics? I propose that we eliminate as much as possible the explicit use of racial categories in the conduct of public affairs. This will, of course, not erase ethnic identity as an important factor in society, but a conscious effort to achieve a humanistic, universal public rhetoric and policy will redound to the social, political, and psychological benefit of the minority poor in America. Racialists, of course, will dispute this. Stubborn economic inequality between groups, they argue, gives the lie to the ideal of *e pluribus unum*. But why should we focus on group inequality, per se? Why not focus on inequality among individual persons and leave it at that? The answer is not obvious.

The preoccupation with group inequality is usually defended on the grounds that group inequalities reveal the oppression of individuals based on their group identity. This rationale is ultimately unconvincing. The Chinese in Southeast Asia, the Indians in East Africa, and the Jews in Western Europe, although subjected to oppression, have economically surpassed their oppressors.[7] The lesson of history is not that, absent oppression, all social aggregates must reap roughly equal economic rewards. Indeed, that view ignores the economic relevance of the historically determined and culturally reinforced beliefs, values, interests, and attitudes that define ethnic groups. "Historically specific cultures," political theorist Michael Walzer has observed, "necessarily produce historically specific patterns of interest and work."[8]

Nor can we claim that the very existence of distinct beliefs, values, and interests among groups proves oppression. If anything, this argument claims that, except for historical oppression, all groups would achieve equal or similar economic success. But if group differences that bear on economic achievement are the fruit of oppression, then so are those differences in group styles celebrated by the cultural pluralists. To put the matter simply by way of concrete example: if poor academic performance among black students reflects "oppression," then does not outstanding athletic or artistic performance spring from the same source? No. Obviously, the existence of group disparities is not a moral problem ipso facto. In any case, to the extent that inequality is a problem, it can be dealt with adequately without invoking group categories. American society has for thirty years pursued government, corporate, and academic policies as if the necessity of using racial categories were a Jeffersonian self-evident truth. The great costs to our sense of national unity arising from this fallacious course are now becoming evident.

Martin Luther King, Jr., is justly famous for his evocation of national unity in his 1963 speech "I Have a Dream," in which he said: "I have a dream that my four little children will one day live in a nation where they will not be judged by the color of their skin, but by the content of their character."[9] Today, it is mainly conservatives who recall King's dream.[10] And to evoke, with any passion, King's "color-blind" ideal is, in some quarters, to show a limited commitment to racial justice. In the face of formal equality of opportunity, liberals cling to race-conscious public action as the only remedy to the persistence of racial inequality. How deeply ironic that a vigorous defense of the color-blind ideal is regarded by the liberal mind as an attack on blacks.[11] I submit, to the contrary, that establishing the color-blind principle is the only way to secure lasting civic equality for the descendants of slaves.

Honor and Identity

In his 1982 study *Slavery and Social Death,* Orlando Patterson rejects a property-in-people conception of slavery. Instead, he defines slavery as the "permanent, violent domination of natally alienated and generally dishonored persons."[12] The novelty of Patterson's definition lies in its emphasis on the systematic dishonoring of enslaved persons. Patterson argues that hierarchical symbolic relations of respect and standing between masters and slaves are the distinguishing features of the institution of slavery. He finds it a common feature of slavery that masters parasitically derive honor from their power over slaves, while slaves are marginalized by virtue of having no social existence except that mediated by their masters.

Patterson's insight into the nature of slavery implies that emancipation—the legal termination of the masters' property claims—cannot by itself suffice to make genuinely equal citizens of slaves (or their descendants). Freedmen must also overcome a historically generated and culturally reinforced "lack of honor"—a matter that formal legal resolutions alone cannot dispel. How are the deeply entrenched presumptions of inferiority, of intellectual and moral inadequacy, to be extinguished? How are the doubts of former masters and the self-doubts of former slaves to be transcended?

This "problem of honor" is a tenacious ideological remnant of our origins as a slave society. It must be faced if we are to live up to the ideal of *e pluribus unum.* Securing the respect of whites and enhancing self-respect has been a central theme in black American history. The late historian Nathan Huggins clarified the matter by noting that blacks, unlike the various American immigrant groups, are not an alien population in this society, but an alienated one—an essentially indigenous people by birthright entitled to all the privileges and immunities of citizenship.[13] The political history of black Americans may be instructively viewed as the struggle to secure an acknowledgment of this birthright. Our goal has always been to belong to the *unum*. Despite various separatist movements, the wisest African-Americans have known inclusion is the only way. But the pursuit of freedom and inclusion is a very hard road. Booker T. Washington understood that blacks would have to confront the "problem of honor," and its demands, in their efforts to achieve true emancipation. Washington argued:

> It is a mistake to assume that the Negro, who had been a slave for two hundred and fifty years, gained his freedom by the signing, on a certain date, of a certain paper by the President of the United States. It is a mistake to assume that one man can, in any true sense, give freedom to another. Freedom, in the larger and higher sense, every man must gain for himself.[14]

Washington also knew that blacks could make progress in our democracy only by being sensitive to the concerns of whites. Indeed, every black leader of any influence has worked within such a context. Only in our time has the notion been advanced that "authentic" black leadership should be unencumbered by the need to consider white opinion. Only in our time, to repeat, are electoral districts drawn so that blacks may be assured of election without the inconvenience of winning white votes.

Persuasion or Extortion?

The old civil-rights activism sought to persuade; the new activism seeks to extort. Martin Luther King, Jr., and his followers protested vigorously on behalf of clear principles of social justice. Their use of nonviolent civil disobedience drew forth the affirmation of common principles from their fellow citizens. Their reliance on the humanity and decency of the American majority showed respect for the moral integrity of their fellows. King was thus rightly a leader of both black and white Americans. His stature in each community depended upon his influence in the other. The dramatic public confrontations he and others in the movement engineered were viewed by white and black audiences—each aware that the other was watching. The morally persuasive nature of King's appeal mobilized the conscience of the white majority. By so doing, King also convinced many blacks that there was realistic hope—at long last—that their essential interests would be accommodated. King thus confronted the most crucial task of any leader who seeks to promote racial harmony in our divided society: to assure the "good people" of each race that counterparts on the other side do, in fact, exist.

That so many young blacks see in Malcolm X and Martin Luther King, Jr., a legitimate polarity of philosophic alternatives is a telling commentary on the moral confusion of today's orthodoxy. Yet Malcolm X is an exceptionally poor guide, especially concerning blacks and the American *unum,* since the interests of blacks, properly understood, are inescapably intertwined with the concerns and sensibilities of whites. But it is to the radicalism of Malcolm X that Afrocentrist, rejectionist rabble-rousers like Al Sharpton look for inspiration. And it is precisely because the civil-rights establishment has itself lost sight of the need to take whites' fears and revulsions seriously that it falls mute in the wake of the excesses of Sharpton, Jeffries, Farrakhan, et al., who, rather than persuade on the basis of a common humanity, issue demands from their racial bunkers.

We see the consequences of this insularity in the events of Crown Heights, New York. Murderous mobs of black youths rampaged, openly incited by Sharpton and others, who then claimed status and prestige for themselves as brokers of the peace. Leaders like Sharpton have emerged because more respectable black advocates have abandoned that cardinal principle that Booker T. Washington understood so well. The dominant message of these new leaders is that blacks have abjured persuasion, hold white opinion in contempt, and seek to frighten and extort. Such "leadership" apparently intends to ensure that bad people of both races will find each other, the better to keep conflict alive.

The truth is that whites do not need to be shown how to fear black youths in the cities. Instead, they must be taught how to respect them. An effective, persuasive black leadership must project to whites the image of a disciplined, respectable black demeanor. That such comportment is consistent with protest for redress of grievance is a great legacy of the civil-rights movement. But more than disciplined protest is necessary. Discipline, orderliness, and virtue in every aspect of life will contribute to creating an aura of respectability and worth. Such an aura is a valuable political asset, and the natural by-product of living one's life in a dignified, civilized manner.

Because racial oppression tangibly diminishes its victims—in their own eyes and in the eyes of others—the construction of new public identities and the simultaneous promotion of self-respect are crucial tasks facing those burdened with a history of oppression. Without virtuous character and public citizenship, there can be no genuine recovery from past victimization. But thankfully, overcoming the accumulated disadvantages of past victimization is not an experience unique to black Americans. It's not just "a black thing, which you wouldn't understand."

A prominent civil-rights leader teaches young blacks the exhortation "I am somebody." True enough. But the next and crucial question is, "Just who are you?" The black youngster should be prepared to respond: "Because I am somebody, I will not accept unequal rights. Because I am somebody, I will waste no opportunity to better myself. Because I am somebody, I will respect my body by not polluting it with drugs or promiscuous sex. Because I am somebody—in my home, in my community, in my nation—I will comport myself responsibly, I will be accountable, I will be available to serve others as well as myself." It is the doing of fine things, not the saying of fine words, that proves that here is somebody to be reckoned with. A youngster is somebody not because of the color of his skin, but because of the content of his character.

3

Black-White Relations: Tales From a Tenement

Jim Sleeper

Would we have the multiculturalist movement of the depth and virulence that we do were it not for the African-American experience in the United States? If the problems of black-white relations were solved, would we still be talking about the "diversity" and multiculturalization of American society? A few experiences of my own may shed some light on these questions.

In 1977, at the age of twenty-nine, I finished a doctorate at Harvard, put it in my back pocket, and never used it again. I moved to New York, into a predominantly black neighborhood in Brooklyn. I was interested in seeing what the city was like outside Manhattan, what life was like in the vast, proletarian, interracial New York that is always in such turmoil. And I became immersed in that world. Al Sharpton and I now have lunch once every few months, and in between I attack him in the *New Republic* or in my column in the *New York Daily News*.

I moved into a tenement building in 1977. The tenants were predominantly black, somewhat Latino; there was only one other white person in the building. Most of the tenants were hard-pressed

---

Jim Sleeper is a political columnist for the *New York Daily News* and the author of *The Closest of Strangers: Liberalism and the Politics of Race in New York* (Norton, 1990).

economically and were not very well educated. The range of occupations included a couple of bank tellers, some school cafeteria workers, and some welfare mothers. These people lived under unremitting and often capricious pressures. There was a lot of violence in their lives —familial-violence, criminal violence, and the accidental violence that comes with living in a shoddy structure that had half burned down.

In terms of cultural identity, most of these people were in a state of what I would call arrested assimilation. They were not particularly attracted to the racialist line that Al Sharpton and other academics or demagogues put out. But neither were they confident of their ability to move forward and upward into a common culture or economy. They felt trapped in situations that they regarded as being primarily of their own making, rather than the result of some omnipresent, malevolent white racism.

On the same block, across the street from my tenement, lived a number of Italian-American working-class families who had been there for thirty or forty years. There was a lot of conflict between the two sets of residents, with miscommunications ricocheting about. By 8 A.M. every day, the sidewalk in front of the Italians' brownstones was hosed down, the laundry was hanging out back, and fathers had gone off to work. In front of the building where I lived and a couple of the larger buildings nearby that were tenanted mostly by black and Hispanic families, there would be a lot of litter, including broken bottles and things that had been thrown out windows during the previous night's conflicts. Only a small minority of the tenants were responsible for these conditions, but the contrast was oppressive and bedeviling to both sides of the block.

Two black boys who lived with their mother in my building had taken to harassing and even mugging people on the streets. One night they made the mistake of crossing the racial line and mugging an elderly Italian-American woman, whereupon a few Italian-American youths took it upon themselves to administer rough justice: they firebombed the door of the black family's apartment off its hinges. Down the hill came all the liberals from other blocks, announcing that this had been a racist firebombing and a major outrage; most New York newspapers covered it in that way. No one reported that other *black* tenants in the black boys' own building had long ago petitioned the landlord to evict them.

The irony was that most Italian-Americans and other white ethnics on the block took a certain amount of pride in saying, "I take each person as he comes; it doesn't matter what his color is." And unlike a lot of white liberals who wring their hands over things like the "racist firebombing" that I described, many of these Italian-Americans worked with blacks in their jobs at ConEdison or on the Long Island Railroad. They carried on friendly bantering—not intimate relationships, perhaps, but certainly cordial ones. There was a certain degree of mutual respect. Of course, among some of the white ethnics there was certainly the Don Corleone culture that Paul Rahe has described so compellingly elsewhere in this book, and there were also instances of familial and cultural breakdown. The white out-of-wedlock birth rate in the United States has now reached the level of the black rate when Daniel Patrick Moynihan sounded the alarm in the 1960s. And in Brooklyn, Italian-American teenagers are dropping out of high school at a rate that is second only to that of blacks and Latinos. For a number of reasons, the monolithic juxtaposition of racist, tightly knit white ethnics with a misbehaving black underclass really didn't exist. The picture was much more complex.

A Displaced Liberal Racism

Here are a few reflections about the people who came down the hill with their placards and leaflets after the firebombing: I think that white liberals who do not themselves interact with blacks on a daily and equal basis—except as consultants and in academic settings where the stage is already set for a certain kind of rhetoric—may fear their own reactions were they to be immersed in a situation like mine for ten years. There's a lot to get angry at: I was furious at the people who broke bottles on the street at night and threw mattresses out the windows. I was furious at those two black youths who were out harassing people. Too many white liberals keep such anger imprisoned behind an elaborate racial etiquette that they dare not violate—for fear of what might come flooding out. In short, they fear their own racism. Their inability to make distinctions frustrates them, and that accounts for much of the torturous etiquette we find in discussions of race. They also displace their own unacknowledged racism—if I may call it that—onto the white ethnics whom they equally misunderstand and whose complexity they equally ignore.

Another vignette, a poignant and painful one: In 1985 some white youths from the Howard Beach section of Brooklyn attacked three black pedestrians and chased one of them onto a busy parkway, where he was struck by a car and killed. It turned out that the ringleader of that band of white boys, one John Lester, was a busboy at a diner on the borderline between Howard Beach and a predominantly black neighborhood in East New York. As a busboy, he had become friendly with a number of black politicians—including Congressman Ed Towns—who would often come to the diner late at night after their political and community meetings. The black politicians called John "Elvis" because his hairstyle reminded them of Elvis Presley. John would always make sure they had good seats. Once when he got into trouble for having an unlicensed, illegal gun, one of the black lawyers became his attorney; this was about six months before the Howard Beach incident. After Howard Beach, Ed Towns and his late-night political colleagues had the distressing experience of opening the *Daily News* and seeing a picture of the young man they knew as Elvis, portrayed as a racist of the kind that they couldn't believe he was. Complexities of this sort are continually lost in the public recounting of racial incidents.

Orlando Patterson, a sociologist at Harvard, had a terrific article in *Transition* magazine on black gender relations, the Clarence Thomas–Anita Hill hearings, and the role of racism in such *intra*racial, male-female relations ("Backlash," Summer 1994 issue). Patterson writes that a lot of whites went through a kind of internal reckoning during the civil-rights movement, that they were shamed by their own sense of what their higher values should be, and that they are open to being appealed to and called to account. The civil-rights movement was a watershed in the consciousness of this country, and a lot of white working people now pride themselves on being willing to take each person as he is. Acknowledging this makes it *easier,* not harder, to acknowledge the depth of racism in our earlier history and the extent to which many blacks still are bedeviled by a kind of prenatal alienation. Orlando Patterson says this alienation spills over from generation to generation—as an internalization and recapitulation of previous oppressions in father-to-son and male-to-female relationships.

Some of these problems can be solved only by blacks themselves. That is what my black neighbors in Brooklyn felt. They didn't really see an omnipresent white racism as the cause of the battles they were having within their own four walls every night—the family breakdown, the inability of their teenagers to stay in school and graduate at a decent skill level. There was a certain grudging acknowledgment that a lot of internal stuff had to be worked out within the community.

To recognize this in no way diminishes the severity of the legacies of slavery, racism, and Jim Crow. Although the Holocaust did not happen to Jews on our soil, our country *was* the locus of the primal violation of blacks: millions of people were stripped of their own culture and denied the kind of choice and self-selection that figures in every other stream of immigration. The irony we often miss is that African-Americans were more committed to America's living up to its own stated creed than were any of the subsequent immigrants, who came with their own cultural resources, not to mention the advantages of being white. When America failed to live up to its creed, blacks, in compensation, grabbed onto the Old Testament as the primal, metaphysical, theological metaphor for themselves. Similarly, figures like W. E. B. DuBois learned to use the King's English with a facility that most whites never matched. And jazz—a strange marriage of surviving black African and quintessentially European musical forms —has become America's own classical music.

Recall the spectacle of young black men in clean white shirts sitting at the lunch counter at Woolworth's in the 1950s, demanding admission to the civic culture: "We are ready, our behavior is good, our aspirations are undeniable." This was an epochal moment for all of us. Recall the nobility of Rosa Parks, refusing to move to the rear of that Montgomery bus. She didn't call the bus driver a racist; she said her feet were tired, reminding us, in effect, that she was a hard-working, upstanding citizen.

What has happened to the black community and racial activists since that time? Why has everything declined? In the 1940s, when blacks began, with the support of white liberals, to demand admission to the civic culture on that culture's own terms, when they began to insist that they were part of the *unum,* proportionately more young black men got married than young white men. Even under conditions of worse segregation and, in some ways, worse economic discrimination than now, more black families stayed intact. Why has the situation deteriorated? For one thing, the kinds of blue-collar manufacturing jobs that did not require a high school diploma, jobs that many blacks held faithfully and performed well—these are precisely the jobs that are disappearing. White industrial workers, often by virtue of better education and better networking, more easily make the leap into white-collar service jobs. As William Julius Wilson has noted, this economic decline undercuts the marriageability of black men.

The Debasing of the Common Culture

But without doubt the demagoguery of the Al Sharptons, the misconstruals of "racism" by academic racialists and racial legal theorists, have prevented us from examining the internal communal dynamic that, as Orlando Patterson says, must confront itself and somehow work itself through. Multiculturalism in this context becomes a sad parody of culture. In the well-known 1989 Central Park jogger case, a young, white, female investment banker was bludgeoned and raped by a group of young black and Hispanic youths. During the deliberation by a mostly black and Hispanic jury, one of the Puerto Rican jurors slammed his fist on the table, faced a couple of the black jurors, and said: "All right, if you'll vote to convict the black guys, I'll vote to convict the Hispanic guys." This racialization of justice is an emblem of what multiculturalism has become: an uncaring parceling out of bargained-for resources and defenses.

Among those who don't share the unique black experience, multiculturalism is a defensive circling of the wagons, the self-fulfilling prophecy of a civic culture in decay. We no longer feel that people look out for one another or will protect one another. We can no longer count on a certain modicum of civil behavior and discourse. The breakdown of the patterned behavior that a common culture enforces is not, I submit, a function primarily of the deep racial fault line that once compromised civic culture so deeply. There is a new fault line, a contradiction that I think conservatives must begin to wrestle with. To some extent the private market system not only facilitates and accommodates but also *engenders* the feeling that people are no longer looking out for one another. Corporate capitalists market to fragmented niches, whether through cable TV or other kinds of product differentiation. They find crass multiculturalism surprisingly congenial.

Consider this case: In 1994, three white teenagers from a small, exclusively white working-class town in north-central Massachusetts went on a joyride to Florida. There they broke into the home of an elderly Hispanic man and murdered him in the course of mugging him. What was that about? The violence by those kids certainly can't be blamed on going to school with black gangsta rappers. Why is the white teenage out-of-wedlock birth rate at 22 per cent in the United States? This is not a product of the kind of phoney multiculturalism spewed forth by racial demagogues. The loss of confidence in mainstream culture has to be confronted, even if we leave aside blacks and talk just about whites.

Market forces, corporate forces, the collusion of liberal democrats with favorite corporate contributors through publicly subsidized boondoggles—and maybe other things that really have nothing to do with these—are subverting politics in both its Aristotelian and its Madisonian sense, and this is causing a big problem. It's hardly surprising that blacks would be most vulnerable to the ensuing shocks, aftershocks, dislocations, and upheavals. They have the fewest independent cultural resources. Meanwhile, whites may be coping with the upheaval only by living on their borrowed and overextended moral and cultural capital.

4

Affirmations of a Multiculturalist

James Counts Early

R einventing the American People: Unity and Diversity Today" is a timely topic that warrants discussion all across the country in formal and informal settings, in electronic and print media, in schools and homes. This urgent and complex topic requires deeper attention than the brief and limited focus it will receive here. My intention is simply to identify key issues in the national debate of culture and present some evaluative perspectives about the debate. To be fruitful to the real-life aspirations of our diverse citizenry and resident populations, the discussions must be inclusive and civil. Polite, one-sided discussion should not be employed to stifle or misrepresent needed debate; but neither should intense debate be used to impose views and practices that will stifle the broad public engagement necessary to resolve old and new challenges to our national health.

Despite our many problems as a nation, I am optimistic about the public debate and the innovative responses to the fundamental national questions: What unites us as a nation? What are our common values? How will we characterize national identity? Where are we headed? I assert my optimism as a multiculturalist, as someone who subscribes to one of at least five paradigms of Afrocentrism, and as

---

James Counts Early is assistant provost for educational and cultural programs at the Smithsonian Institution. The views expressed here are his own, not those of the Smithsonian.

53

one who is also a part of the living traditions of the West. And I vigorously and directly challenge opposing views that would narrow the plane of debate, limit the breadth of participation, and refuse to expand beyond canonical philosophy and traditional ways of practicing democracy.

During the seventeenth and eighteenth centuries, civil society in Europe changed. People began to move away from looking at external phenomena as the determinants of how society should operate. It was a movement away from the notion of an omnipotent God who orchestrated reality and toward the freedom of the individual to mediate distinctions of interest based not just on individuality, but rather on the idea of the commonwealth. Although present-day change mostly addresses the virtually unlimited influence of Eurocentric perspectives over national life, we nevertheless continue towards an expanded commonwealth mediated by the movement towards freedom of expression and participation by various cultural groups.

What is happening in the United States today is partially analogous to what was going on in Europe in the seventeenth and early eighteenth centuries. There is a crisis of order. The way the country used to "look" and function no longer holds us together in relatively stable ways. So now we are challenged to find new ways of negotiating conflicts and building public community. This is why the reemerging discussion of the nature of civil society is so important. We share a common rhetoric about America, but if we put our common ideas to the test of history, we have to deal with racism, a *fundamental* organizing principle in the founding of this republic, and with the nation's multicultural makeup, a suppressed factor that has now fully emerged in the public sphere.

High-flown philosophical concepts and absolutist ideological judgments about the primacy of nationality over and against race, ethnicity, gender, class, or sexual orientation; syrupy romantic outpourings about "the nature of America" and "the universality of American democracy"; sharp-edged and exclusive racial and religious constructs of "who are the true Americans"; and cataclysmic warnings about "the threat of multiculturalism to national identity and the wholeness of the American nation"—are all brought to bear against multiculturalism. Against all this, I wish to invoke some sense of history and contemporary reality. I also speak with simultaneous optimism and criticism of the American democratic project and its complementary modern capitalist market system (an unbridled economic system that produces social dislocation and thus deserves fuller examination in relationship to the practice of democracy, especially in the post–Cold War era).

My optimism and criticisms are informed by the ongoing struggles, throughout the history of the United States, of those who were not included in the polity or who were treated as less than potentially equal, to live up to and to improve upon the nation's creed of "liberty, equality, and justice for all."

I was born in the continental United States and educated here primarily in the English language, in the Euro-American-centered texts. I am a student of foreign languages, and I have some sense of what is going on elsewhere in the world. My optimism is born of the historical and contemporary efforts of African-Americans to democratize American life, generally and more specifically. Generally, through the crucible of anti-racist/pro-constitutional movements, and specifically, through American education—the continuum that connects the affirmation of Negro History to African and African-American Studies, to humanistically grounded Afrocentrism, and to an integrative multiculturalism.

I am from a community called African-American, whose members have struggled to make the constitutional ideals *living principles,* not rhetorical principles. Not ideals that hang above us as an ideal or abstract unity as we face each other in our inequalities, but rather ideals that are mediated and struggled over and refashioned by us so that they are manifest in our actual social existence. Through social struggle and social compromise about civic culture and civil practice, I do think that we all share something.

Not all people in the various communities I am a part of will think as I do. But our national political-cultural context gives us ground for discussion and debate to try to come to some resolution that—*Yes!* —there are transcendent values in the national culture, as well as in our respective ethnic cultures; and that these values can contribute to national stability and development. These contributory principles to meaningful democracy are not simply to be found in some static notion of Western civilization—consisting of Plato, Pericles, John Donne, John Locke, and whomever. Ideals of justice and commonwealth exist in all societies, however small, archaic, traditional, or pre-literate they are or may have been. Thus, I am part of a historical trend of increasingly broader racial, cultural, class, gender, and ethnic segments of the American population who seek to better understand and appreciate the multiple social and cultural currents that have shaped and continue to shape the meaning and content of the United States of America.

Contradictions and failings notwithstanding, the American democratic project has been positively characterized, thus far, by a society that has lived and struggled with its contradictions of racial, economic, gender, and other social inequalities. And thus far, this society has gradually changed to include some of the people and ideas heretofore excluded or simply not contemplated. This change has sometimes been painful or bloody; but we have not met the national demise that has beset so many other nations in the last decades of the twentieth century.

This is the real-life context for "Reinventing America" that must embolden us to seek a reformed future and expanded democracy for our nation in contrast to the ultra-conservative, atavistic vision entombed in philosophical rhetoric that fails to reckon with both the virtues and inequities wrought from lived and living experiences. So this is the nation where I choose to be, not simply by birthright, but because this nation is where I and others of many ethnic and cultural backgrounds, but of similar understanding, have contributed to making the United States of America the living democratic example that it is today—and the improved example that it must and will be in the future.

Multiculturalism and the Common Space

Some may dispute or disagree with my commitment to multiculturalism and to Afrocentrism. Both subjects provoke heated, and at times uncivil, discourse. Ironically, both subjects have spurred widespread experimentation and innovation with respect to standards for representation and participation in public and private institutions, and in government and economic institutions. The developmental linkage between the noisy, strident, deprecatory style and content of the public debate about multiculturalism and Afrocentrism among pundits, politicians, and ideologues, and the dramatically shifting standards of assessment and practices of inclusion under way in American society, has yet to be explored. Why is so little attention given to the hundreds of socially productive and nationally beneficial adaptations of multicultural principles and practices in workplaces, schools, and other mainstream activities throughout our nation? Is it a wonder that the culture of democracy as it has been understood is not fully in sync with changed and changing cultural demographics among our citizens and resident populations?

Multiculturalism emerges at this juncture in our national history (and in part informs similar developments abroad) as a democratic thrust for total inclusion of all those who have been unjustly excluded from the democratic project. Multiculturalism is not a panacea. It is not the end of American history. Nor will multiculturalism irreparably divide the nation, or lower the cultural standards of democracy or the nation. Rather, multiculturalism is—for this transitional moment in the nation's development—a framework for new/(re)inventions. It is a new stage of democracy in action, and a new stage for potential democratic growth and development that will also produce its own limitations which we are all challenged to overcome.

A brief examination of the contention and confusion around the use of the term "culture" is a good starting place to delve beneath the canonical smoke of the combatants in the so-called cultural war. We need to see what is really happening in the various fields of life where the social principles and content of multiculturalism and Afrocentrism are being played out. The extensive back-and-forth about these terms has neglected to identify and focus on the causal factors that have brought the nation to this moment of portentous discourse.

Amidst the salvos about culture in general, and multiculturalism and Afrocentrism in particular, too few have tried to clarify how these subjects are defined or what content or values are presumed or dismissed. One dimension of shared culture is national identity—those learned and shared beliefs in such concepts and principles as freedom, liberty, justice, equality, fairness, tolerance. Tenets of democracy such as freedom of speech, voting, a free press, I would argue, are certainly commonly held values.

What is it that makes us citizens of this country called the United States of America? Do we share values? Meanings? Patterns of interaction? My response is, absolutely yes. The freedom anthem of the world is "We Shall Overcome"—a song that came from a group of African-American women in a labor movement in South Carolina. It is now sung (shared) by liberation movements around the world, and by different cultural and political groups throughout the United States engaged in protest or petition to their government or employer. "We Shall Overcome" is an African-American contribution, a touchstone of a living, vibrant, Western tradition that inspires others and fosters shared civic lessons about "we the people."

Multiculturalism—distinct from the cultural polemic about national identity—is a movement opposed to the monocultural hegemony of Eurocentric values, which has generally resulted in the marginalization of other ethnic cultural values. All too frequently throughout history, this hegemony has led to the conscious, systematic denigration of other ways of knowing and ways of doing; it became the rationale for enslavement, confiscation of land and property, mayhem, and murder. Cultural elements such as language, visual and musical aesthetics, religion, group social values, and social practices frequently differ among ethnic groups who otherwise share many human traits, values, and even national identity. At this moment in history what makes multiculturalism a welcome prospect for some and a matter of foreboding for others is its implications of change in how we perceive and practice national identity and democratic principles, heretofore subsumed under Eurocentric interpretations of Western civilization.

Now, there are some who will say everything Europe produced was evil and devil-like. I make no concession to critics of multiculturalism by acknowledging that such criticisms are shallow and extreme, even though they are rationalized as necessary or true reactions to real historical and contemporary inequalities spawned by white prejudice, selfishness, and outright greed in a socially irresponsible capitalist market. But those tendencies are not the dominant perspectives in multiculturalism. Critics of multiculturalism, Afrocentrism, and other integrative centric perspectives who raise shrill alarms to "protect us from this onslaught against American civilization" should be—must be—required to measure the real-life implications of their narrow Eurocentric concepts of American democratic principles, culture, and identity against principles, perspectives, and practices being forged all across the country by pre-collegiate and collegiate educators, museums, local and federal government agencies, civic organizations, and even corporate entities.

The more challenging arguments of multiculturalism, in contrast to, and in some instances against, "traditional" concepts and practices of American culture, nationality, and capitalist enterprise, are not about separation but about inclusion. Rather than looking at the democratic thrust of multiculturalism, some critics argue (really, in my view, a rationalization that simply continues and, to some degree, gives countenance to racial and other forms of social discrimination and inequity) that we are all different, that our virtue is our ability to live together, but apart. That is not the American project I subscribe to, nor the concept of national access and interaction in civil society to which most proponents of multiculturalism subscribe.

Multiculturalism has become a main organizing principle in every aspect of American life. The business community, corporate America, higher education, even select politicians are talking about multiculturalism. They are trying to figure out how to sell to consumers and deal with workers who come from ethnic-specific cultural backgrounds, who do not necessarily have shared contexts and meanings. Rather than *denying* them the opportunity to speak Spanish, how do we provide the opportunity for them to learn to speak English? That is our new democratic challenge.

According to a District of Columbia judge, nearly 150 of the city's judicial codes have been translated into Spanish. Here is a radical new development of democracy. Whether we like it or not, a lot of immigrants cannot communicate effectively in English. What is the responsibility of a just society to these people in public spaces like hospitals, libraries, schools, and government departments? It is to help them understand and participate, even if in another language, and to provide them the opportunity to learn English. I have spent a lot of time in Latino communities in this country and throughout the Americas. When I am dealing with working-class immigrants, I do not hear them say that they do not want to learn English. It is the upper class that says, "We will be the first immigrants to the United States who won't give up our Spanish language" (though they say this in excellent English).

The working people want to learn English. We must provide them the community and public institutions to do so. They are intelligent people. Back in their home countries, when a village gets one television set, the people get an image of Washington, D.C., and two months later there are ten or fifteen cars in that village. Meanwhile, those who are here are not living in apartments any more; they have bought homes. They are living a trans-national cultural identity. With the globalization of economic relations such new cultural factors are emerging with respect to national identity.

Miami—one of the sixteen cities that have passed an English-only law—did not at the time reveal it was sending home all official documents from the school system in three languages: English, Spanish, and Haitian-Creole. That is a radical democratic development that will serve this nation well. While it does not solve the problem of one common language (an issue still to be resolved), it does avoid making scapegoats of the children. Miami accepted its public responsibility to communicate with parents and guardians in order to educate their children. We must find new structures for the twenty-first century, not just defend or completely reject the templates that have brought us this far.

The new civil society needs to find a new civil conversation, a better culture of discourse. We really do have a problem. If you turn on your radio or television, basically you hear the old tug of war between liberal-left and conservative-right, rather than reasonable, civil debate. People are dismissed because they belong to one subgroup or another. We won't get anywhere with that kind of dialogue. We need to take more time to find the common ground among us for reasonable debate and compromise. Western civilization in the United States of America is a formative process, not some Hegelian philosophical idea to which we must all bow down and try to return. Our formative process must be renewed every day; it must include the new African, Asian, Pacific Islander, Latin American, Caribbean, Eastern European, and other immigrants who will give new meaning to "Western civilization," even as they are attracted by historic meanings of the "West." If we lose this understanding, we will lose one of the most important strengths of this nation, which is our ability to confront our differences, to embrace them with vigor, and to try to negotiate them in the best interests of aggrieved individuals, not abstractly on the principle of majority rule.

The Meaning of Race

The subject of multiculturalism cannot be fully comprehended short of unraveling its connection to the pivotal factor of race in the founding and evolution of this country. Race is not synonymous with culture. This distinction seems to befuddle both proponents and critics of multiculturalism and Afrocentrism. Simply put, race is a social construction of assigned (defining) value based on our outward appearance. Uses and meanings of racial constructions change over time through the mediation of involved social groups. That I am racially called (and self-identified as) African-American is because someone said way back in history, "You will be 'black' because I'm 'white.'" That reveals almost nothing about my symbols, my values, or how I look at the world. This computer called the mind allows me to be multicultural, to learn, appreciate, and even practice different traditions of knowing and doing.

When some people use the term multicultural, they really mean by it multiracial: "There's an African-American, there's a white person, there's a Native American, there's an Asian. There's a gay person, there's a lesbian person." Acknowledging visual or perceived behavioral differences is somehow supposed to represent multiculturalism. All too often, the social meaning behind such designations is not located in cultural meaning but in highly defined physical (racial) distinctions. When we really mean "race," we're not talking about culture, despite the overlap between the two in our national culture.

I use the term multicultural in a different way. I am a multicultural person by virtue of my attitude, my will, and my ability to examine and step inside those intrinsic patterns, those shared ways of meaning of other cultures, to try to understand what is common amongst us all, as well as what is distinctive. "Attitude" is the prerequisite factor. When you use the Spanish word *iglesia,* meaning church, the image is not of a wooden A-frame church building with a tin roof—characteristic of the Baptist and Methodist churches where I grew up in Florida. The *iglesia* would likely be a more open-spaced, more decorative structure, even if it were in a rural area. I can understand and appreciate both those cultural vantage points. I can read an ancient Greek poem, study it, step inside the internal logic of it, and if it is a lament, I might be brought to tears. This does not mean I am alienated from my primary, learned African-American aesthetic tradition; it means that I am multicultural in my orientation. I am open to learning and even incorporating other points of view into my identity. Do I therefore find all cultural values relative? No! I would not, for example, condone female circumcision or patriarchy in any culture.

If multiculturalism, in part, reflects a united front of cultures against the hegemony of Eurocentrism, then Afrocentrism is its cutting edge.

Its centrality in this new development is seen in three areas: prece-
dent-setting frameworks in government, employment, and education
philosophies, policies, and practices; adaptation by other aggrieved
groups; extreme reactions from the status quo, and extreme,
frequently shallow assertions from Afrocentrists.

Racism and the preoccupation of the national psyche with the
"black-white" social relation produce a contradictory unity in Afrocentrism. Afrocentrism, in its varied paradigms, is a catalyst for educational and national cultural enrichment; it is also a point of stagna-
tion in the national discourse. When Lani Guinier called for a national
discussion of race, she was dismissed as left-wing and a "Clintonite"
—an indictment from which the president quickly distanced himself.
But we need that discussion, which may take us yet further along to
forging shared values.

Proponents of multiculturalism and Afrocentrism are now critiqu-
ing and challenging some of its perspectives in an effort to find common space. Our terminology will no doubt change, constructs will be
refined; but the essence of cultural recognition and participation in
the ongoing process of developing a national cultural identity and
shared national values will not cease or be stopped.

We all would do well to heed the words of the nation's presidential
poet, Maya Angelou:

> The Horizon leans forward,
> Offering you [us] space to place new steps of change.

5

The One-Out-of-Many Blues

Stanley Crouch

People who are in some striking way unlike us are an American obsession. That is because our history has demanded that we address and learn from the "other," either to enrich this culture's resilience, or to wage struggles against adversaries within our borders, or against threats abroad. Absorbing the influences of Europeans, Indians, Negroes, Mexicans, Chinese, and others into our national corpus has put everything to a test—our Declaration of Independence, our Constitution, our local laws and customs. Yet we have succeeded.

But now this hard and endless feat is threatened. For in our shrill, cloudy, contemporary era, we have naively embraced a polluted and separatist version of pluralism—usually referred to as multiculturalism. Our most shining history has often come from a bluesy wrestling with the impulses to exclude, on the one hand, and to adapt, on the other, the new and strange. Always before we have modestly extended our basic principles, and in the process weathered the storms of putrid xenophobia. Now, though, under the guise of "inclusion," we must suffer through a politics of resentment, one based on ethnic and gender franchises instead of the former goal of "a fair chance."

Stanley Crouch is a recipient of the MacArthur Foundation Genius Award and the author of *Notes of a Hanging Judge* and the forthcoming *All-American Skin Game*.

Our politics of resentment has much in common with the adolescent passions of popular culture, where all authority is flawed Grand Canyon deep. Like the yowling and stomping of hostile rock music, this political vision makes use of very sophisticated technology to reduce all complexity to the blunt and the simple-minded. Where the rock musician counts on innovations in electronic amplification, the purveyor of bitterness and envy draped in political rhetoric calls upon statistics, historical guilt, and elaborate theory to shift the complex realities of human engagement into a melodrama of good versus evil as inaccurate as the lollipop trees drawn by children.

The politics of resentment is based most deeply on a denial of individual responsibility. The history of groups, or as the vastly overestimated W. E. B. DuBois would have it, the history of races, is all. In this regard, the politics of resentment that lies directly behind "multiculturalism" is built on the sense of having been had by some larger external force or by "society" in general. If the resentful one is from a racial minority, the culprit is "white racism"; if female, one may blame "political testosterone poisoning." All of these are variations on the child-abuse defense—a dysfunctional family as the root of all wrong. As the comedian Dennis Miller recently observed on his cable show, "Thanks to the notion of dysfunction, every zipperhead in this country can tap himself with a Freudian wand and go from failed frog to misunderstood prince."

This posturing amounts to nothing more than frying the rotten fish of self-pity and blame on a griddle made hot by opportunism, and greased with scoops from the bottomless Crisco can of white guilt. It is another manifestation of the ethnic hustles that have become so big since the 1966 arrival of Black Power, that first stinking catch of what became a huge market. We are now accustomed to various groups hypnotized by the tone of their skin, their genitalia, and whatever else—all seeking positions of high honor as victims supposedly lacerated by the sharp blades of the cultural blender, their shouts of psychic agony even louder than the icy-hard electronic drone of the machine they claim is liquefying them into faceless Americans. The separatist struggle against absorption is also founded on muddled discomfort with the fact of our crisscrossed Americanness: the reality that the entire nation is a protean composite of everything we find adequate for adaptation. This discomfort is basic to our history, and it demands clarity of thought and courage to discern the difference between enriching charisma and reductive contamination. Therein lies the difference between vitality and decay.

The most provincial among us always warn against contamination by others. The so-called whites have spoken of the mongrelization that comes of race-mixing. We have long been given images of "mission Indians" who have lost contact with their own people and exist in some nether region of identity crisis between the white world that won't completely accept them and the red world they cannot understand or feel comfortable in. There are many terms for the "Oreo," the Negro who is black on the outside but "white" on the inside. Years ago, when Mexican-American nationalism imitated Black Power, the term was "coconut": brown without and pale within. We even hear of the woman who thinks or acts or votes "like a man." These are all dreams of an authenticity so at odds with our real history that we should understand it for the paranoid discomfort it truly is.

The Indian and the Woodsman

Beyond xenophobic discomfort is the historic fascination with things different and things foreign. At first we were entranced by the Indian who was here when the rest of us arrived. Constance Rourke points out that Robert Rogers, the author of *Ponteach*—the very first American play on an indigenous subject, written the same year as our Declaration of Independence—was a frontiersman and "merciless destroyer of Indians," who set down "episodes from his own ruthless career" with a bitter self-satire. Uncomfortable with his destructive victories, and equally disturbed by his familiarity with Indian butchery of white men, the playwright finally makes the Indian chief Ponteach his hero. "The Indians had somehow imposed their own view on this first imaginative embodiment of the two races," Rourke notes. "The noble savage emerged; and strangely enough this concept fitted a body of philosophical thought emerging in Europe . . . as to the damaging effects of civilization."

So perhaps in Robert Rogers we have the beginning of something that looms large in our consciousness—the non-white functioning as an aspect of social morality. We might also consider this work the beginning of a tradition central to the ways in which Americans have criticized themselves. Ponteach attempts to represent a purity beyond the reach of the westward settlement that was then dismantling existing natural and traditional orders.

The professors of ethnic studies and the professionals working for segregated minority cultures are thus all sons and daughters of Robert Rogers, repentant Indian-slayer. Whenever we invoke dastardly "white male power" and hail the importance of separatist franchises, we are reaching for a version of Rousseau's romantic and remarkably inadequate mantle of nobility. Modern exponents draw a line through the word "savage" but otherwise appropriate the logic. This hand-me-down protest is but another example of how material, ideas, and styles are democratized in our country—sometimes for the better, sometimes not.

Soon after the Indian, we were taken by the woodsman, because in certain fundamental ways the men in buckskin were our first full-fledged cultural mulattos. In his ways and in his being, the frontiersman was a hybrid of white and Indian existence. He combined the light of European-derived information and the wild black of America's ancestral night—where history had no forward motion, no written language. The closest thing to crystal in the woodsman's world was the thin frozen surface of a lake at the beginning of winter. While his rifle, powder, and round lead bullet connected him inextricably to the Western technology that would determine the future of the country, his hair was worn Indian-style, his ear was dog-tuned to the inaudible music rising from the deep, and his knowledge of the land, the native tribes, and the ways of the birds and the beasts was imitative of, and often directly derived from, America's aboriginal peoples. The mixture of technology and reason with traditional blood and lore made the pioneer American a white man unlike any the other side of the Atlantic had ever produced. Those who would thrive on this continent would have to draw experimentally upon more than what they brought with them from Europe. They would mix in their consciousness, and sometimes in their blood, the richest national resources available.

These improvisational mixtures made popular the minstrel show, the dime-novel western, the Buffalo Bill circuses of cowboys, leftover Indian chiefs, sharpshooters, and rodeo clowns, the interest in the "heathen Chinee," Nanook of the North, various hillbilly doings, the Southwestern lore of Texas and Mexico, the underworld of gangsters, the yakety-yak of Jewish humor, and much else that made its way up the invisible cultural gully separating convention from the swamp water of superstition and odd custom. We all know how much American music, comedy, and dance were influenced by the minstrel show, where even the imagery of insult had a vitality that addicted Americans to the dark people from the other side of the tracks. If we understand that, we can recognize Fred Astaire as an Afro-American dancer, an artist as much a mulatto as the frontiersman, one whose combination of styles and information springs him beyond any sort of ethnic "purity."

Didn't Carl Jung observe that white Americans walked, talked, and laughed like Negroes, and don't Africans tend to think of black Americans as dark-skinned whites? Isn't it obvious to outsiders how much we have made each other what we are?

D. W. Griffith's *Broken Blossoms* (1919) makes a tragic hero of the Chinese lover of a white woman—a miscegenation theme we might not expect from the director of the 1915 film *Birth of a Nation*. But perhaps we should, if only because Griffith was an American of genius, and one perhaps so repulsed by what his racist Reconstruction fable had wrought that he lost his shirt making 1916's *Intolerance*—the four-themed cinematic fugue that prefigured subsequent improvisations on the overt and covert meanings of miscegenation. In the films of John Ford, we also see an evolution of the images of Indians and Negroes that moves them further and further away from tools of comic relief or dread until they at last reach a tragic complexity. Ford's *The Last Hurrah* (1958) is a lament for the old Hollywood, plus a gloomily comic acknowledgment that traditional political machines of flesh and blood will be replaced by the real machines of the media; and, to add another row of shark's teeth to Ford's cinematic saw, it is also a drama of symbolic racial integration in which the dependents of the lower-class Irish and the upper-class British talk of their children going to the same schools and "intermarrying."

The American Dream Machine

This development of heroic figures within even the stereotyped works of Hollywood proves that American life is far from the closed book of atrocities imagined by our country's sternest critics. In one instance after another we have seen our legendary dream machine shift its sympathies and elevate the downtrodden and the excluded. Minorities and women continue to move into fresher areas of characterization, functioning so often in narrative positions of complexity and authority that people new to America are convinced that the country is truly a multiracial enterprise in which the sexes stride closer and closer to equality. In our real world, many black mayors and women executives and minority experts, advisors, and intellectuals make obvious the inspiration.

Even the sex symbol and matinee idol has gone far beyond an enclosed idea of refined looks to include individuals like Woody Allen, Spike Lee, Barbra Streisand, Madonna, and Whoopi Goldberg—none of whom has traditional good looks but each of whom has somehow hooked into the national appetite for charisma. A poll taken ten years ago revealed that most Americans, if they couldn't have their actual father, would choose Bill Cosby! In a more recent poll, American teenagers said that the woman they respected most after their mothers was Oprah Winfrey, and the man Denzel Washington. Whether these figures represent high quality or mediocrity or trash, they are all aspects of unexpected democratic evolution.

Of course, the kind of imbecilic balkanization that was put in motion by the celebrated numbskull Malcolm X and progeny has also been received surprisingly broadly. But it shouldn't be, because it threatens to undermine the moral basis of our central social contract. When we become obsessed with race, we forget that in Europe and many other places, class was like race is today. We must remember just how young the idea of equality is in the world—even among whites.

What the American and French revolutions did was boot the idea of royal blood from the Western lexicon. Definition by blood—that fenced-in idea of aristocracy—was a way of making class a form of race. The royals considered themselves a genus separate from the poor. This freed them from identifying with human tragedy beyond the palace or the estate. Part of the brutality that came after the fall of Louis XVI was the bitter result of a hatred that George Bernard Shaw described as the anger felt by those once awed and intimidated. It is a kind of anger we have foolishly revived in these United States over the last thirty years. We have encouraged each other to put on the mask of the martyr, or the martyr's descendant.

In some fundamental way, racism has been a form of protest against the implicit depths of democracy—the central idea of which is that greatness can come from anywhere, that virtue knows no innate limitations, that genius and courage arrive where they will, that every group or class is as vulnerable to the shortcomings of the human species as any other. The ethnic or sexual separatist—like the racist —wants to reassert a monarchy of blood. He or she wants to draw a line in the dirt, to hide from the grandeur and pressure of democracy and avoid the tragic knowledge of human frailty. At the bottom of too many of the multiculturalist's complaints is a feeling of being overmatched by the sophisticated demands of this wide open society.

This strategy is destined to fail. It now enjoys its moment at the microphone, so we must watch one nut after another fill the airwaves with complaint, each dressed in a more outrageous get-up designed to express hostility or warlike readiness to the television audience. But these new-moon yahoos will mean nothing in the long run. Just why has already been laid down by our best writers, musicians, and filmmakers—by people like Constance Rourke, John A. Kouwenhoven, Ralph Ellison, and Albert Murray.

Here is the reality, straight, no chaser: The American is an incontestable mix of blood, style, and tradition. Part Yankee, part frontiersman, part Indian, part Negro, part Hispanic, part Asian, part Christian, part Jew. We hear this in our talk, we see it in the way we walk and the way we laugh, the gestures we use, the facial expressions we pass over ethnic fences, the foods we eat, and even the dreams we have. We will continue to reinterpret our interrelationships, regularly stretching the heroic into the angelic and turning the vile into the demonic. Yet we will continue to respond to each other's stylization of sensibility. Some narrative will come our way that allows us to be lyrically touched to the quick by an individual superficially unlike us. We will continue to reinvent our diets and make spiritual searches. We are hopeless experimenters and improvisers, just as we are hopeless suckers—never given an even break by those who wish to manipulate us through our curiosity and our willingness to engage in that good old American self-criticism.

Not for very long will we be able to accept the visions of the separatists, however, because our history, public and private, has proven to us over and over that we were made for each other. We will sometimes be knocked down to one knee. But we are too shot through with shared personal and historical resonances to separate. We are now and forever Americans, which means that we are in some very specific ways parts of all other peoples. Our culture and our bloodlines are cosmopolitan. No matter how hard we might try, we can't have it any other way.

6

Diversity Is Not a Virtue

Mark Helprin

Of all the divisions in the politics of the Western world, the clearest and most consequential are those between corporate or communal rights and the rights of the individual. Other questions, though they may be all consuming, are often restatements of this fundamental issue.

Socialists steadfastly champion central planning, despite its monotonous failures, because they cannot abide individual liberty, even if it accomplishes their goals of material advancement. And proponents of the free market who rest their case upon the market's performance forget that ultimately they are its advocates, not because of its operational superiorities, but because it is a necessary precondition of a free society.

A dispassionate look at the twentieth century reveals, amid the smoke of distant battles, that the great alliances were ultimately what our propagandists held them to be. For all its pathos, the First World War was a struggle between liberal democracy and a state system in which legitimacy flowed merely from the success of executive action. In the Second World War, the conflict between raw state power and the idea of individual rights was amplified by Fascist enthusiasm for

---

Mark Helprin is a columnist for the *Wall Street Journal* and the author of numerous books, including *Soldiers of the Great War* and, most recently, *Memoir From Antproof Case.*

71

corporate rights, in which group identity was the basis not just of monstrous systems of government but of death warrants for whole peoples. The West then engaged the Soviet bloc in a half-century proxy war, with millions of casualties, over the same division.

Though the Soviet apparatus disintegrated, the communalist ideal escaped. It is still with us, harbored by the old guard in the East and the intellectual elites of the West, who, now that their enthusiasms seem no longer a matter of national betrayal, are more fervent than ever.

A Dangerous Principle

At the founding of the nation, in the Civil War, and in the authentic struggle for civil rights, the corporatist idea was found wanting and the rights of the individual affirmed. Once again we are faced with this choice, but in a different cultural context. Today the churches, the president, the universities, and the press endorse rather than condemn the idea that we are most importantly representatives of a class, a tribe, or a race, and that we are to treat others and expect to be treated as such.

They do so to make amends and to "celebrate diversity," without concern that the recipients of their largesse may not themselves have been wronged. As they see it, they need only find people of the same type, and the deed is done. And what amends! To atone for having wrongly judged people by race, they will now rightly judge people by race. To atone for segregated accommodations, they offer separate dormitories. To atone for having said "colored people," they say "people of color." What they do now is as wrong as it once was—not merely because of the effect, but because of the dangerous principle that individuals do not transcend the accidents of birth.

Almost every scholastic body in the country now considers itself a kind of Congress of Vienna with the special mission of making its students aware of race and ethnicity. The students are forced to dwell on a half-dozen categories and told that this is diversity. The reduction of 250 million individuals to a handful of racial and ethnic classifications is not a *recognition* of differences but their brutal *suppression*. This is a triumph of the academic impulse to classify, a triumph of the bureaucratic need to categorize, a triumph of reductionism, and a triumph of utilitarianism. But it is a defeat of the human spirit. The debit or credit now furiously assigned to membership in various communities; the federal laws that in requiring complex racial assessments embarrassingly parallel Hitler's Aryan Decree; the virtual *numerus clausus* in the American university, this time directed against Asians; the regrowth of racial segregation; the computerized homelands of congressional redistricting—these are a long way from equal justice under law.

Many well-meaning liberals now deal carelessly with the stock in trade of Nazism and apartheid. What they advocate is racism plain and stupid, no different from the laziness of mind and deficiency of spirit of the old-time segregationists—"There goes a white one, there goes a black one, that one's an octoroon." They are comfortable with what they once abhorred, because it is part of the good work of promoting communal rights, and in the past few years they have expanded their purview with the voraciousness they attribute to corporate raiders. Accelerating far beyond the relatively simple matter of race, they have included absolutely everyone in their systems of grievance, publicity, manipulation, and reward.

The Communal Maelstrom

The sucking sound (the phrase is Melville's) is that of the entire population disappearing into a communal maelstrom. No longer is the family supposed to be the fundamental unit of society. The wife and female children owe their allegiance to womanhood. The children's loyalties lie not with their oppressive parents but with the class interests of children. If one of them is adopted, he must cleave to his ethnic or racial group, unless she is a girl, whereupon she may be a woman first. Even the dog has a union card, and if he feels abused will summon the defenders of animal rights.

This damage having been done, the next step is the promotion of diversity as a political value, and the institutional proclamation of ethnic differences ("We're so proud to have Melanie in our class, because she's an Eskimo"). Even were this somehow to further diversity, neither diversity nor unity is a virtue, and both should be left to find their own balance without stilted prodding. Freezing acculturation to keep each contributing element pristine would have been impossible even in the age of steam. It is much less possible now, when things change faster than we can register. Why the useless, shallow, and patronizing acclaim for the great tributaries of this new stream that goes its own way and will not be made to back up? Why the interminable school programs in which parents are forced to listen as their hostage children sing Indonesian Christmas carols? Am I really a European-American? The hell I am.

All the hyphenation, all the saccharine praise of differences (in which any politically useful subdivision becomes a "culture"), serves to organize and divide the otherwise unmanageable, unplannable chaos of a society of individuals, and thus to augment the power of the state. When you want to control a complex social situation, the first thing you do is make categories and award privileges. But, as in any statist system, for every entitlement there is an equal and opposite obligation. When, in the flush of class action, entitlements are compassionately granted to groups, obligations are cruelly drawn from individuals. Over all, the state is the decisive arbiter. Its power increases as it manufactures new rights and new relations, shifting them in an ever-changing shell game in which the players have the illusion that they are winning but it is the dealer who goes home with the money.

A Portent of Fascism

Those who see individualism as selfishness and narcissism—for which the only remedy is state planning and intervention—are in full agreement with Mussolini, a bit of a narcissist himself, who said (as if anticipating the failed Clinton health-reform guru Ira Magaziner), "The more complicated the forms assumed by civilization, the more restricted the freedom of the individual must become." Bringing rights and powers over the bridge of tribe and class into the hands of government does not diminish world narcissism; it merely concentrates narcissism in the people who think the rest of us should improve our characters by letting them tell us what to do.

They always mean well. Communalists, multiculturalists, the politically correct always want to do good, but they always, always require power to do so; and as their appetite for doing good is limitless, so is their capacity for acquiring power. Intent, as history shows, is a poor bulwark against despotism. As a nation we have never failed to understand this, rightly refusing to accept either a benign despotism or a pernicious one, for at heart they are the same.

If I have not done so already, let me make myself absolutely clear. The contemporary passion to classify and divide the American people is a portent of fascism both red and black. Where the communal approach rules (Yugoslavia, the Middle East, Northern Ireland, Soviet Central Asia, Hitler's Germany, Stalin's Russia), blood flows and no one is treated fairly. We, on the other hand, have fought many times for the sake of being apprehended not as classes of people but as individual souls.

Six generations ago, my forebears left Russia after the Kishinev Pogrom. They left behind the weight of a thousand years for a future that they thought sparkled and shone like a diamond, because it was fair, because the great, euphoric gift of America—its essential condition, its clarity, its purity, and its decency—was that, looking past the accidents of birth and the complications of history, it took them for what they were, just as God would. I cannot imagine that we would willingly leave this behind, and I, for one, will not.

PART TWO

Politics, Constitution, Law, Institutions

7

The Crisis of Constitutionalism

Richard E. Morgan

The birds were singing and the ice cubes were tinkling and the canapés were circulating briskly. It was a garden reception following a June wedding, one of those "legal weddings"—both the bride and groom (one a former student of mine) were young attorneys, and many of the guests were young attorneys too, the couple's friends from law school, clerkships, and first jobs. I found myself chatting with one of these guests, an obviously able recent graduate of one of our elite law schools. Well on his way to success at the bar was my chance acquaintance, and after learning that I taught constitutional law he confided that while he had never been a terribly hard-working student in law school, he had won the prize in constitutional law the year he had taken the course. The subject had turned him on, he said, "because it had so little to do with law." "Constitutional law," he announced brightly, "is moral philosophy, pure and simple"; no one with any pretense to sophistication could think otherwise. And, he continued, "all that stuff about the Framers and their intentions—well, all that the past really tells us is to try to do the right thing!"

It was in that spirit, he told me—obeying the injunction to "try to do the right thing"—that he wrote his final examination in constitu-

---

Richard E. Morgan is William Nelson Cromwell Professor of Constitutional Law and Government at Bowdoin College. He is the author of *Disabling America: The Rights Industry in Our Time* (Basic Books, 1986).

tional law, for which he received the top grade in the course. I do not mean to mock my chance acquaintance. While his chosen field is something harmless, like estate planning, his outlook is shared, if truth be told, by most practicing constitutional scholars and commentators. His expression of it was remarkable only for its insouciance. This is the measure of our difficulty. The twin notions that constitutional law is "moral philosophy pure and simple," and that our constitutional tradition is so multifaceted and ambiguous that all that can be extracted from it is "try to do the right thing," have become the conventional wisdom into which several generations of constitutional experts have been socialized. Unless we achieve some considerable resocialization, and rather quickly, the American republic will be in for increasing, serious trouble. We are facing nothing less, I think, than a crisis in American constitutionalism.

In our supremely verbal but decreasingly literate age, there are many previously serviceable words that one is almost embarrassed to use. "Crisis" is one of these. By resorting to it I am saying more than that there is conflict at present over the direction of American constitutionalism, or that there are some particularly interesting intellectual problems with respect to it. I use "crisis" according to its first meaning in the *Oxford English Dictionary:* "The point in the progress of a disease when a change takes place which is decisive of recovery or death. . . ." It is precisely the case that over the next few years the principled core of traditional American constitutionalism either will be reasserted or will be finally abandoned and become archaic. If the outcome is abandonment, the consequences for the nation will be grave.

These consequences are already apparent—even if their mordant potential is not yet fully appreciated—in the degraded quality of much recent constitutional law (understood as the decisions of the Supreme Court). Further, we have seen lower federal courts, state supreme courts, and even administrative agencies increasingly straining to get into the business of making bad law illegitimately. Finally, and most seriously, as a consequence of the breakdown of our constitutional tradition, we are experiencing a blurring of American political identity —of our perception of ourselves as a people defined by our involvement in a common and uniquely worthy governmental enterprise.

Thus my concern is on a more fundamental level than the usual complaints about "judicial activism" or interest groups that seek in the courts what they cannot get from legislatures. When I say constitutional law is degraded, I do not mean simply that particular policy results are wrought by unelected judges rather than elected legislatures and executives; I mean that the substantive policy embodied in the decisions is often at odds with our political culture, that it contradicts the American constitutional tradition, and that it cannot command broad and deep respect.

The use of the definite article in connection with the words "American constitutional tradition" will appear radical to far too many people today. But it is precisely the point. Our past is not an intellectual buffet from which we may pick what is to our taste of the moment and leave the rest; neither is it bland pap, without distinctive taste. It must be insisted that embedded in our past are substantive political teachings and choices of constitutional dimension that should be accorded continuing respect in our governance. Should we fail to give this respect, we betray our identity and prejudice our claim of participation in the distinct moral enterprise of the American republic.

"Naive!" says the historical sophisticate. What about all that famous diversity of American opinion during the revolutionary, constitutional, and formative periods? What about the distance between a John Dickenson and a Thomas Paine? Or between Hamilton and Jefferson in their constitutional views? Or, notoriously, what about the disagreements of James Madison with himself? After all, whole sections of libraries are given over to learned discussion of theoretical nuances separating the Founders from one another and distinguishing the English, Continental, and classical authors on whom they often relied for either inspiration, justification, or example.

Such crosscurrents are not without interest to specialists, but they are not really very important for the practical work of establishing constitutional meaning. Those charged with construing and applying constitutions (at least American constitutions) turn to the past in different ways and for different purposes than the scholar. For the would-be interpreter, the *central intellectual tendencies* and the areas of *general agreement* are important. For the scholar it is almost the opposite.

Professional scholarship today, organized around departments in colleges and universities, is a sprawling industry. And like all industries, it has requirements. A core requirement of that part of the scholarly industry concerned with the American past is that the historical record be rich enough to support the historians, political scientists, law professors, and others who depend upon it. Furthermore, scholars, because they are a species of intellectual, rejoice in subtlety and ambiguity. Academic careers are built by invoking complexity and celebrating paradox. And this is exacerbated by the ways in which shifting ideological tides within the intellectual community create demands for new images of our past. Taken together, the natural and healthy striving for novelty and the often morbid striving to remake the past in conformance with contemporary fashion have been sufficient, over time, to obscure our view of what was central, widely agreed upon, and broadly shared in America's founding era and through most of our history.

THE FOUR AUTHORITATIVE PRINCIPLES

I suggest that when one thinks about it, undistracted by the sirens of fashion, four political principles emerge as authoritative from the American founding, and that these concepts were confirmed by the understandings of those generations closer in time to the founding than we. This does not mean that *everybody* subscribed to them in precisely the same way. What it does mean is that there was a broad agreement on these matters at a level of specificity high enough to insure they had real meaning as the basis of the rules for doing political business.

It cannot be stressed too firmly that these principles are interconnected. None can be understood independently of the others. These four interlocking concepts do not constitute a systematic theory of politics in the academic sense, but they were (and are still) an internally consistent set of propositions; and they are still serviceable as a practical matter, for orienting constitutional interpreters. Obviously they did not eliminate arguments; there were some bitter ones. What they did was to constrain argument—to limit what could be argued seriously. Through most of our history the corpus of constitutional law was quite modest. Its dramatic growth over the last thirty-five years coincides almost exactly with the decline of the four authoritative principles as a discipline on constitutional interpretation.

Principle One: Liberty

There can be no reasonable doubt about where to begin an account of the political theory that undergirds and makes comprehensible the

Constitution of the United States. It is with a particular conception of liberty. For the revolutionary, founding, and formative generations, which overlapped, the purpose of government was to protect individual liberty, and the distinctive pathology of government—tyranny—occurred when the government interfered with the kinds of interests it was established to protect. The contractarian liberalism of John Locke provided a convenient vocabulary for expressing this core commitment.

On this fundamental point there was consensus, broad and deep. Herbert Storing, the most distinguished student of the Anti-Federalist critics of the Philadelphia product, concluded that Federalist and Anti-Federalist were as one in "the decisive sense" of seeing "the end of government as the security of individual liberty, not the promotion of virtue or the fostering of some organic good."[1] As Martin Diamond demonstrated in an influential article published twenty years ago, the "crucial point" from which an American theory of constitutional interpretation must begin is the priority of liberty as the end of government.[2]

But right here is a pitfall. For "liberty" is just a word. Even with the addition of the qualification "individual" (which in the American context should always be there), little of significance is conveyed. Standing alone, "individual liberty" might be understood in the sense of doing anything one damn well pleases.

In fact, the founding generation and its successors (at least until fairly recently) were committed to a *particular vision* of individual liberty, not to liberty as an abstraction, or as some kind of universal value. As Daniel Webster once put it: "Our inheritance is an inheritance of American liberty. That liberty is characteristic, peculiar, and altogether our own." Not all claims to individual autonomy or free choice were cognizable under this version of liberty. And as a contemporary scholar, Rogers Smith, has put it:

> To a surprising extent, early liberals conceived of popular governance, religious tolerance, the rule of law, . . . only as a means to their basic goals. They did not equate liberalism (liberty) with . . . the pursuit of the maximum freedom imaginable, as many modern liberals do. Instead, liberals originally held that only a *specific and limited conception of liberty* deserved to be an end in itself.[3]

There is nothing mysterious about this understanding of liberty. It is anchored to *selectively* limited government. Certain types of individual choices were placed beyond government's capacity to control, and these are most obviously displayed in the familiar prohibitions contained in the declarations of rights in the state constitutions and in the federal Bill of Rights. I have never found a more concise summary of them than in Fisher Ames's letter to Thomas Dwight of June 11, 1789, commenting on the introduction into the First Congress of the package of proposed amendments that become the federal Bill of Rights:

> It contains . . . the right of enjoying property, of changing government at pleasure, freedom of the press, of conscience, of juries, exemption from general warrants . . . this is the substance. . . . Oh! I had forgot, the right of the people to bear arms.[4]

What strikes the modern reader is how perfectly routine and well understood these things appeared to Ames. If pressed, no doubt he would have recognized the possibility of disputes at the margins over the meaning of these limitations; but basically he regarded them as unproblematical, and this was because they were understood as *limited*.

This was the most important thing about the traditional American conception of liberty: it was bounded, not comprehensive. Certain aspects of individuals' lives were routinely considered fit subjects for regulation through law. For the framers and ratifiers of the Constitution there was no question that the police powers of the states would extend to the regulation of public order and the morals of the community. "Licentiousness," defined as idleness, aggression against property, or an affront to public morals, was punishable by the community acting through the agency of government—there was no offense to liberty in that. As for knowing the difference between liberty and license (something that might seem problematical to many contemporary intellectuals), an inherited and broadly shared moral code could be counted on to sort things out, always allowing for a few hard cases at the margins.

For most of our history, we, as a people, had no difficulty with this understanding of liberty. It is an understanding from which contemporary libertarians can take little comfort. The liberal polity was not a night-watchman affair, ever forbidden to regulate people and property in the general interest. Nor was government, at least local government, required to hold itself in lofty isolation from the moral life of the community, especially those aspects having to do with sexual behavior. Government was not responsible for the ultimate moral fate or spiritual destiny of the citizens, but their conduct in the here-and-now was subject to its policing. Persons were at liberty to steer their own political and religious courses, but sexual activity and the protection of public order was understood to be very much a matter of community concern. Similarly, liberty included freedom of speech to engage in reasoned expression of ideas, but it did not imply *license* to libel, exhort to violence, or scandalize by lewd expression. To attempt to comprehend what the Founders and their successors understood by "liberty" without at the same time coming to grips with their conception of "licentiousness" inevitably leads to misunderstanding.

Principle Two: Equality

For the founding generation, liberty was primary. For us late-twentieth-century Americans, however, concerns about equality approach the obsessive; we are so concerned with it that we assume the Founders also were. Equality, indeed, is often advanced as a substitute for liberty at the core of the American constitutional tradition. Furthermore, the kinds of ideas that often parade today under the banner of "equality" have very shallow rooting in our history. For this reason it is important to focus on what the founding generation conceived equality to mean, and the relationship of equality to the other orienting principles of our constitutionalism.

Here again Martin Diamond is helpful. Diamond debunked the progressive historiography of the early twentieth century in which writers such as J. Allen Smith, Charles A. Beard, and Vernon L. Parrington argued that the Constitution represented an oligarchic reaction to a more radically democratic and egalitarian political theory underlying the Declaration of Independence. While never doubting that there were important differences between the political tenor of 1776 and that of 1787, Diamond re-established what any nineteenth-century American historian would have taken for granted—that both the Declaration and the Constitution assume the centrality of the idea of liberty to the political enterprise. "The social contract theory upon which the Declaration is based teaches not equality as such but equal political liberty."[5] What was affirmed was an *equality before the law.* There were no estates and no hereditary ruling class. The citizens of colonial New York were the equals of a British citizen in London. It was because London denied this, as the balance of the Declaration goes on to detail, that the break from Britain became inevitable. This distinctly American conception of equality appears in the protest of the "frontiersmen" west of the Schuylkill at the pretensions of their more comfortable Pennsylvania brethren to the east.

> We apprehend, as Free-Men and English Subjects, we have an indisputable Title to the same Privileges and Immunities with his Majesty's other Subjects, who reside in the interior Counties of Philadelphia, Chester and Bucks, and therefore ought not to be excluded from an equal Share with them in the very important Privilege of Legislation.[6]

What citizens were *equal in* was the right to have their liberty respected by government and to take part, if they satisfied certain neutral criteria of property, in the process of self-government. Diamond concludes: "The equality of the Declaration, then, consists entirely in the equal entitlement of all to the rights that comprise political liberty, and nothing more." In other words, equality before the law.

This does not imply social leveling, and it certainly does not imply economic equality. Nor is it a canon of "equal dignity and respect" (a neo-Kantian concept beloved by some contemporary legal theorists). Men were understood in America to differ in their dignity and respectability just as they did in their talents, intelligence, and industry —in all the ways Madison recognized in *Federalist* No. 10. What equal liberty did mean was that citizens possessed equally the legal capacity to acquire and dispose of property; to enter into voluntary agreements and associations with others in order to advance their ends; to establish families; and to have the state follow their wishes in concluding their affairs after death. It meant that men were equally entitled to due process of law (the regular, established procedure of the courts) before they were sentenced to death, incarcerated (deprived of liberty), or fined (deprived of their property).

The congressional debates over what became the Fourteenth Amendment are remarkable for the extent to which the meaning of equal liberty, which was now being extended to former slaves, was unchanged since the 1780s. States were forbidden to deny basic civil rights, in the sense of equality of legal capacity (the capacity to acquire property, convey it, invoke the courts to protect it, and so on). States were forbidden to execute, to imprison, or to fine without due process of law (the familiar restriction imposed on the national government by the Fifth Amendment). More fundamentally, the states were required to accept as citizens all born and naturalized citizens of the United States. No longer could there be a legally inferior class based on race. Reconstruction saw the extension of the American social contract, not the creation of a new one.

Principle Three: Self-Government

Locke was prepared to accept any form of government that adequately protected liberty and was consented to by the governed. But the American Founders were clearer as to their choice of governmental form. Liberty would be safeguarded best by a system of republican government—that is, self-government through representative processes. Not only would this *safeguard* liberty: self-government was *required* because it was *inseparable from* liberty. That is, one of the liberties of free men was the potential to participate in their own governance.

It was not that the Founders were enamored of democracy—certainly not of anything like mass democracy as it is understood today. They wrote often and eloquently of the dangers and the dismal track record of democracy as a form of government. The liberties of the people were never safe in a pure or mass democracy because the mob and the demagogue inevitably carried the day. How then to achieve self-government while at the same time avoiding the pitfalls of democracy?

The answer was to be found in what Alexander Hamilton called "improvements in the science of politics." There was to be popular government through representative institutions, with those powers of government most directly touching the lives of ordinary people exercised at the state and local levels—federalism. At the national level there was to be a separation of powers guaranteeing against consolidated government. Nothing was ultimately removed from the authority of the people, nor could any appeal be made to any other source for the legitimation of public policies. Governmental power would be dispersed and checked.

So much is familiar. But it is one thing to doff one's intellectual cap to the proposition that there is no source of governmental authority other than the people, and quite another thing to confront its contemporary implications. The Founders' Constitution was not a

mixed government in which multiple sources of authority operated
—a divinely ordained monarch, hereditary aristocracy, a priestly caste,
a council of wise men. Instead there were multiple institutions at
various levels, and various attenuated representational arrangements,
of which the provisions for the election of senators and the choosing
of the president are obvious examples. But only a vote of the people's
representatives could get the system going, and nothing but a vote
could be appealed to in explaining to any citizen why he was bound
to obey. That vote might be the legislative division on an ordinary bill,
or the nose count in a town council, or that most solemn and fundamental kind of vote—the approval of a constitutional amendment by
two-thirds of the national Congress and the people of three-fourths
of the states. These voted outcomes, or settlements, with the constitutional settlements "trumping" all others, are the rules by which we
are to live our public life.

The rub, of course, is that the terms of past settlements, especially
the constitutional ones, are never pellucid. While contemporary interpreters of votes are not bound by the *precise things* the winning side
in some past political struggle had in mind, they must be limited to
the *objectives* that the winning coalition was seeking. Yet a fair construction of the purposes of some past political coalition may not yield
a result that strikes contemporary advocates as just or decent.

Very well then, might one not argue as follows: The winners in
some past vote were surely seeking a more just society; the limitation
on the majority we want to impose today is required as a matter of
natural justice; and even though this limitation was not in any historically demonstrable way implicated in that old constitutional or
statutory outcome, we are authorized to impose it on the authority of
that old vote because the historical actors on the winning side aspired
to a greater justice than they could envision.

The fatal problem with "natural justice" as a guide to public decision-making is that it adamantly refuses to reveal itself to all of us in
the same way. Being on the losing side of the vote binds one morally,
but no one is morally bound to accept someone else's idea of what is
"just" or "fair." We abide by what the community—acting through
procedures it has previously agreed to—adopts as public policy. We
properly rebel at anything based on an appeal to overarching or revealed truth. That is not necessarily because we disbelieve in the
existence of objective standards of justice and fairness (although some

may). It is because our obtuse neighbors can be counted on not to share our understanding of these things and to make trouble if ignored.

The principle of self-government, therefore, denies resort to a certain kind of argument in support of a governmental decision—the argument that the result is compelled by natural justice or objective moral "rightness" even though no "vote" can be plausibly identified as dictating the result. However, this sort of argument from moral authority has immense and continuing attraction. The temptation is omnipresent—especially for judges—to impose on the political community limitations that the political community has not in any meaningful sense decided to impose upon itself. It is the judicial failure to resist this temptation to traduce self-government that, more than any other factor, has brought us to a crisis in American constitutionalism.

Principle Four: Decentralization

Early in 1986 a distinguished law professor addressed the Attorney General's Conference on Federalism, assembled in Williamsburg, Virginia. He concluded that federalism was dead:

> American Constitutional Federalism has expired; . . . many causes have contributed to its death; but . . . the national courts—by which I really mean the Supreme Court—bear a special responsibility for the demise, because it was into their hands that the fragile compromises worked out in the national and state conventions were placed.[7]

I think this obituary premature, but not, perhaps, by much. While grievous wounds have been inflicted, the damage is not irreparable. Indeed, there have been certain encouraging signs of late.

The matter is crucial, because federalism was not only a useful, if fragile, compromise: it is the theoretical linchpin of that new American science of politics. For most constitutionally literate Americans, through most of our history, federalism was thought to have important normative significance. It reinforced both liberty and self-government. It advanced limited government in the obvious way (by constraining the power of the central government), and insured a built-in decentralization and counterbalancing of power within the system. Federalism also advanced self-government by confirming in those governments closer to the people the most basic and sensitive power, the police power—that is, the power to act to protect the health, welfare, and morals of the citizens in the general community interest. The people of the states would decide, through their own constitutional provisions, what internal limits they would place on state governments and on the structure of political participation within their borders.

Furthermore, although it does not figure formally in our constitutional scheme, it was well understood by the founding generation that as a practical matter much of this state police power would devolve on the localities. While local governments are, technically, mere creatures of the states, the framers of the national Constitution and of the successive state constitutions could rest assured that much of the important work of government—that which impinged most directly on the individual—would be performed at the local level, where the republican check on its exercise would be most immediate and effective. This would allow for the powerful and regular involvement of the people while still avoiding the dangers of mass democracy. The founding generation was painfully aware of the evidence that large, consolidated republics could not adequately protect liberty. That is why they created an "extended republic"—a hybrid of multiple governmental levels.

Today, at least among much of the American intelligentsia, this core doctrine has been stood on its head. The localities and the states are seen as the more likely engines of tyranny, and a consolidated national government is seen as the agency most likely to protect the liberties of the people. Federalism—at least as a judicially enforceable constitutional doctrine—is thought of as an embarrassment. Whatever the good intentions and generous motives that drive this heresy, it is destructive of our constitutional order.

Properly understood, decentralization does not imply a rigid formalism in the division of powers between the nation and the states (that was a late-nineteenth-century distortion). Even less does it imply some insular "state sovereignty" orthodoxy (that was early heresy, manifested in the Kentucky and Virginia Resolutions, and recurred to by politically desperate men in later times). What it does imply is the acceptance of local *differences* as the necessary consequence of a hybrid constitutional form—not sweet, trivial little differences in speech, or architecture, or food, but important differences in laws and government. To recognize that an entity has considerable power of self-government is to accept that it may outrage us by the ways it exercises that power.

We should suspend decentralized decision-making by imposing a uniform national rule only on a powerful showing of need. Mere convenience will not do, nor will a sense that a national dispensation will be superior as public policy to the state and local rules it displaces. There are sometimes good reasons for creating national rules in areas formerly left to local control. Often, in recent decades, these reasons have had to do with protecting individual rights. But the value on the other side of the scales is constitutionally weighty as well. Liberty and self-government are both implicated, and there is no way, within the theory of the Constitution, that judges can discount "federalism questions" as less compelling than questions of civil rights. Federalism is precisely a matter of civil rights, and the extension of national power in the name of "rights" will always extract prices in liberty and self-government.

We have lived now through six decades of rapid, massive extension of national power into the states and localities. While some of this was surely necessary and justifiable, we would have honored the principle of decentralization better by aggressively questioning, challenging, and selectively resisting some aspects of this nationalizing surge. Instead, with a few exceptions, there has been supine acquiescence—by that very Supreme Court that the Framers envisioned as a protector of the constitutional division of power.

THE THREAT TO NATIONAL IDENTITY

These, then, in brief, are the underpinnings of American constitutionalism. Throughout most of our history they served to bound and constrain the enterprise of interpreting American constitutions. Indeed, the fact that these principles were generally understood and broadly shared made the enterprise of constitutional interpretation *plausible*. The breakdown of these traditional American constitutional understandings was a consequence of certain powerfully deconstructive intellectual forces (e.g., legal realism), loosed early in this century. These forces worked their mischief slowly but pervasively, undermining confidence in and respect for constitutional forms.

To reaffirm the tradition and to reestablish its authority will require extraordinary effort. Yet it is a great mistake to suppose that the crisis of American constitutionalism is only a crisis of constitutional law. For, should we fail to resolve it in the direction of American constitutionalism as traditionally understood, the gravest consequence will be for our national identity. This is because of the special importance of constitutionalism in defining Americans as a people. A country with a long history and a homogeneous population may be able to slip in and out of different constitutional arrangements without great stress or risk of moral dissolution. But it is the commitment to a particular political vision—a vision of a specific kind of relationship between government and society—that defines us as Americans.

What core commitment or common approach to living unifies our otherwise ethnically, regionally, and now even linguistically diverse population? For a student of American history, the answer would once have been easy: a commitment to a specific theory of constitutional government was the powerful and sufficient force that united us in a coherent national enterprise. (Indeed, when we came to disagree fundamentally over the nature of our constitutional arrangements, we fought a bloody civil war to settle the issue.) Today, no one can speak this answer with anything like confidence. American constitutionalism is commonly thought of (to the extent that it is thought about at all) just as my chance acquaintance at the garden party thought of it: as a collection of lofty abstractions about freedom and justice and liberty and equality, and a collection of historical precedents pointing in different directions. Since this "constitutionalism" is without specific content, opportunists can grasp it and claim to see in it whatever is their heart's desire at the moment. And who is to say them nay? What one observer sees is no more or less valid than what another sees—providing that they are both persons of "good will" (which means, I guess, something like being sincere).

But this is nowhere near good enough. When identity is based on a self-conscious experiment with a particular form of government, to lose the sense of the particularity of that form—of its distinct characteristics and requirements—is indeed to risk becoming little more than a collection of ethnic groups huddled around a standard of living.

8

The Founding and American Unity

Charles R. Kesler

What unifies the diverse races, religions, and ethnicities of Americans and allows us to think and act as a single people? In trying to answer this question for our own time, we can seek guidance from the doctrines and experience of the statesmen who first had to grapple with it—our country's Founding Fathers. In what follows, I shall make a few general observations about their principles and the setting in which they applied them, and then three related points about their designs for achieving national unity.

To begin with, in the mid-1780s American unity was sharply challenged both within and without. From without, the Union was challenged by the foreign policies of England and Spain, whose irredentist hopes would have been advanced by the nation's dissolution into partial or separate confederacies of states. England still had a vital presence on the continent, thanks to its control of Canada and its garrisoning of posts on America's western frontier, and the Spanish empire pressed against the new nation from the south. Internally, the United States faced challenges, even then, from immigration problems—Benjamin Franklin, for example, was quite worried by the high percentage of German speakers in Pennsylvania (at least a quarter of

Charles R. Kesler is director of the Henry Salvatori Center at Claremont McKenna College. He is the editor of *Saving the Revolution: The Federalist Papers and the American Founding* (Free Press, 1987).

the population, by most estimates). And it also was challenged by the far more serious problem of states' rights and powers under the feeble Articles of Confederation. The congenital weakness of any federal system, as the Federalists warned, is the centrifugal tendency of its constituent parts. This problem of "anarchy in the members" was solved in theory by the "firm Union" created by the Constitution of 1787; and *e pluribus unum* meant, of course, in the first place, that out of the thirteen states one country or people had been born. But this problem was solved in fact only by the Civil War and by the adoption of the Civil War amendments.

Today, American unity is challenged not by the claims of foreign princes or fractious states (though in a federal system the latter are always potential problems) but by the acid criticisms of the so-called multiculturalists, who charge that American unity has come at the expense of diversity. According to them, the American Founders launched the nation on a continuing crusade to impose white, male, heterosexual, property-holding, Eurocentric culture on the diverse cultures that then existed, or later sprang up, or should have sprung up, in the United States. Partly in response, some American conservatives insist that the problem with our civic culture is not so much that it is oppressive but that it is uninspiring: it is so lax and low that it virtually opens the door to multiculturalism. In contemporary debates on law, education, race, religion, and immigration, many conservatives therefore call for a more exclusive or rigorous definition of our civic culture—sometimes along ethnic or ethno-cultural lines.

Thus prominent segments of the left and right seem to agree today that American unity is or ought to be based more on culture—on ethnicity, customs, and history—than on the abstract principles of the Declaration of Independence or the form of government established by the Constitution. These critics make the provocative point that for better or worse the nation began as, and long remained, a White Anglo-Saxon Protestant bastion; and therefore that our historic national identity is actually much more the result (to use *The Federalist*'s language) of "accident and force"—the accident of our British origins, and the force used to keep out, or down, any competing cultures—than of "reflection and choice." To put it succinctly, they assert that America is a people, not an idea, though both liberal and conservative critics admit that sometimes America seems to be a people masquerading as an idea.

The Origins of Our Unity

From the standpoint of the American Founding, however, this is a profound misunderstanding of the origins and purposes of American unity. To say this is not to deny, of course, that the Americans began as the "British North Americans," that is, as an offshoot of the British people and as a part of the British Empire. But the American colonists made a revolution against that empire and chose as "one people" to "dissolve the political bands which have connected them with another," thereupon assuming their "separate and equal station" among the nations. The governments that they substituted for the British monarchy were exclusively republican, based not on the rights of Englishmen but on the rights of man. These two kinds of rights overlapped, to an extent, but the crucial consideration was that the revolutionaries retained or adopted the former (e.g., common-law procedural guarantees) only insofar as they did not contradict the latter. Natural rights provided the ultimate standard.

In making these decisive political choices, the Americans remained a people profoundly shaped by British culture, by the traditions of colonial self-government, and by the experience of the Revolution itself. John Jay overstated the point for effect in *Federalist* No. 2. "Providence has been pleased," he wrote, "to give this one connected country to one united people—a people descended from the same ancestors, speaking the same language, professing the same religion, attached to the same principles of government, very similar in their manners and customs, and who, by their joint counsels, arms, and efforts, fighting side by side through a long and bloody war have nobly established their general liberty and independence."

America began, then, as a people—but as a people with an idea. In thinking through the idea of natural rights and of natural-rights constitutionalism, this people made a revolution with "no parallel in the annals of human society" and gave itself new forms of government "which have no model on the face of the globe," to quote *Federalist* No. 14. And therefore this people bearing an idea soon found that its idea was creating a new, American people. Abraham Lincoln expressed this fact beautifully in a speech in July 1858, reflecting on his own generation's connection to the men who had declared America's independence on that first Fourth of July. The passage is worth quoting at length:

We find a race of men living in that day whom we claim as our fathers and grandfathers; they were iron men, they fought for the principle that they were contending for; and we understand that by what they then did it has followed that the degree of prosperity that we now enjoy has come to us. We hold this annual celebration to remind ourselves of all the good done in this process of time, of how it was done and who did it, and how we are historically connected with it; and we go from these meetings in better humor with ourselves—we feel more attached the one to the other, and more firmly bound to the country we inhabit. In every way we are better men in the age, and race, and country in which we live for these celebrations.

But after we have done all this we have not yet reached the whole. There is something else connected with it. We have besides these men—descended by blood from our ancestors—among us perhaps half our people who are not descendants at all of these men; they are men who have come from Europe—German, Irish, French and Scandinavian—men that have come from Europe themselves, or whose ancestors have come hither and settled here, finding themselves our equals in all things. If they look back through this history to trace their connection with those days by blood, they find they have none, they cannot carry themselves back into that glorious epoch and make themselves feel that they are part of us, but when they look through that old Declaration of Independence they find that those old men say that "We hold these truths to be self-evident, that all men are created equal," and then they feel that that moral sentiment taught in that day evidences their relation to those men, that it is the father of all moral principle in them, and that they have a right to claim it as though they were blood of the blood, and flesh of the flesh of the men who wrote that Declaration [loud and long continued applause], and so they are. That is the electric cord in that Declaration that links the hearts of patriotic and liberty-loving men together, that will link those patriotic hearts as long as the love of freedom exists in the minds of men throughout the world. [Applause.]

Neither Lincoln nor the Founders maintained, however, that simply because the United States stood for certain principles, anyone who professed to share those principles was *ipso facto* eligible to be an American citizen. For one thing, the very principle of equal natural rights required that just government be derived from "the consent of the governed." According to this notion, civil society was based on a social contract, and no new members could be added to that contract without the consent of both the would-be immigrants and civil society itself, as expressed by a majority vote of its representatives. In deciding who should be admitted to citizenship, a people had every right, therefore, to consider the moral and political qualities needed to sustain its way of life. In this connection, three peculiarities of the Founders' statecraft demand our attention.

The Fathers as Founders

First, the men who made the Revolution and wrote the Constitution understood themselves to be engaged in an act of *founding*. This seems obvious, perhaps, but its significance needs to be remarked. Every discussion of American unity is sooner or later driven back to a consideration of our national beginnings. The American nation *has* a founding, complete with "fathers," and so America is not just a social contract among equal contracting parties, or a bit of British culture that broke off and floated across the Atlantic like an iceberg. We have a conscious beginning, with certain intentions or principles in mind, above all in the minds of those great men whom Jefferson called "demi-gods." There are no such "founding fathers" in, for example, John Locke's description of the social contract in his "Second Treatise." For Locke, the notion of "founding fathers" might sound too much like the paternal power that he wants radically to separate from political power. The confusion of paternal with political power is for him the origin of political despotism. There is still a role for unequal men in Locke's political theory, to be sure: in leading revolutions, in capitalist acquisition, perhaps in the exercise of executive power. But the central role of "founding fathers" seems to be a peculiarly American variation on the liberal theme of the social contract.

Certainly some who were among the leading figures of the 1770s and 1780s did not think that founding in this strong sense was really necessary. Tom Paine, for instance, held that all one really needed for decent and good government was to keep politics very close to the people, to the people as they are in their pure republican simplicity. But the more thoughtful American Founders rejected the notion that an act of founding was unnecessary, for they saw two critical problems with the simple social-contract model of political authority. One was in its beginnings, the other in its perpetuation.

First was the problem of beginnings. James Madison, for example, rejected the conceit that the people could find their way to good government through their own spontaneous virtue or even through pursuit of their individual self-interest. The people, he wrote in *Federalist* No. 40, cannot move "spontaneously and universally" towards their object. Hence some "informal and unauthorized propositions" —i.e., the Constitution—had to be proffered by "some patriotic and respectable citizen or number of citizens," which plan of government the people might then deliberate on and choose whether to ratify. But the people could not draft the Constitution themselves: so, if good government on the basis of social-contract theory were possible, founders "unauthorized" by the theory itself were indispensably necessary.

Secondly, there was the problem of perpetuating the republic once it had been established. Here the social contract in its crudest sense promised merely that individuals would keep their promise to obey the law out of their sense of enlightened self-interest. Madison objected that such a calculated attachment to the law could not sustain republican government over the long run. The law, especially the "fundamental law" of the Constitution, required a certain "reverence" or "veneration" from the people if they were to obey it when, as would eventually happen, their self-interest or passions would come into violent conflict with it.

Now, it is important for American unity that we as a people trace our nationhood to "founding fathers," to ancestral lawgivers as it were, somewhat in the manner of the ancient city. For the enduring greatness of the Constitution surely rests not only on its legal claim to be "the supreme law of the land" but also on its reputation as the excellent handiwork of truly outstanding men. As the product of their wisdom, it partakes both of the majesty of the "higher law" and of the admiration that subsequent generations have felt for a human law that could be so brilliantly defended and expounded by the genius of James Madison, Alexander Hamilton, and others.

Separating Citizenship From Church Membership

This brings us to a second distinctive feature of the Founders' strategy for American unity. Although the American Founding resembles ancient foundings in its need for fathers, or its need for great men to legislate for the republic, the American founding is not an ancient founding. The principal difference between them is religion. In the ancient world, every city had its own gods, and every city had divine or semi-divine founders. But the American founding occurred in a world decisively transformed by Christianity—by the presence of universal religion—in which there was one God of all men everywhere, but of no city or country in particular. Thus was created the endemic conflict or separation between the city of man and the city of God, civic loyalty and religious loyalty, that ever after loomed so large in the history of the West, and that led to the bloody religious wars of sixteenth- and seventeenth-century Europe.

America in its founding attempted to resolve this problem, not by imposing a political establishment on religion or a religious orthodoxy on politics, but by separating church and state. Americans did this in the name of civil and religious liberty, not virtue, because disagreements over the definition of godly virtue had helped produce the theological-political wars that had sundered Christendom. These were the kinds of disputes, in the Americans' view, that had to be carried on at the highest level among good friends. Such disputes should not, must not, be conducted in politics, where any attempt to decide what was true religion, whether by force of arms or majority vote, was bound to be tyrannical, not to mention foolish.

So the American Founders took a different path, proclaiming a new ground for citizenship, on the one hand, and a rule to separate citizenship from church membership, on the other. Both doctrines emerged from their understanding of natural rights. The basis of political obligation they found in the consent of free and equal individuals—the social contract. But this contract had to exclude the highest questions of revealed religious truth from the political realm, from determination by political majorities: the contract had to be for limited government. In the modern world, the Founders argued, minority rights and majority rule could be made consistent only on this basis, for otherwise trust between minority and majority, and thus the rule of law, was impossible.

These principles of civil and religious liberty marked the United States as a liberal or modern republic, in that unlike an ancient city, the American regime did not aspire to dictate a comprehensive or total way of life for its citizens. One might say that this was the original and highest American multiculturalism, the requirement that each citizen should have a realm of privacy in which he would be free to nurture his relation to God.

Cultivating a Public Morality

Yet the other side of this realm of privacy—and the final aspect of the Founders' statecraft to be considered here—was the emphatic recognition of a public morality, based on the natural-rights and natural-law doctrines of the Declaration of Independence. This morality consisted of the commonsense teachings of reason and revealed religion alike, the meeting ground indicated by the very phrase "the laws of nature and of nature's God." American unity rested above all on the cultivation of this public morality, which necessarily extended into many areas of private life, too. The condemnation of slavery as contrary to natural law, for example, had implications not only for state and federal governments but also for households, churches, and civil associations. Toward the establishment of such a public and private consensus on morality the Founders devoted all their best efforts. Two in particular deserve mention here.

In the first place, the Constitution was itself designed to create what Harvey C. Mansfield, Jr., has called a "constitutional space" between the American people and their fundamental law. The Founders made the amendment process arduous enough to discourage all but the most persistent efforts to change constitutional writ. Moreover, the Constitution's structure prevented the people from directly administering the government, though in return it gave them regular occasions to evaluate the conduct of the officials elected to administer it. This arrangement encouraged Americans to think of the Constitution as authoritative law and to hold themselves and their representatives to its standard. As a consequence, a politics of public opinion, loyal to the Constitution and to the ends of limited government, could develop, and a political party system could be devised to guard the Constitution against abuses.

Second, the Founders undertook a far-sighted effort to cement the Union and to prepare future generations of Americans for republican citizenship through an unprecedented campaign for public education. Beginning in the 1780s, primarily at the state level, the Founders (including some Anti-Federalists) launched efforts to establish public primary and secondary schools. Public education had long existed in

Connecticut, Massachusetts, and the other New England states, but now it began gradually to spread southward and westward. Thomas Jefferson drew up his plan for public education in Virginia in this decade, and Benjamin Franklin, Benjamin Rush, and others were working along similar lines in Pennsylvania. The federal government assisted the states in their educational undertakings: the Northwest Ordinance, passed first under the Articles of Confederation and then re-passed by the first Congress under the Constitution, called for setting aside one-sixteenth of each township formed in the Northwest Territory in order to finance public schools for that township.

By the early part of the nineteenth century, the public-schools movement had spread to all thirteen original states and to many of the new states formed out of the Northwest Territory. The principle of the Northwest Ordinance was subsequently applied to the admission of every other territory to the Union. Indeed, beginning with the admission of California in 1850, the proportion of each township reserved for public education was increased to two-sixteenths, and later was raised even higher.

One of the chief goals of these new common schools was, in Benjamin Rush's words, "to conform the principles, morals, and manners of our citizens to our republican forms of government." This educational project, he declared, was the *real* American Revolution, as distinguished from what he called "the late American war," which was just that, a war for independence. The real revolution—the forming of the new people's habits, character, and principles—was achieved principally through the educational efforts of the Founders and succeeding generations. One might say that these common schools, the most novel and in some ways the most distinctively American of such efforts, functioned as the American equivalent of common meals in Sparta, or common property in other ancient cities, in powerfully unifying the citizen body through the inculcation of common habits and precepts.

Efforts to unify the American people did not end with the Founding, of course, and many other factors came into play, from the geography of the North American frontier itself, which was such an important part of Frederick Jackson Turner's interpretation of the American character, to the role of commerce, to the effects of war. Above all, in facing contemporary divisions within the American public, we might ponder the fact of the great Civil War, fought to vindicate the Founding Fathers' ideas of liberty and union. This war, perhaps more than any other event in our history, goes to the heart of the question of what it is to be an American. For this was the war fought over the very definition of Americanism.

9

The Twofold Meaning of "Unum"

Harvey C. Mansfield

The challenge of multiculturalism to the oneness of American culture is in a sense nothing new, thus in a sense not even a challenge. The motto on the Great Seal of the United States—and what could be more official than that?—is "from many, one" *(e pluribus unum)*. The design of the Great Seal was adopted in 1782, before the Constitution, by the Continental Congress under the Articles of Confederation. It seems to imply that oneness or union in America comes from its contrary, manyness or diversity. The oneness is, therefore, not *imposed on* the many — it has arisen *out of* the many.

Multiculturalism avers that the oneness of our culture has in fact been imposed on us; the *unum* does not come *e pluribus*. Perhaps it implies, further, that oneness always has to be imposed. The oneness in question is culture, and the imposition is made by politics. The multiculturalists say that the dominant culture reflects the dominant political power, that of white males. White males use a traditional patriarchal, racial, and bourgeois culture to justify and secure their rule over the rest of society. But their culture is not the only one available. The multiculturalists point to many cultures that have grown up "naturally," without the advantage of political dominance,

---

Harvey C. Mansfield is the William R. Kanan, Jr., Professor of Government at Harvard University. He is the author of *America's Constitutional Soul* (Johns Hopkins, 1995).

to nurture and express the values of the oppressed. Thus they accept the view that culture is broader than politics, and they add that politics has the effect of narrowing culture. Political dominance makes culture exclusive, which for the past few centuries has meant Eurocentric.

One might object that all culture is exclusive; all of it is "centric" in some way, such as Afrocentric. To this the multiculturalists would probably agree, but they would reply that Eurocentric culture is more exclusive than other cultures. European culture regards itself as civilized and progressive by contrast to other cultures, which consider themselves to be rooted in tradition. The basis of the European claim is modern science especially, but also the whole tradition of rationality and philosophy beginning with the Greeks from which modern science derives. It is superiority in science that gives the West the power to judge other cultures, and that allows it to feel so superior to them. Its exclusiveness expresses itself paradoxically in a professed openness to other cultures, in a so-called scientific objectivity that claims to study others without passing judgment. But of course "scientific objectivity," whatever it says, cannot help giving preference to the culture that has science, since scientific objectivity cannot survive without valuing, or "valorizing," itself. The result of the West's pretense of openness is, then, an exclusiveness that is especially rank because it considers Western culture universal, on a plane above all the other cultures, and is therefore blind to itself.

We can see now why multiculturalism is part of the phenomenon of postmodernism. Although it is opposed to tradition, it is even more opposed to reason; indeed, it is against the tradition of reason. According to the Enlightenment (which burst into view in the eighteenth century but began earlier), the tradition of reason, culminating in the twin discoveries of modern science and the rights of man, was what mainly distinguished civilization from barbarism. Eighteenth-century philosophers were not ignorant of other nations; Montesquieu, for example, writes of the Persians, the Chinese, and the Indians. They might even speak of non-Western nations like these as civilized, if they had laws and polished manners. But until Rousseau, such philosophers had no doubt of the superiority of the rationalism of the West. Rousseau, invoking the image of the noble savage, was the first or at least the most powerful philosophical critic of Enlightenment rationalism, and he was the founder of postmodernism. His successors in the nineteenth century developed the notion of culture over against the rationalist idea of civilization. The multiculturalists today are feeble stragglers at the end of a parade led by Rousseau.

The Two Meanings of "Culture"

What is the meaning of the transformation of civilization into culture? In common parlance, "culture" has two meanings: high art, and an ethnic group with common origins or roots. These are the artistic and the anthropological senses of the word. They differ in that while not everyone is cultured in the first sense, everyone has a culture in the second sense. But they resemble each other in that both substitute history for human nature. High art, both the artistic creations and the sophisticated taste for them, is created over time. It represents not a perfecting of a benign human nature but rather an improvement over man's brutish nature. Ethnic culture is also historical, the result of gradual growth that has come to be considered natural. Whereas human nature in the Enlightenment view is something fixed, in the opposing cultural view it is growing from its roots. The "natural" becomes nonviolent growth, and seeking one's identity becomes a search for one's roots. High culture descends to ethnic roots, a single process despite the distinction between the two meanings of culture, and a historical process despite the reference to nature.

The two meanings of culture are separated by the bourgeoisie, the class of those guided by rational self-interest who represent the Enlightenment. High culture looks down on the bourgeois as a vulgarian; popular culture looks up at him as an oppressor. In the nineteenth century, the romantics sought to make contact between high culture and low in such a way as to circumvent the bourgeoisie in its embodiment of rational self-interest. Both the creative artists and the uncalculating people have "soul," in contrast to the narrowing, soul-destroying selfishness of the bourgeoisie. So the artists celebrate the popular soul.

One can see this alliance at work even as late as T. S. Eliot's *Notes Towards the Definition of Culture* (1949), which defines English culture as the particulars of English popular life: "Derby Day, Henley Regatta, Cowes, the twelfth of August, a cup final, the dog races, the pin table, the dart board, Wensleydale cheese, boiled cabbage cut into sections, beetroot in vinegar, nineteenth-century Gothic churches and the music of Elgar." Eliot is known as a "modernist," an opponent of romanticism, but this is just romanticism in a new guise. It is repeated in conservatives today, such as John O'Sullivan and Peter Brimelow, who oppose further immigration to America by ethnic groups too far diverse from those that originally populated the country. For them, and for the nineteenth-century romantics, culture is something exclusive.

From Exclusion to Inclusion

It is then quite remarkable that the multiculturalists want to produce a culture that is inclusive. The cultural outlook, heretofore on the political right, has traveled over to the left as the political consequence of culture shifts from exclusion to inclusion. The multiculturalists somehow regard themselves as progressives while refusing to believe in progress. Progress would go toward the triumph of Western rationalism, which the multiculturalists think impossible and undesirable. They embrace the notion of the decline of the West put forward by Oswald Spengler in 1918 and endorsed in less ponderous fashion by Eliot, who speaks of a "total decline in culture" in our time. But they do so without the gloom and pessimism of these men of the right. They believe that by being multicultural and inclusive, we can save our culture from decline. The very mixing that appears to the right as jumbled confusion looks like healthy diversity to the left.

To save itself from despair, the multicultural left elevates the role of politics and simultaneously lowers that of religion. For the culturalists of the right, culture reaches its height in religion, where creators and peoples meet. Since they think that culture grows on its own, "naturally," they do not want politics to interfere with it. Eliot, for example, says that culture is not an end one can aim at; hence politics cannot have the aim of improving culture. When politics makes the attempt to foster culture, at least in a democratic age, it stifles genius and cultivates mediocrity. The same people that the conservatives patronize for their culture, they condemn for their politics. An English multitude cheering at the cup final is not so pretty when gathering at the polls to vote for the Labor party.

But the multiculturalists are more hopeful and less coherent. They are, to be sure, small fry in comparison with Eliot and even Spengler. They concede that a culture must be exclusive because the exclusiveness follows from its particulars, and the particulars keep it from being dully rational and universal. Such is the *unum* of culture. It is *one* in the sense of unique, or supposedly unique; but it has no answer to the question, one *what*?

The multiculturalists believe it is possible to indulge the exclusiveness of culture without endorsing it. Others may be exclusive, but we must be inclusive. Others may be, must be, conservative, but we can transform their conservatism into liberalism merely by offering our patronage. Our patronage is available quite without the harsh criticism required of those in the past who needed to maintain the standards of civilization. Multiculturalism is non-judgmental toward other cultures—the Other—while reserving its condemnation for those in the West who hold the West to be superior.

A Fixed Human Nature?

Progress toward civilization was based on a fixed human nature that served as a standard by which to judge progress. How far have we progressed in the relief of man's estate (in Francis Bacon's phrase)? What qualities of security, comfort, liberty, and science have been procured to propel us toward this end? In this fundamentally liberal view, human nature is impossible to change but possible to manipulate so as to bring about progress. What, then, is the ground of the multiculturalist belief that Western culture can be improved through the politics of multiculturalism? How can culture, which grows on its own without political direction, suddenly be changed by deliberate policy?

The same difficulty occurs in the idea of affirmative action, which is really multiculturalism in application. According to that idea, your background or history, not your human nature, is your identity. If you were once a slave, you carry that "social construction" on your back, passing along the burden for generations so that freed men never walk —or run the race, in Lyndon Johnson's metaphor—without feeling the imaginary weight of the original shackles. You have, according to the affirmative-action idea, no spark of freedom in your nature enabling you to shrug it off. And yet at some point, after you have received affirmative-action admission, affirmative-action hiring, and affirmative-action promotion, your natural faculties take over, enabling you to continue without help from the government. It is a sudden revelation of potentiality that occurs—quite distinct from what is called "empowerment," which is an implanted power. The same transformation occurs in any person or group thought to be victim by virtue of its social background: the explanation is abruptly cast aside when a remedy is proposed.

So the political optimism of the multiculturalist is based on an illicit return to human nature. All of a sudden it appears that we have the capacity to learn from another culture, a capacity that we did not get from a culture and that cannot be distinguished from the capacity by which we judge cultures. Learning is inseparable from becoming critical, and being critical of our own culture is indistinguishable from being critical of other cultures. How can one denounce the oppression of women in America and not be critical of their mistreatment in Africa, Iran, and India?

An illicit return to human nature is necessary to prevent multiculturalism from surrendering to the conservatism of any particular culture. The illicit return constitutes the illicit *unum* of multiculturalism. Multiculturalism is not in fact multicultural, not at all. Its egalitarianism is far stronger than its relativism. It uses the relativity of culture to argue for the equality and equalization of individuals, rather than using the equality of cultures to dispute the equality of individuals. It cares little for religion, giving no attention to the appreciation of religion in the better postmodernists, such as Jean-François Lyotard or Gianni Vattimo. Nor do the multiculturalists give evidence of having read the better novelists of the Third World, who do reflect on the relation of culture to humanity. Their cosmopolitanism comes to a focus on cuisine, and they make themselves expert in various spicy foods. Their type is the bored yuppie-liberal seeking variety in life to make up for a lack of seriousness in thought, feeling, or accomplishment.

The Liberal Ideal

Since multiculturalism cannot explain or even admit its *unum,* let us return to the earlier liberal idea of civilization. Liberal civilization means progress toward an end by certain means. The end is material and scientific improvement, and the means is a free society that makes free choices partly as individuals, partly together. The free society culminates in the free politics of a liberal democracy, in which choices are made together and choices are facilitated for individuals. To qualify as *progressive* or *civilized,* however, it is doubtful that a society needs to have reached any particular stage along the way to the end. It can be civilized even if it is in the horse-and-buggy era. What matters is that the society be progressing in the proper manner. Thus the *means*—free speech, free elections, free markets—are an end in themselves, good for their own sake, and qualifying a society that respects them as civilized even though it might be backward in comparison with the attainments of civilization at its most advanced. Indeed, since the desired end, civilization, seems to recede into infinity, no society could ever be declared truly civilized in the sense of having achieved material security and intellectual comprehensiveness. Yet it is true that progress is progress toward that end. The means of liberal democracy are not neutral instruments useful for any way of life; they are means to a particular end.

So the question arises: Which is more important, the end or the means? Or, since the means, as we have seen, are also an end, the question is: Which is the *unum* of liberal civilization, the end of improvement or the end of self-government? For example, we were instructed by Presidents Carter and Reagan to ask ourselves, in choosing a president: Are we better off now than we were four years ago? That question implies that the purpose of elections is to check on progress toward that end. But is not the act of electing, almost regardless of the choice made, the practice of the end? Are we not made better off, or better, by the exercise of self-government than by the attainment of prosperity?

I conclude that the *unum* of liberal civilization is twofold. It is to be found in the connection and the tension between the progressive end and the progressive means. To explain the situation, it is not enough to go back to the original liberal thinkers; we must return all the way to Aristotle, who (in the third book of his *Politics*) asks what it is that makes a city or a society the same, what gives it its oneness. The answer is not, he says, its culture (as we would say)—not its people, nation, or race. What chiefly defines a society is its form of government, a *form* that becomes its *end*. Having a democratic *form of government* produces, over time if not right away, a democratic *way of life*, a living democracy. The end of democracy as a form of government is democracy itself, not something external to democracy, such as being better off. The democratic assumption is that one is better off in a democracy. Thus the *end* is the *form*. The twofold *unum* of liberalism is united in the Aristotelian regime or constitution *(politeia)* that refers to both form of government and way of life.

The Rights of Man

The original thinkers of the Enlightenment, who lived a century or more before it, saw trouble in the Aristotelian union of form and end. Their view of Western political history, sharpened by experience of the religious wars in the sixteenth and seventeenth centuries, showed them that the Western way of life can become captive to what we might call either the Christian Right—the Catholic and Anglican churches—or the Christian Left—Puritans, Congregationalists, and other more democratic movements. Their solution was to frame a new political science that would not allow the government to define a society's way of life.

The new construction was a philosophy of the rights of man, and it was designed to limit government by splitting the Aristotelian notion of regime then regnant. A right of the individual leaves the exercise of the right to the individual. For instance, the right of free speech or consent does not prescribe—on the contrary, it purposely leaves open —what the individual will say or how he will vote. Government gets the function of protecting formal rights—formal because their content is not specified—and individuals in society exercise the rights as they please, supplying the content or the way of life. They live, of course, within the limits of law; the law now has the purpose not of telling people how to live but of facilitating their right to live in freedom.

Thus in John Locke's political science, as opposed to Aristotle's, the form of government and the end of society are separated, as required for liberal progress. The constitutional regime can be justified on its own as the exercise of self-government, but it will also be judged from the outside by the people as a means to their self-preservation. Their right to judge their constitution amounts to an extra-constitutional right of revolution against it, something impossible in the pre-liberal dispensation.

The Impartial Republic

The separation of the form from the end of society makes possible the framing of a single form of government viable for all free societies, which might be called the impartial republic. In Aristotle and in his tradition, several forms of government are possible and legitimate, and there is no single form suitable for all situations. Aristotle believed that a distinction between the few and the many can be found in every political situation, and that politics is characteristically an argument and a conflict between them. The argument is unending because each party can reasonably appeal to those things in human nature that make us equal or to those that make us unequal. Democracy and oligarchy are both partly right and partly wrong—therefore *partisan*. A regime might be conceived that mixes the virtues of both, but it is very difficult to accomplish and hence unlikely. In practice, all regimes will be partisan.

The political science of the Enlightenment conceived the ambition of harmonizing the interests of the few and the interests of the many so as to construct an impartial republic. Essentially, the few were made to compete with one another bloodlessly (if not harmlessly) in politics through the separation of powers and in society through commerce and the market, while the many were removed as direct actors on the political scene and constituted as an electorate with powers to choose and to judge their government. The electorate would judge politics from outside politics, and being as it were uninvolved, would judge among the parties of the few without partisan bias. Such a regime, being impartial because it does justice to all tendencies in human nature, would not be subject to the instability of Aristotle's partisan regimes. If the people choose to replace their present government with a new one, this is an election, not a revolution.

One great revolution is needed to establish the impartial republic, however. It will be the last great revolution because it is irreversible; once it occurs, the impartial republic will make further revolution on this scale unnecessary. The revolution will found *the* republic in order to give liberal civilization its lasting form and to set liberal society surely, if not always steadily, on the way of progress. Actually, of course, there were several attempts at the one great revolution—the British, American, French, Russian, and Chinese—all of which were intended not merely for the peoples of those countries.

The American "Unum"

America, then, was and is yet part of the great attempt of the Enlightenment to rationalize politics by constituting one impartial republic. That republic is the *unum* in our motto, identifying an experiment in political union that is being carried on by one people on behalf of mankind. Although it will not be imposed elsewhere, it is applicable elsewhere, at least under favorable circumstances. It is not confined to one culture, because it was conceived by a political science using an analysis of human nature and seeking a new formulation not dependent on previous practice or past culture. Although the motto originated under the Articles of Confederation, in which the *plures* were several states, it applied better to the Constitution. There a complicated structure assures a more lasting union by building on the *plures,* understood as both states and individuals. Thus the *unum* not only comes *e pluribus* but also reacts upon the *plures* from which it was composed. The American people living under the Constitution is not the same people that made the Constitution; it has been reordered and improved. Its way of life or culture has been changed *ex uno plures.* Or, better, the American people, formerly the many, has become a multitude, *one* multitude, by virtue of its Constitution. The Greek philosophers, occupied with the famous question of the one and the many, pondered how it was that *many* things, say 260 million of them, could also be *one* thing. The American Constitution is a solution in politics.

The *unum* of America remains twofold and ambivalent in accordance with its original nature and ruling principle. It both affirms and denies that Americans have a common way of life. Although what makes us one people is our form of government, that form of government does not seem to impose one form of life. Yet we have a way of life, one that arises indirectly from a society of individuals possessing rights, a way of life that is consonant with our form of government though not imposed by it. The duality of government and way of life is fashioned for us by our form of government, which is said by the Declaration of Independence to be open to change whenever the people decide for it. But America is not really conceivable without its Constitution. Such a country would be a different America from the one we know, in which the only changes ever proposed, political or social, are changes made under the Constitution. When we get upset, we amend the Constitution rather than overthrow it.

Multiculturalism is disguised liberalism, sick of itself but unable to think of anything new. It is rightly called "postmodern" because it is still involved in the modernity it rejects and cannot find any replacement. Instead, it flirts with the notion of culture and the nihilism it represents. With a culture, we have the blind leading the blind in feckless change in which the only identity we have is in the past and our only sure knowledge is that we cannot return to that past. By contrast, in our impartial republic we have our Constitution as guide. We can ask whether any recommended change is consistent with its principles and with our motto.

10

Don Vito Corleone, Friendship, and the American Regime

Paul A. Rahe

The opening scene of Francis Ford Coppola's classic film *The Godfather* is justly famous, but unjustly neglected for what it tells us about the kind of political society in which we live. Connie, the daughter of Mafia Don Vito Corleone, has just been married, and a celebration is taking place in the ample backyard of her parents' Long Island home. Inside the house, her father is doing business, conferring with a series of visitors who have come to ask for his help. They know that a Sicilian can deny no one's request on the day his daughter is married. In any case, Connie's father is known to be a generous man. As Mario Puzo puts it in the book that inspired the film:

> Don Vito Corleone was a man to whom everybody came for help, and never were they disappointed. He made no empty promises, nor the craven excuse that his hands were tied by more powerful forces in the world than himself. It was not necessary that he be your friend, it was not even important that you had no means with which to repay him. Only one thing was required. That you, *you*

Paul A. Rahe is the Jay P. Walker Professor of American History at the University of Tulsa. His book *Republics Ancient and Modern: Classical Republicanism and the American Revolution* has been reprinted in a three-volume paperback edition by the University of North Carolina Press (1995).

yourself, proclaim your friendship. And then, no matter how poor or powerless the supplicant, Don Corleone would take that man's troubles to his heart. And he would let nothing stand in the way of a solution to that man's woe. His reward? Friendship, the respectful title of "Don," and sometimes the more affectionate salutation of "Godfather." And perhaps, to show respect only, never for profit, some humble gift—a gallon of homemade wine or a basket of peppered *taralles* specially baked to grace his Christmas table. It was understood, it was mere good manners, to proclaim that you were in his debt and that he had the right to call upon you at any time to redeem your debt by some small service.[1]

Among Don Corleone's visitors is an undertaker whom the Don greets with a marked lack of enthusiasm. He is at the wedding because his wife is a close friend of Don Corleone's spouse; Mrs. Corleone is, in fact, godmother to their daughter. But the two men do not share the affection that unites their wives.

The undertaker has a story to tell. "I raised my daughter in the American fashion," the man begins. "I believe in America. America has made my fortune. I gave my daughter her freedom and yet taught her never to dishonor her family." But eventually a problem presented itself. "She found a 'boy friend,' not an Italian. She went to the movies with him. She stayed out late. But he never came to meet her parents. I accepted all this without a protest, the fault is mine." The results were all too predictable:

"Two months ago he took her for a drive. He had a masculine friend with him. They made her drink whiskey and then they tried to take advantage of her. She resisted. She kept her honor. They beat her. Like an animal. When I went to the hospital she had two black eyes. Her nose was broken. Her jaw was shattered. They had to wire it together. She wept through her pain. 'Father, Father, why did they do it? Why did they do this to me?' And I wept."

"Why did I weep?" he asks. "She was the light of my life, an affectionate daughter. A beautiful girl. She trusted people and now she will never trust them again." Then, after a pause, he continues:

"I went to the police like a good American. The two boys were arrested. They were brought to trial. The evidence was overwhelming and they pleaded guilty. The judge sentenced them to three years in prison and suspended the sentence. They went free that very day. I stood in the courtroom like a fool and those bastards smiled at me. And then I said to my wife: 'We must go to Don Corleone for justice.'"

Throughout, Vito Corleone has remained silent. When he speaks, it is only to ask, "Why did you go to the police? Why didn't you come to me at the beginning of this affair?" The undertaker carefully side-steps the question. "What do you want of me?" he asks. "Tell me what you wish. But do what I beg you to do." And when the Don inquires as to what he has in mind, he whispers something in his ear, and the Don responds, "That I cannot do. You are being carried away." Then, the undertaker brings the conversation to an abrupt halt with the statement: "I will pay you anything you ask."

In a voice that Puzo compares with "cold death," the Don replies, "We have known each other many years, you and I, but until this day you never came to me for counsel or help. I can't remember the last time you invited me to your house for coffee though my wife is godmother to your only child. Let us be frank. You spurned my friendship. You feared to be in my debt." When the undertaker murmurs, "I didn't want to get into trouble," Don Corleone stops him.

The Don held up his hand. "No. Don't speak. You found America a paradise. You had a good trade, you made a good living, you thought the world a harmless place where you could take your pleasure as you willed. You never armed yourself with true friends. After all, the police guarded you, there were courts of law, you and yours could come to no harm. You did not need Don Corleone. Very well. My feelings were wounded but I am not that sort of person who thrusts his friendship on those who do not value it—on those who think me of little account." The Don paused and gave the undertaker a polite, ironic smile. "Now you come to me and ask, 'Don Corleone give me justice.' And you do not ask with respect. You do not offer me your friendship. You come into my home on the bridal day of my daughter and you ask me to do murder and you say"—here the Don's voice became a scornful mimicry—"'I will pay you anything.' No, No, I am not offended, but what have I ever done to make you treat me so disrespectfully?"

"America has been good to me," the undertaker then exclaims. "I wanted to be a good citizen. I wanted my child to be American."

This elicits ironic applause from the Don:

"Well spoken. Very fine. Then you have nothing to complain about. The judge has ruled. America has ruled. Bring your daughter flowers and a box of candy when you go visit her in the hospital. That will comfort her. Be content. After all, this is not a serious affair, the boys were young, high-spirited, and one of them is the son of a powerful politician. . . . So give me your word that you will put aside this madness. It is not American. Forgive. Forget. Life is full of misfortunes."

When the undertaker once again asks for justice, the Don responds contemptuously, "The court gave you justice." And then Vito Corleone nods as the undertaker denies the claim. "No," says the suppliant. "They gave the youths justice. They did not give me justice." And when asked what he means by justice, he replies, "An eye for an eye." But, says the Don, "you asked for more. . . . Your daughter is alive." And then the undertaker gives way: "Let them suffer as she suffers." And in despair he adds, "How much shall I pay you?"

This last interjection is more than Corleone can bear: he turns his back on the man. But the undertaker stands his ground and silently refuses to withdraw. The Don eventually turns around. "Why do you fear to give your first allegiance to me?" he asks.

"You go to the law courts and wait for months. You spend money on lawyers who know full well you are to be made a fool of. You accept judgment from a judge who sells himself like the worst whore in the streets. Years gone by, when you needed money, you went to the banks and paid ruinous interest. . . . But if you had come to me, my purse would have been yours. If you had come to me for justice those scum who ruined your daughter would be weeping bitter tears this day. If by some misfortune an honest man like yourself made enemies they would become my enemies . . . and then, believe me, they would fear you."

Finally, the undertaker concedes: "Be my friend. I accept." With his hand on the man's shoulder, Don Corleone replies, "Good . . . you shall have your justice. Some day, and that day may never come, I will call upon you to do me a service in return. Until that day, consider this justice a gift from my wife, your daughter's godmother."

Contract Versus Friendship

The moral of the story is easy to draw: one cannot be "a good American" and be "armed" with what Don Corleone calls "true friends." Puzo brings this home by naming the undertaker "Amerigo" — after the Italian who discovered America — and by giving him the surname "Bonasera," which in Italian means "Good night." By accepting Don Corleone's "gift" and agreeing to become his "friend," Amerigo Bonasera says good night to America.

Of course, none of this would matter were there not some truth in the claim intimated by Puzo and reiterated by Coppola. Can one be "a good American" and be "armed" with "true friends"? On the face of it, the answer should be yes. But we may well wonder. Clearly there is a radical difference between the republics of classical antiquity and our own, and that difference turns, in part, on the status of friendship within the public realm.[2]

No one steeped in ancient history can watch Coppola's film or read Puzo's novel without recalling the role of friendship — *amicitia* — and what we now call "patronage" in the public life of ancient Rome.[3] Amerigo Bonasera wants to confine his relationship with Vito Corleone to the contractual realm: he wants to pay up front for services rendered; he wants his freedom and autonomy, the independence required of a "good citizen"; he wants distance from the man about to act on his behalf; he has no desire to incur a moral obligation, for he knows all too well that obligations of this sort can be crippling. Keeping a distance and retaining one's independence is part of what it means to be "a good American." Bonasera would easily understand why Americans might cringe at a waiter who simultaneously presents the menu and himself by his first name — thus intimating friendship. In the modern republic, dignity in the exchange of services depends on the distance established by formalities, on the impersonality of a relationship regulated by contract.

Don Corleone insists that there is more at stake in the doing of a service. He is about to confer a favor — what the ancient Romans called a *beneficium* — and he asks for no payment in return. His services cannot be bought. When they are rendered, they are rendered solely as a "gift." Instead, he exacts reciprocity for this "gift" in a form perfectly familiar to students of anthropology.[4] In return, he expects the offices that a client owes a patron: respect, deference, undying gratitude and its outward signs. Don Corleone insists that Bonasera's "first allegiance" be to him. He asks of Bonasera what the Romans called a *deditio in fidem*—his *surrender* to Corleone's *faith, loyalty,* or *trust.* Puzo summarizes this ancient order of relations in the scene with which Coppola ends his film, the passing on of succession to Vito Corleone's youngest son, Michael. As Michael's wife sees her husband accepting "homage" from his subordinates, she is reminded "of statues in Rome, statues of those Roman emperors of antiquity, who, by divine right, held the power of life and death over their fellow men."

If we are to understand Don Corleone—and the premodern order of political life he represents—we must remember that our English word *patron* descends from *pater,* the Latin word for father. Don Corleone is very much the Roman *paterfamilias.* The Don claims paternal authority over his family and his subordinates, the true friends who entrust themselves to his care. The Don's preferred term "godfather" is, of course, a usage of the Christian Church, and the authority the Don claims is something akin to the Christian notion of "divine right."

Don Corleone insists—and his status depends on his insisting— that the relationship between himself and his subordinates is more than merely contractual. In fact, it is not contractual at all. It is moral and quasi-familial. In the classical understanding, friends are like kin —they are one's own *kind.* In Homer, the word for friends can be used to describe the members of one's own body. In the Greek and Roman worlds, one's friends, first of all, were members of one's own family, and then those outside the family whom one most loved. We still say of a man's familiars that they are like family.

The question is whether what I here call "the politics of friendship" is appropriate or acceptable to the modern pluralistic political regime. If Don Corleone embodies the Old World ethic of "true friendship" and familial politics, as I think he does, the answer is clear: this kind of friendship and politics is foreign to the New World. The American regime is grounded in what I call "the politics of distrust."

In what follows, I will examine the role of friendship in the political order of premodern society; and, with the help of Niccolò Machiavelli, Michel de Montaigne, and Sir Francis Bacon, I will look at the suspicion of friendship that underpins impartial governance in the modern republic. The comparison will make manifest some of the roots and political dangers of modern attempts—such as the program put forward by the advocates of multiculturalism—to base public policy on group membership rather than on an equality in individual rights.

Politics and the Family

No civil society possessed a more fully developed understanding of what I will call "the politics of friendship" than classical Rome. Nowhere is the tradition of patronage exemplified by Don Corleone more visible. Our most important terms for this politics of friendship derive from the Latin: patron from *patronus* and client from *cliens*. As early as the Twelve Tables (circa 450 B.C.), patronage was given public sanction at Rome. In Roman primeval law, a patron who betrayed a client was said to be *sacer* or sacred. To grasp what this means, we must consider the etymology of our word "sacrifice"—which derives from two Latin words, meaning "to make sacred." To sacrifice an animal on an altar, to roast and distribute the flesh, to burn and offer up the fat and the bones—this was to make the animal *sacred*. At Rome, the betrayal of a client was a matter of supreme seriousness. It was a political and religious infraction that rendered the perpetrator *sacer*— worthy of death. It was comparable to betraying a member of one's own family. Indeed, the client was a marginal member of what the Romans called the *familia*. The politics of friendship is the politics of family, involving one's *familiares*—those who are near and dear.

Roman legend conceived of the *familia* as the bulwark of liberty. Thus, to avenge the rape of Lucretia by Sextus, son of Tarquinius Superbus, Brutus led her father and husband in ousting the monarchy of the Tarquins and then founded the Roman Republic. Another story recounts how Verginius, in order to preserve his daughter Virginia's virtue against the lust of Appius Claudius (one of the ten extraordinary ruling magistrates or decemvirs), took his daughter's life and then employed this public act to stir up the plebeian secession that restored political freedom to Rome.[5]

There is a sense in which the republic—the public thing or *res publica*—comes into existence for the sake of the household—the private thing or *res privata*. The public order does not just fulfill needs that the private order cannot meet, but it preserves and defends the chastity essential to the integrity of the private order. To say that the family takes precedence over the political community would be to exaggerate. After all, when Brutus caught his sons plotting to over-throw the republic, he saw to their execution.[6] And if the story of Lucretia teaches anything, it is that the *res privata* depends for its very survival on the *res publica:* Brutus cannot prefer his sons to Rome without at the same time undermining the foundations of his rela-tionship with them.

What is the *res privata,* or household? As its name suggests, it is a realm of privation or deprivation because it cannot satisfy all needs, such as friendship and virtue (which in Aristotle are closely linked), the practice of virtue, and the happy life. Aristotle makes clear in the *Politics* that the political community may come to have a public pur-pose that transcends the private reasons for which it came into exis-tence in the first place.[7] But as Aristotle's critique of the community of wives and property in Plato's *Republic* reminds us, the *res publica* depends for its continued existence on the integrity of the *res privata:* it cannot be cut loose from its origins; and, as a purposive entity, it remains suspended forever between the mundane needs that called it into existence and the noble activities that its existence makes possible.[8] The *res publica* is neither fish nor fowl.

The Politics of Friendship

Friendship is everywhere in the ethical and political writings of the ancients. Homer makes it a central theme in *The Iliad.* Sophocles explores it in depth. Plato, Aristotle, and Cicero give it careful con-sideration. No one seems to doubt that understanding the nature of friendship is vital to understanding what it means to be a good citizen, to be a good man, and to live the good life.

In Greece, one frequently encounters "the politics of friendship." In Plato's *Republic,* when Socrates asks Polemarchus what justice is, he has a ready answer: justice is helping one's friends and harming one's enemies.[9] This was the common sense of the matter—strange as it may seem to us—and Sophocles devotes a great deal of attention in his surviving tragedies to exploring its implications.[10] Aristotle distinguished between friendship grounded in pleasure, friendship grounded in utility, and friendship grounded in virtue, while tacitly conceding that most friendships are at least in some measure grounded in all three. Patron-client relations may not have played the prominent role in Greek politics that they did in Roman life, but there is no doubt that friendship was central to Greek popular ethics. Perhaps it would be best to say that in Greece the politics of friendship took another—perhaps, *the* other—form.

Here again foundation myths are revealing. The Athenian analogue to the legends of Lucretia and Virginia is the story of the two lovers, Harmodius and Aristogeiton. Despite the best efforts of Herodotus, Thucydides, and Aristotle to persuade the Athenians otherwise, the man in the street persisted in tracing the origins of Athenian liberty to these two homosexual lovers who were putatively responsible for expelling the Peisistratid tyrants from Athens.[11] The Athenians set up statues of these men in the *agora* or public square. In the cities of ancient Greece, the role allotted Lucretia and Virginia at Rome seems ordinarily to have been assigned to adolescent boys. In verses that would be sung at symposia for generations, the poets of Hellas celebrated the feats of lovers—subjected to torture or killed in the end—who fought to protect their young favorites from the lust of tyrants. Antileon was so remembered in south Italy; in Agrigentum, Melannipus and his young beloved, Chariton, were honored for their plot against the tyrant Phalaris and for their steadfast refusal, when caught, to divulge the names of their fellow conspirators.[12] By the same token, tyranny was thought a direct assault on the skein of personal relations that made of the city a men's club.[13] Political participation was supposed to foster friendship, while the stereotypical tyrant seemed as incapable of having friends himself as he was of allowing others that much-treasured possession.[14] To be a *good* Spartan, a *good* Theban, a *good* Athenian, a *good* Roman was to be "armed" with "true friends."

The Politics of Distrust

In modern times, the subject of friendship is hardly ever discussed. Apart from Montaigne and Bacon, no thinkers of the first rank ever bother to address the question.[15] And neither of these two essayists can be listed among the advocates of friendship in politics. Montaigne treats true friendship as a phenomenon so rare that in ordinary life it cannot be relied on, while Bacon intimates that is it chimerical.

Montaigne's discussion of friendship begins as a lament concerning its virtual absence in the world. True friendship is "so perfect and entire that few such can even be read about, and no trace at all of it can be found among men today." It is so rare, he observes, that "Fortune can achieve it once in three centuries."

What of family? The family—far from forming a natural society of friends and allies—is in Montaigne's view an obstacle to perfect friendship. Between fathers and their children, murder is more likely than perfect friendship. Perfect friendship cannot exist between parent and child

> because of their excessive inequality; it might also interfere with their natural obligations: for all the secret thoughts of fathers cannot be shared with their children for fear of begetting an unbecoming intimacy.

Nor, he adds, can children presume to counsel their fathers. Indeed,

> there have been peoples where it was the custom for children to kill their fathers, and others for fathers to kill their children to avoid the impediment which each can constitute for the other: one depends naturally on the downfall of the other.

Similar obstacles bar true friendship between brothers. As Montaigne puts it, "sharing out property or dividing it up, with the wealth of one becoming the poverty of the other, can wondrously melt and weaken the solder binding brothers together." In any case, the relationship of brothers—and, for that matter, all relationships of consanguinity—is dictated by convention and lacks the crucial element: "willing freedom."

What of marriage? Montaigne grants that "willing freedom" no doubt plays a role in marriage, but marital friendship suffers from other burdens:

> Apart from being a bargain where only the entrance is free (its duration being fettered and constrained, depending on things outside our will), it is a bargain struck for other purposes; within it you soon have to unsnarl hundreds of extraneous tangled ends, which are enough to break the thread of a living passion and to trouble its course.

According to Montaigne, the effectual truth of friendship is mutual utility. Even outside the family, where "willing freedom" can be presumed, friendship in virtually all cases turns out to be defective. Except with regard to "the unique, highest friendship," which "loosens all other bonds" and "is moreover the rarest thing to find the world," Montaigne argues that "you must proceed with wisdom and caution, keeping the reins in your hand: the bond is not so well tied that there is no reason to doubt it." He even cites with approval the adage: "Love a friend . . . as though some day you must hate him: hate him, as though you must love him."

With rare and negligible exceptions, Montaigne believes that alliances "only get hold of us by one end." In these circumstances,

> we need simply to provide against such flaws as specifically affect that end. It cannot matter to me what the religion of my doctor or my lawyer is: that consideration has nothing in common with the friendly services which they owe to me. And in such commerce as arises at home with my servants I act the same way: I make few inquiries about the chastity of my footman: I want to know if he is hard-working: I am less concerned by a mule-driver who gambles than by one who is an idiot, or by a cook who swears than by one who is incompetent. It is not my concern to tell the world how to behave (plenty of others do that) but how I behave in it. . . . For the intimate companionship of my table I choose the agreeable not the wise; in my bed, beauty comes before virtue; in my social conversation, ability—even without integrity. And so on.[16]

By the time Montaigne concludes this discussion, his lament concerning the virtual absence of true friendship in the world has become an argument hinting that religious toleration and civility can best be sustained in a society in which utility—not moral judgment—dictates the pattern of human relationships. That an experienced soldier in the midst of a religious civil war entertained such a proposition should not escape our attention. Montaigne's contemporaries and successors through a number of generations were acutely aware of the historical context within which he penned this passage. Figures such as Montesquieu, Voltaire, and Adam Smith took care to articulate in full the case for commercial society that Montaigne obliquely pointed out.[17]

Like Montaigne, Francis Bacon set out to debunk the classical understanding of friendship. Bacon modelled his essays on those of Montaigne, and he devoted two chapters to friendship. In the first, Bacon contests Aristotle's suggestion that someone who "delighted in solitude" might be a god rather than a wild beast. In denying to man the possibility of achieving a godlike capacity for serene and solitary contemplation, Bacon denies to man the capacity for *logos*—for speech, for reason, for reflection—that he must possess, at least in some measure, if he is to be capable of a friendship transcending utility and the desperate craving men feel for a "discharge of the fulness and swellings of the heart." Bacon emphasizes throughout the degree to which "those that want friends to open themselves unto are cannibals of their own hearts." Thus, when Bacon writes that "a natural and secret hatred and aversion towards society in any man, hath somewhat of the savage beast," and when he contends that "it is a mere and miserable solitude to want true friends," he depicts what he takes to be man's natural state.

Bacon ends his second essay on friendship with a blunt admission that echoes Montaigne:

> There is little friendship in the world, and least of all between equals, which was wont to be magnified. That that is, is between superior and inferior, whose fortunes may comprehend the one the other.

The examples Bacon presents in the first essay—the friendships between Sulla and Pompey, Caesar and Brutus, Augustus and Agrippa, Tiberius and Sejanus, and Septimius Severus and Plautianus—illustrate the conclusion of his second essay. Among other things, these examples suggest that he recognized perfectly well what Aristotle had in mind when he suggested that inequality is an obstacle to friendship and noted the relative friendlessness of kings. Each friendship cited involves a relationship between "superior and inferior, whose fortunes" do, in fact, "comprehend the one the other"—at least for a time. Each friendship is, naturally enough, fraught with tension; all but that of Augustus with Agrippa ends in betrayal.

Bacon's approach is oblique. Like Montaigne, he accepts provisionally the inherited presumptions of his readers and then by indirection subverts those prejudices. His rhetoric is aimed at dispelling illusion and bringing home to his readers "what solitude is, and how far it extendeth. For a crowd is not company; and faces are but a gallery of pictures; and talk but a tinkling cymbal, where there is no love."[18]

The Perils of Friendship

Why the project to debunk the classical understanding of friend-ship? To understand, we must ponder the implications of Bacon's allusion to the fifteenth chapter of *The Prince*, in his acknowledgment that he is "much beholden to Machiavelli and others, that write what men do, and not what they ought to do."[19] In that famous chapter of *The Prince*, in which he presented his shocking suggestion that virtue and vice should be distinguished solely with an eye to "security and well-being," Machiavelli attacks the moral imagination. He is writing "a thing useful for one who understands it," and so it is "more profitable" for him "to go behind to the effectual truth of the matter rather than to that matter as represented in the imagination."

Machiavelli thus dismisses as worthless the efforts of the "many" —his classical and Christian predecessors—who "have imagined republics and principalities which have never been seen or known to exist in truth." He will expose the dichotomy of results between how men really live and how they have been taught they "ought to live": "he who abandons that which is done in favor of that which ought to be done learns rather his ruin than his preservation." The prince who would survive or "maintain himself" must "learn how not to be good," as that term is conventionally understood, and "use this knowledge or not as necessity demands." Such are "the modes and government" appropriate for dealing "with subjects or with friends."[20]

The foundation of Machiavelli's teaching on politics and friendship —that one treat subjects and friends as enemies—is his Heraclitean claim that "all the things of men are in motion and cannot remain fixed: they must either rise or fall; and necessity leads you to things to which reason does not lead you."

By this he means something akin to what Thomas Hobbes and David Hume had in mind when they asserted that reason is the slave of the passions. As Machiavelli put it: "the human appetites are insa-tiable"; "by nature" human beings "desire everything" while "by fortune they are allowed to secure little"; and since "nature has created men in such a fashion" that they are "able to desire everything" but not "to secure everything," their "desire is always greater than the power of acquisition." As a consequence of this doctrine, the Floren-tine rejected Aristotle's doctrine of the mean, arguing that the pursuit of moderation is a species of folly; in a world in constant flux, there simply is not and cannot be "a middle road."[21]

His position, which he slyly attributed to "all who reason concerning civic life," is that anyone intent on setting up a republic and ordaining its laws must "presuppose that all men are wicked and that they will make use of the malignity of their spirit whenever they are free and have occasion to do so."[22] Machiavelli thus advises rulers in ordinary circumstances to use against subjects and friends the very weapons that Cicero thinks a political community should employ only against enemies—and at that, only in time of war.[23] On friendship, in the conduct of public life, one simply cannot rely.

Bacon summarized the moral consequences of Machiavelli's understanding of the passions quite elegantly when he ascribed to his Florentine mentor two great principles. First,

> that virtue itself a man should not trouble himself to attain, but only the appearance thereof to the world, because the credit and reputation of virtue is a help, but the use of it is an impediment.

And second,

> that a politic man should have for the basis of his policy the assumption that men cannot fitly or safely be wrought upon otherwise than by fear; and should therefore endeavour to have every man, as far as he can contrive it, dependent and surrounded by straits and perils.[24]

In short, in rejecting the politics of friendship, Machiavelli preached the politics of distrust. In *The Prince,* as one would expect, when he speaks of friends, he nearly always has clients, dependents, and partisans in mind.[25] It is telling that he follows the same practice in his *Discourses on Livy.*[26] Never does he explore or even acknowledge the possibility that a friendship might exist between equals or be grounded in a common dedication to human excellence rather than in utility narrowly understood. In tacitly repudiating that possibility, he rejects the common-sense understanding of friendship articulated and probed in the writings of Homer, Sophocles, Xenophon, Plato, Aristotle, Cicero, and their medieval successors. Machiavelli scoffed at friendship, except the species of association that is derivative from calculations of self-interest.

A Productive Disunion

In the political sphere, this debunking of friendship had two implications. To begin with, it led Machiavelli to reject as a chimera the classical and medieval quest for concord and to embrace, in its place, a politics of conflict. Those who are inclined to denounce political turmoil and to argue for social and political harmony, he wrote, "have not considered how it is that in every republic there are two diverse humors—that of the people [*popolo*] and that of the great ones [*grandi*] —and that all the laws that are made in favor of liberty are born from this disunion." He insisted that "good examples arise from good education, good education from good laws, and good laws from the tumults which many so inconsiderately condemn."

The appetites of the two classes, the people and the great ones, vary. The people "have less of an appetite for usurpation" than the *grandi*. "The nobles" are motivated by "a grand desire for domination," and the people act "solely from a desire not to be dominated." The former "desire to acquire" while the latter "fear to lose what they have acquired." "The demands of a free people are seldom pernicious and rarely endanger their liberty," Machiavelli argues. "They arise from oppression or from the suspicions they entertain that they are about to be oppressed; and when these opinions are false, there is a remedy in the public assemblies where a good man can stand up and, in speaking, demonstrate to the people that they are in error." He therefore recommended that "every city . . . have modes by which people can vent their ambition."[27]

Machiavelli's debunking of friendship caused him to deny respectability to the role hitherto played by friendship in public life. In an important and as yet insufficiently appreciated passage in his *Florentine Histories,* he distinguishes between salutary and unhealthy political conflict, linking the latter with the acquisition of "reputation" by "private modes," which, we know, were prevalent in Rome. Public reputation, he writes,

> is acquired by conquering in battle, acquiring a district, conducting a legation with care and with prudence, counselling the republic wisely and to good effect. Through private modes, it is acquired by doing favors for this or that other citizen, defending him from the magistrates, aiding him with money, securing for him undeserved

honors, and by gratifying the plebs with public games and gifts. From this mode of proceeding are born sects and partisans, and the reputation thus earned wreaks harm as much as reputation helps when it is not mixed up with sects, because that reputation is founded on a common and not on a private good.[28]

Much could be said concerning this passage. What I want to stress is Machiavelli's misrepresentation of Rome. For in denouncing "the private modes" by which citizens acquire reputation, Machiavelli is silently condemning as "corruption" much that is visible in the actual conduct of political affairs in republican Rome. In so doing, he severs the time-honored link between civic virtue and friendship—a link as visible in Plato and Aristotle as it is in Cicero. And he prepares the way for the extraordinary emphasis that the moderns place on impersonal governance and on political, moral, economic, and intellectual independence.[29] The Rome depicted in his *Discourses on Livy* is neither classical nor Christian—and in it there is no place for Ciceronian *amicitia*.

The Modern Res Publica

One might ponder, in light of the question of friendship, the character of what is excluded from the world of public concern by modern social-contract theory. The absence of the theme of friendship, indeed the debunking and banishment of friendship as a mode of politics from the modern political order, including that of the American regime, is more than merely striking.

Friendship is found nowhere in that critic of early modernity, that apparent admirer of antiquity, that advocate of romantic love, Jean Jacques Rousseau. What is the role of friendship in the thinking of the greatest of the modern moralists, Immanuel Kant? What is the notion of virtue implicit in the peculiar selection of classical subjects made by the painter David?

One might also consider the link between Machiavelli's critique of the classical politics of friendship and John Adams's emphatic claim that

there must be a positive Passion for the public good, the public Interest, Honour, Power, and Glory, established in the Minds of the People, or there can be no Republican Government, nor any real Liberty. And this public Passion must be Superior to all private Passions. Men must be ready, they must pride themselves, and be happy to sacrifice their private Pleasures, Passions, and Interests, nay their private Friendships and dearest Connections, when they Stand in Competition with the Rights of society.[30]

One might similarly explore what Benjamin Rush had in mind when he expresed the hope that the proliferation of colleges and schools throughout America would make it "possible to convert" his countrymen "into republican machines" and then added:

Our country includes family, friends and property, and should be preferred to them all. Let our pupil be taught that he does not belong to himself, but that he is public property. Let him be taught to love his family, but let him be taught, at the same time, that he must forsake, and even forget them, when the welfare of the country requires it.[31]

In this light, one might also examine Thomas Jefferson's attribution of virtue to agriculturalists, and of vice and "corruption" to those dependent on "the casualties and caprice of customers."[32] In the same fashion, we should consider the welcome that this model American extended at the time of Shays's Rebellion to what he called, in language pioneered by Machiavelli, "the tumults in America."[33] And then we can ponder the counterintuitive contention, advanced in *Federalist* No. 10 by James Madison, that the division of a society into a multiplicity of rival religious sects and contending special interests may serve the cause of promoting a more perfect union characterized by domestic tranquillity.

The Ultimate American Virtue

What does the banishment of the politics of friendship tell us about the American regime? I will restrict myself to a series of assertions.

First, I suggest that the ultimate American virtue is independence —of mind, of means, of temperament; that we can stand together only in so far as we can stand apart. Consider in this connection the last public communication of the quintessential American democrat Thomas Jefferson, in a letter he drafted to decline an invitation to festivities for the fiftieth anniversary of America's Declaration of Independence:

May it be to the world, what I believe it will be, (to some parts sooner, to others later, but finally to all,) the signal of arousing men to burst the chains under which monkish ignorance and superstition had persuaded them to bind themselves, and to assume the blessing and security of self-government. That form which we have substituted, restores the free right to the unbounded exercise of reason and freedom of opinion. All eyes are opened, or opening, to the rights of man. The general spread of the light of science has already laid open to every view the palpable truth, that the mass of mankind has not been born with saddles on their backs, nor a favored few booted and spurred, ready to ride them legitimately, by the grace of God.[34]

Not only does Jefferson reject tutelage: he also makes it clear that republican "self-government" is inseparable from the intellectual liberation brought about by modern science.

Second, the practice of this virtue of independence requires of Americans the species of public prickliness that I have labeled the politics of distrust. This explains why Thomas Jefferson could look favorably on "tumults" such as Shays's Rebellion and remark to Abigail Adams that "the spirit of resistance to government is so valuable on certain occasions that I wish it to be always kept alive."

While in Europe, Jefferson had become persuaded by the force of Machiavelli's distinction between the *grandi* and the *popolo*. There, he observed, "under pretence of governing they have divided their nations into two classes, wolves and sheep." It was his fear that the same could only too easily happen in the infant republic in America. Once the people "become inattentive to the public affairs," he warned a friend, "you and I, and Congress, and Assemblies, judges and governors shall all become wolves. It seems to be the law of our general nature, in spite of individual exceptions; and experience declares that man is the only animal which devours his own kind."[35]

The American regime was not founded on a *deditio in fidem*: when we choose our rulers, we do not surrender ourselves and make to them a promise of faith, loyalty, and trust. With Jefferson, we are inclined to the view that "confidence is everywhere the parent of despotism," that "free government is founded in jealousy, and not in confidence," and that "it is jealousy and not confidence which prescribes limited constitutions, to bind down those whom we are obliged to trust with power."[36]

Third, the spirit of modern American republicanism requires impartial governance. It precludes the notion, taught by Don Corleone to Amerigo Bonasera, that there is a genuine distinction between his "justice" and the "justice" due his daughter's assailants. It rules out the legitimacy of using government to help one's friends and harm one's enemies. And it thereby condemns as "corruption" a practice which is perfectly normal in all premodern societies and which is all too common in polities that have not yet fully completed the transition to modernity.

Fourth, I believe that impartial governance is virtually impossible in the absence of a pluralism of the sort suggested by Montaigne's discussion of "alliances" that "only get hold of us by one end." What I have in mind is that our unity as a people depends upon an acceptance of our diversity: that it rests on an abstraction of citizenship from religion, ethnicity, gender, and—to some degree—even moral ideals. In our public and, to a large degree, even in our professional lives, except with regard to questions of utility such as competence and reliability, we quite rightly pay little attention to whether we are doing business with Catholics, Protestants, Unitarians, Muslims, Jews, agnostics, or atheists; with individuals of European, African, Asian, Native American, or mixed origin; with men or women; with adulterers, homosexuals, transvestites, monogamous heterosexuals, or the strictly celibate; with drunkards, gluttons, drug abusers, cigar smokers, or the abstemious.

True Civic Virtue

Above all, our understanding of civic virtue is inconsistent with the species of multiculturalism embraced by Don Corleone and advocated by an increasing number of disaffected intellectuals hostile to, or alienated from, our liberal democratic society—a phenomenon that is characterized by one left-liberal feminist critic of multiculturalism as the "construction of 'difference' as a form of group homogeneity that brooks no disagreement or distinction *within* and can maintain itself only as a redoubt *against* threatening 'enemies' from without." "The language of opposition," she laments,

> now appears as a cascading series of manifestos that tell us we cannot live together; we cannot work together; we are not in this

together; we are not Americans who have something in common, but racial, ethnic, gender, or sexually identified clans who demand to be "recognized" only or exclusively as "different." Think about how odd this is on the face of it: I require that *you* recognize that *we* have nothing in common with one another.[37]

One need not be so pessimistic: the fact that intellectual and cultural apartheid is inconsistent with the spirit of American republicanism explains why what began in America as a radical, *postmodern* attack on the spirit of the melting pot has a tendency, when put into practice, to be transmuted into a renewed commitment to our *modern* ethic of pluralism.

Let me add that the all-pervasive power exercised by the spirit of our peculiar form of republicanism explains as well why the Old World ethic of "true friendship" represented by Don Corleone tends gradually to wither and die when imported into the New World. Think about the initial intentions of Amerigo Bonasera: in attempting to hire Don Corleone to kill the boys who disfigured his daughter, is he not trying to form one of those "alliances" that, as Montaigne puts it, "only get hold of us by one end"?

That we fall short of meeting the standards I have outlined—that dependency is a problem in our society; that over the last half century we have been insufficiently jealous and have tended to place too much confidence in government; that favoritism is by no means unknown; that religious, ethnic, sexual, and moral convictions sometimes dictate discriminatory public and professional behavior—all of this goes without saying.

There was a time, not so long ago, in American society, when we had as an establishment what the Romans called *ordines* or "orders": we distinguished in law between castes comparable to the patricians and plebeians of early republican Rome. Members of one legally defined group were accorded special advantages as such, while members of another legally defined group were subjected to special disadvantages as such. It was illegal in many states for those of African descent to marry those of European descent. There are elements—relics, I would say—of a similar partiality evident in our public policy today; affirmative action comes to mind. Our failures need to be acknowledged: the politics of friendship and of religious, ethnic, sexual, and moral favoritism come easily—I would even say, naturally—to us. To discover the roots of this, one need only reflect on the behavior of parents at Little League games.

But our failures are largely beside the point. Human frailty is a given, and La Rochefoucauld was certainly right when he argued that "hypocrisy is a homage that vice pays to virtue." Given the weakness of human nature and our remarkable capacity for self-delusion, the absence of hypocrisy is more likely to mean the absence of virtue than a liberation from vice. In any case, when pushed to the limits, the ethics of impartiality and distrust seem cold and inhuman. What matters is that we give these standards lip service, that we deny public respectability to their breach, and that to a degree we feel awkward and ashamed when we connive in their subversion. We must honor and admire citizens who fight to establish and maintain their independence, who strive to be impartial, and who, in their public and professional dealings with others, give meaning to the American adage "live and let live."

In American public life, the politics of distrust is still very much alive. That much should be obvious from the widespread anti-incumbent mood in politics. But it is hardly peculiar to this moment. Among other things, its prevalence helps explain what Harry Truman had in mind when he said some years ago that, if you live in the District of Columbia and really want a friend, you should save up your money and buy a dog. Can anyone doubt that Don Corleone would have understood what he had in mind?

11

The Post-Constitutional Era

Gerard V. Bradley

In 1878 William Gladstone delivered what historian Michael Kammen has called the most commonly quoted observation about the United States Constitution, *ever*, by anyone. Gladstone, who was then a member of Parliament, wrote that as the British Constitution is "the most subtle organism which had proceeded from the womb and the long gestation of progressive history, so the American Constitution is, so far as I can see, the most wonderful work ever struck off at a given time by the brain and purpose of man." The one was grown, Gladstone added, the other was made.[1]

Never mind that Gladstone may have paraphrased without attribution. Kammen noted an uncanny resemblance to the remark, forty-five years earlier, of Supreme Court Justice William Johnson: the Constitution was "the most wonderful instrument ever drawn by the hand of man."[2] At least neither Gladstone nor Johnson claimed that the Constitution was found in a burning bush, or that it was delivered from heaven on a spirit-propelled juristic meteor.

The interesting point is that by so contrasting the deep cultural roots of the British Constitution with a shining self-consciously

---

Gerard V. Bradley is a professor of law at the University of Notre Dame Law School. He is the author of, among other works, *Church-State Relationships in America* (Greenwood Press, 1987) and is currently at work on a book on constitutional theory.

nationalist moment in 1787, Gladstone (and the many who have quoted or echoed his view) raises the *unum* question in an acute way: Is America an idea, or a people? Or neither? Were Americans constituted *as* Americans by the Constitution? In the beginning, there was the law, and it was good, and it was the *unum*?

Ardent nationalists in the young republic (like Webster and Story) held that an American nation preceded and brought forth the Constitution. But even they could not place the date of birth before 1774, with the meeting of the First Continental Congress. Their successors, including not a few historians, have found America in the further reaches of the past, but in a way reminiscent of the *New Yorker* cover depicting, beyond the Hudson, an undifferentiated and featureless someplace else. In the search for social and cultural oneness antecedent to the Constitution, New England is surrounded by a blank expanse. The American mind is the Puritan outlook. All roads worth taking lead back to the Mayflower.

Further argument for the proposition that America has always been more diverse than the Mayflower may be unnecessary. Those inclined to argue for an early American ethno-cultural unity may point to the first words of the Constitution, "We the people of the United States." But the citation, with its declaration of a unified "we," is not decisive proof of an *unum*. After all, ratification of the Constitution proceeded state by state, on a winner-take-all basis. In Article VII of the Constitution, we see clearly another view of the Union's constituency: "The Ratification of the Conventions of the nine States, shall be sufficient for the Establishment of this Constitution between the States so ratifying the same."[3] Many, perhaps most, of the Founders understood the Preamble to mean: "We, the people(s) of the (several) United States," do hereby associate for some important but limited purposes via these articles of compact.

Surely the Southern states ratified the Constitution according to the latter understanding. It is germane to note that the Confederate Constitution was very similar to the Constitution of the United States, save for greater clarity about states' rights and, of course, slavery. It was professedly the work of "the people of the Confederate States, each State acting in its sovereign and independent character." Little wonder that Jefferson Davis appealed in his inaugural to the verdict of God, and of history, to vindicate his view that Southerners were the true Americans.[4]

The question, of course, is whether the Constitution, like the terms perhaps of a Common Market agreement, basically contained that which unified the many, or whether the Constitution manifested a deeper unity of more consequence and note. The matter was finally settled at Appomattox. Even the seceding Southerners of 1861 thought the Constitution, as intended and understood by their forefathers, was quite sound. Their fundamental criticism was that the Constitution had been perverted by misinterpretation, chiefly by the Supreme Court under the sway of the nationalism of Marshall and Story. In an important sense, the matter led *to* Appomattox: secession as a legal question turned on whether the states were parties to a national compact.

Legitimacy From "The People"

I want to concentrate upon one important aspect of law and the *unum* in the 1990s: the impact—negative, or positive, or both—of the Constitution, or at least constitutional law, upon democratic self-governance based upon truths of human nature. To do so, we must first look at how the Constitution *has* functioned in our political culture, how it *has* bound and loosed the ties that distinguish the American people from others.

There is a lively debate these days among academic scholars of American political thought about natural rights and the Founding. The discussion owes much to the recovery of some texts by the Anti-Federalists—the losers in the ratification struggle. This new scholarly work reminds us just how divided the Founders were about the desirable shape and scope of the proposed national government. The current discussion tends to obscure the fact, however, that after a spirited if not bitter struggle over its ratification, the basic legitimacy of the Constitution was not thereafter questioned, even by former Anti-Federalists. That the Constitution was so widely and peaceably accepted suggests a common commitment to the authority of popular decision-making.

The Constitution, once ratified, established self-government on the basis of a representative system. It gave the inhabitants of this land (at least those with pale skin) an opportunity to become one people—an *unum*—through political deliberation and decision-making. Without anticipating it, the Founders set in place an electoral process that soon generated the trans-sectional political parties that, apart from the churches, have been the great unifying agents in our history.

In any event, our Constitution was self-consciously written in plain and ordinary terms so that the people—as well as those exercising public trust—could understand just what the limits of the latter's authority were. It was enacted by successive special state conventions of the people, not by existing state legislatures. Ratification was all but universally understood as the legal act that validated and enacted the Constitution. That is, the formidable collection of notables at Philadelphia merely proposed a plan of government. They exercised no authority to make law.

The meaning of the Constitution—it was further understood by both the ratifiers and the Philadelphia Framers who reflected upon the proper mode of constitutional construction—was what the ratifiers apprehended the document to mean. Ratification was the operative act of legitimating and enacting the Constitution, and the ratifiers' understanding of the Constitution *was* its content.[5] Courts were not expected to protect people from government, or to protect one group of citizens against other groups.[6] Apart from its role as "umpire" of the federal system—settling boundary disputes between state and federal authorities—judicial review hardly registered as a conception of constitutional theory.

Historian William Nelson expressed this basic point well in an unjustly neglected article. Judges of the early republic, he said,

> unlike judges of today, did not see judicial review as a mechanism for protecting minority rights against majoritarian infringement. . . . Judges of the early nineteenth century viewed "the people" as a politically homogeneous and cohesive body possessing common political goals and aspirations, not as congeries of factions and interest groups, each having its own set of goals and aspirations.
>
> Judicial review as it developed after the 1780s was thought, in sum, only to give the people—a single, cohesive and indivisible body politic—protection against faithless legislators who betrayed the trust placed in them, and not to give judges authority to make law by resolving disputes between interest groups into which the people and their legislative representatives were divided.[7]

Maintaining limited government was a popular—not a judicial— exercise through which the many might act as one. Georgians, New

Yorkers, and Virginians were united in keeping the national government—including federal judges—in line with the Constitution. They kept watch by consultation, frequent elections, organizing into trans-sectional political parties, proposing constitutional amendments, and —ultimately—by resisting. The Bill of Rights, added to the Constitution in 1791, confirms this picture. Contrary to historical claims made by present friends of judicial power, these amendments did not withdraw huge areas of deliberation about the common good (having characteristically to do with "rights") from ordinary political processes. Far from manifesting a lack of confidence in politics, the Bill of Rights was composed of adjuncts to self-government (much of the First Amendment) and contained an instrument for the people to control the governors (the Second Amendment).

Many other amendments in the Bill of Rights (the Fourth, much of the Fifth, the Sixth, Seventh, and Eighth Amendments) reveal a lack of confidence in the judiciary: *they guarantee rights within judicial proceedings;* at their heart is the guarantee of a trial by jury in both civil and criminal cases. Far from diminishing or eliminating democratic deliberation and decision, this guarantee reinforces and adds to the prerogatives of the people. Trial by jury was meant to be a protection against government oppression of the people and an instrument of the local community's self-government.

Discarding the Constitution

The Constitution did not just reflect a previously unified people. Neither was it simply a compact. The Constitution presupposed a "people" capable of keeping the state in line with it. Thus constitutionalism was not the counter-principle to self-government. Much less did constitutional law provide or make provision for judicial governance owing to the felt inadequacies of democracy. In other words, the Constitution did *not* establish a board of nine justices—the Supreme Court —to make law, to formulate "rights," or to revise the Constitution.

But constitutional law today has been reduced to something very much like government by the judiciary. If the preceding observations are even roughly accurate, then the reduction of our popularly ratified form of representative government could occur only if the Constitution, understood as a body of norms capable of guiding decisions, was effaced.

That effacement occurred as early as 1930, when Supreme Court Justice Felix Frankfurter declared that "in good truth, the Supreme Court *is* the Constitution."[8] Or, as Justice William O. Douglas revealed in a 1972 interview: "The Court is really the keeper of the conscience. And the conscience is the Constitution."[9] In 1992, the Supreme Court further articulated this view of the Court and Constitution in *Planned Parenthood v. Casey:*

> Like the character of an individual the legitimacy of the Court must be earned over time. So, indeed, must be the character of a Nation of people who aspire to live according to the rule of law. Their belief in themselves as such a people is not readily separable from their understanding of the Court invested with the authority to decide their constitutional cases and speak before all others for their constitutional ideals. If the Court's legitimacy should be undermined, then, so would the country be in its very ability to see itself through its constitutional ideals. The Court's concern with legitimacy is not for the sake of the Court but for the sake of the Nation to which it is responsible.[10]

Note well: the (old) Constitution has disappeared entirely in this passage in *Casey.* Nowhere does the Court refer to extant, fixed principle(s) as a guarantor of its legitimacy. The word "Constitution"—even a "living" one—is displaced by the lower-case adjective, "constitutional." The Court is concerned not with the "legitimacy" of the Constitution, but with its own legitimacy. Significantly, the Court does not claim a "legitimacy" coextensive with the "legitimacy" of the Constitution, as one might expect. The Constitution, as such, is not at all a part of the new "legitimacy" equation. Nor do the "people" and their "government"—with the Constitution as their bond—supply the Court's "legitimacy." Instead, the Court equates itself with the "rule of law." What legitimates the Court, and its rulings, is now the "court," and "constitutional ideals," and (somewhere) the "people." But the people are now considered more as clients or passive consumers than enforcers of the Constitution and masters capable of lawmaking through legislatures.

Is this passage from *Casey* atypical of contemporary legal reflection on the role of the judiciary? John Rawls, our preeminent political theorist, says about the Court and the Constitution: "The Constitution is not what the Court says it is. Rather, it is what the people acting constitutionally through the other branches eventually allow the Court to say it is."[11]

Rawls here is prescribing, not describing. He is not mimicking that sage judicial observer, Mr. Dooley, who said long ago that the Court follows the election returns. He posits no antecedent legal limit on either the Court's jurisdiction or the content of its law-making. Though Rawls allows for some subsequent check by the people, this check is an illusory one. Who decides whether the people have acted through regular constitutional processes? Judges, of course. In the very next paragraph, Rawls justifies judicial dec-larations of the constitutionality—or lack thereof—of the amend-ments to the Constitution, proposed and ratified according to the procedures for constitutional change as established in the Consti-tution.

Consider also the more arresting assertion of Ronald Dworkin, one of the most prominent legal theorists of our day, in his 1993 book on abortion and euthanasia. According to Dworkin, the Court does not operate under law at all. The "Constitution insists that our judges do their best collectively to construct, reinspect, and revise, generation by generation, the skeleton of freedom and equality of concern that its great clauses, in their majestic abstraction, command."[12] If that does not reduce the (old) Constitution to one breathtaking grant of jurisdiction to nine black-robed guardians to legislate as they see fit, I can scarcely imagine what would.

How might we rein in our guardians? Dworkin holds that "at least theoretically [there] is the power the people retain to amend the Constitution if they believe the Court's decisions are intolerable, or to impeach particular justices."[13] But, Dworkin continues, "these extreme remedies are impractical, and the main engines for disci-plining judges are intellectual rather than political or legal."[14] Accord-ing to this view, judges are not subject at all to the rule of law: they make law; they set their own jurisdiction.

It is apt (but incomplete) to say that the justices have supplanted the people as the Constitution's main enforcer. In our era, there is, in fact, no Constitution to enforce. What we have is a judicial activity called "constitutional law." The "people" figure, somehow, as keepers of the Constitution, or rather of the Court, or at least of constitutional law. But theirs is a shadowy role that is less and less distinguishable from revolutionary action.

Enshrining Autonomy

What is the substance of this new institutional form? The answer is found in what I call the "mystery" passage of *Casey*. This notion now controls our constitutional law of civil liberty. The mystery passage reads:

> These matters [marriage, contraception, procreation, etc.], involving the most intimate and personal choices a person may make in a lifetime, choices central to personal dignity and autonomy, are central to the liberty protected by the Fourteenth Amendment. At the heart of liberty is the right to define one's own concept of existence, of meaning, of the universe, and of the mystery of human life. Beliefs about these matters could not define the attributes of personhood were they formed under the compulsion of the state.[15]

Why is this passage so important? Did the Supreme Court not simply concoct it to provide a way out of the abortion mess for the justices who had misgivings about *Roe?*

Well, it may be that, but it is certainly a lot more. It spells out the elusive rationale for a generation of important judicial rulings in the areas of sexual morality, family life, and education. The "mystery" passage rationalizes, and closes, what I call the "apostolic age" of the new constitutionalism. Warren, Brennan, Marshall, and Douglas are gone. Theirs was the task of bringing the kerygma of "autonomy"— really, moral subjectivism—to the legal world. With the appointments of Ginsburg and Breyer, and with the emergence of the so-called *Casey* centrists, we have entered the post-apostolic era of institution-building, and bricks and mortar have been thrown up to protect and preserve the Great Insight. Personal "autonomy" is to the contemporary American polity what the dictatorship of the proletariat was to Marxian theory.

What, if anything, is wrong with the mystery passage?

The mystery passage raises the decisive philosophical question whether "autonomy"—defined as freedom from external constraints and from internal compulsion and delusion—is a *basic* good or an *instrumental* good. Is autonomy a basic good, like life and knowledge —truly worthwhile in itself and thus an ultimate reason for action? Or is autonomy an instrumental good, like pleasure—when associated with upright choices good, with wrong choices, bad? I believe that autonomy is an instrumental, not a basic, good. (A full treatment of the question would have to show why this is so—a chore I cannot take up here.)

Certainly, no individual can create a world in which he or she assigns idiosyncratic meanings to the entirety of life, experience, and even "the mystery of human life." Individuals naturally constitute groups, whose coordinated behavior secures survival and satisfaction. Thus, the autonomy enshrined by *Casey* is existentially impossible. Besides, for those within the tradition of Aristotle and Aquinas, there are principles of practical reason (reasoning about what to do) that can be ignored but from which no one can escape—just as one can ignore the law of gravity but only at one's peril. One major effect of the mystery passage, therefore, is to partition one's acting self from one's self-understanding. A person in the grip of this construction will not know what he or she is actually doing.

Persons enjoying *Casey*-type freedom *may* decide that meaning comes from a greater than human source—say from the God of Abraham, Isaac, and Jacob, or from the cosmos, or from the Force— but no one *need* do so. Persons may also decide that meaning is found deep within turtles, or trees, or in Punxsutawney Phil's shadow each Groundhog Day. The ground of the so-called right "to define one's own concept of existence, of meaning"—though not necessarily each person's exercise of it—is our human capacity to assign meaning.

The principle of "autonomy" articulated by *Casey* is entirely secular. Its autonomy is freedom *from,* and does not imply anything freedom is *for.* Of course, by calling this autonomy "secular," I do not mean to imply that everybody who would be his or her personal sovereign over what is good and what is evil is a moral subjectivist. From the law's point of view as articulated in *Casey,* however, *all* meaning is derived by persons from a framework of strictly this-worldly human concerns—even to allowing individuals the "right" to define who is a person and who is not ("the attributes of personhood"). I cannot survey here the rise of modern secularism, save to say that constitutional law has played a role (though a more recent one) in the process of secularizing our society, as have science, economics, and the like. I should add that, for whatever reasons, secularizing pressures have not yet entirely eroded traditional, monotheistic faith in the United States, and had not done so when secularism entered constitutional law in 1947, with the case of *Everson* v. *Board of Education.*[16]

Some elements in our political culture and law impede the practical unfolding of the logical implications of this secularism. Some are vestigial remnants of a predecessor culture. Some impulses toward traditional morals in law are also a conscious effort to square the older concepts with the new principles, to pour new wine into old skins. A good example of this is Justice Souter's opinion (joined by Stevens and O'Connor) in Lee v. Weisman, one of the Court's many prayer-in-public-school cases.[17] (This 1992 case involved a benediction at a middle-school graduation.) Souter attempted to explain how state accommodation of religion could be reconciled with the overarching command of the Establishment Clause that government be "neutral" between religion and irreligion; such neutrality is the Court's idea of what the First Amendment protection of religious liberty requires. Souter said that he was sympathetic to the plight of those put "to the choice of taking sides between God and government."[18] He wanted, it seems, to justify alleviating precisely the plight of those who believe in a greater than human source of meaning and value—perhaps God. But he offered a justification for ameliorating conflicts not between God and Caesar but between Caesar and values "central to the lives of certain Americans."[19] These "values" are protected *because* they have been *chosen* by persons. They do not necessarily refer to God. Thus "religious liberty" under the First Amendment is brought into line with the individual right to definition in the mystery passage.

Defaulting on the Common Good

What are the political implications of *Casey?* One problem with any doctrine of "autonomy," such as the one in *Casey,* is that it reduces our various rights to a single mega-right: the right to be oneself. In the more traditional understanding of the moral basis for the duties and responsibilities of public authority towards persons, the different aspects or components of genuine human flourishing corresponded to rights: thus, the right to *life,* the right to freedom of *religion,* and so forth. But the doctrine of *Casey* rules out of bounds the moral evaluations necessary to the traditional understanding, like the evaluation that life is good, that religion is good. Under *Casey,* by default, the common good becomes not the moral requirements that arise from cooperation in pursuit of objective goods—like life, knowledge, and religion—but equal shares of autonomy, at least for those subjects capable of deciphering the mystery of life.

What is public life like under the new dispensation? Let us call *Casey*-type autonomy "liberal freedom." Let us call democratic deliberation on the basis of shared values "civic freedom." Charles Taylor traces the implications of liberal freedom:

> It offers a picture of human life in which common purposes have no valid place, in which they appear more often as potential obstacles to individual self-development. Indeed, what one finds where the culture of liberalism is strong is that the possibility of genuinely common values gets lost from sight. A kind of philosophical atomism becomes widespread by which all public enterprises are construed as based on *merely convergent purposes* [emphasis added].[20]

Taylor is saying that once the notion of a genuine common good is erased by liberal freedom, all there can be to public life is a more or less stable consensus on an agenda, or the more or less harmonious pursuit by individuals of what they happen to want.

The "legitimacy" of political authority is thus thrust forward as an urgent question (cf. *Casey*). Sooner or later, autonomous meaning-givers will wonder: What is the contribution to my well-being of legal constraints upon actions that seem meaningful to me, especially where those constraints are imposed by lawmakers for the apparent benefit of strangers in some other part of town (say, inner-city school kids)? More formally put, the question reads: Why should A respect the rights of B, if respecting the rights of B is not in A's interest, and A could avoid legal retribution for his actions against B's rights? Under the constraints of liberal freedom, there seems to be no satisfactory answer.

Into this unhappy situation the *Casey* court intrudes high-toned encomia about the "conscience" of America, the Constitution, and the justices. Somehow, the justices would be irreproachable sources of norms that, again somehow, compel us because (for the last time) somehow, the norms are ours—almost, but not yet. But the "somehows" are, alas, impenetrable mystifications. Self-government on the basis of truths about human nature is impossible under the doctrine of *Casey*—which the Court presented to us in the name of the Constitution.

We have seen enough of the Founders' Constitution, however, to conclude that *Casey* hardly corresponds to anything the Framers had in mind. Granted, the Constitution is not limited to just what its crafters had in mind. The Constitution specifies a class or kind of acts —search and seizure, for example—which the Court has rightly interpreted to include activities (like wiretapping) that did not exist in 1790. The writers of the joint opinion in *Casey* maintained that they imposed no moral code of their own but simply defined the liberty of all, the liberty guaranteed by the Due Process Clause of the Constitution. Does *Casey* represent a legitimate development of doctrine, a reasonable interpretation of that document in light of the needs of the present?

Not even the *Casey* court thought so. Besides repeating the language of the Due Process Clause, the justices looked almost exclusively to judicial utterances of the last thirty years for support of their annunciation of personal autonomy. According to its judicial authors, the mystery passage does not aspire to be much more than the principle that explains a series of "privacy" holdings, dating back to 1965.

Justices have sometimes claimed warrants for this generation-old project of liberal freedom in the constitutional protection of religious liberty. But I have already argued, albeit briefly, that the Court's church-state jurisprudence is a product of the same drive for autonomy that undergirds *Casey:* it *is Casey,* I conclude, and therefore *cannot justify Casey.*

The Madisonian Dilemma

More often the privacy project is justified by reference to the so-called Madisonian dilemma. This is what Madison described as the problem of "guard[ing] the part of society against the injustice of the other part."[21] The dilemma, therefore, is the problem of faction, which Madison treated in *The Federalist,* particularly number 10. He located the "latent causes" of faction in human nature, and identified "the various and unequal distribution of property" as the most common and durable source of faction.[22] Factions might also be religious; zealots might be moved by the opinions of a charismatic leader. But religious division was for Madison just another type of faction, treatable by the same remedy. Extend the sphere of politics to take in a variety of religious opinions—encompass a "multiplicity of sects"

—and private rights will be more or less effectively secured. Empower the sects. Do not disenfranchise them in favor of judicial resolution of all that the justices call "church-state" matters. "Pluralism" was for Madison the organizing feature of his reflections upon the possibilities of stable self-government, just as it is for our liberal savants. If you explained to Madison just how pluralistic we have become, he would probably rest easy with *Federalist* 10 and 51. We run to the courthouse.

Madison gambled on controlling the mischievous effects of faction because he saw that the alternatives were worse, and "worse" simply meant inconsistent with the basic liberty of self-government. For Madison, the constraints necessary to deal with the problem of faction resulted from the maintenance of that liberty which is essential to political life.[23] Dependence on the people was the mainstay of sound government.

According to the proprietor of the dilemma, there are two methods of protection against the evil of majoritarian oppression. One involves "creating a will in the community independent of the majority, that is, of the society itself."[24] But "in a free government," Madison concluded, "the security for civil rights must be the same as for religious rights"—a multiplicity of interests, as well as a multiplicity of sects.[25] In speaking of a "will" independent of the community, Madison probably had in mind a hereditary executive of some sort—and only maybe more. But "more" is in fact the route taken in the late twentieth century by our Supreme Court. The Court has contradicted what seems to be the central proposition of our Constitution: self-government may be risky business, but the alternatives are far riskier.

The Court has tried to convince us of precisely the reverse proposition: rule by judicial guardians is the only alternative to the unacceptable risks to our freedoms that self-government entails. If liberal freedom is true—if the capacity for self-definition is all that can be affirmed as a basic value—then the justices are right. "We" are a group of subjects seeking the autonomy necessary to create our universes. All that government can be, this side of a brutish state of nature, is a will that imposes restraint from, as it were, outside the struggle.

But "we" are an *unum* in a different sense entirely if we recognize moral truths, reflected in human nature, that include such basic goods as life, religion, family, and so on. Then, the justices are quite wrong.

12

Religious Liberty in a Diverse Society

Terry Eastland

My reflections on law and the *unum* turn on the 1990 Supreme Court decision in what has been dubbed "the peyote case." Perhaps for the plaintiffs in *Employment Division* v. *Smith* that is an accurate way to think about the case. The case was, however, about the First Amendment's guarantee of the free exercise of religion. (As an original matter, of course, the First Amendment applied only to Congress, not the states. In 1940, the Supreme Court extended the First Amendment's free-exercise provision to the states; most of the legal disputes over that provision have come from the states.) And it was also, though less obviously, about the right to self-government and ultimately the kind of *unum* we might create by the exercise of that right.

First, some facts. Alfred Smith and Galen Black were fired from their jobs with a private drug-rehabilitation organization when it was learned that they had ingested peyote during a ceremony of the Native American Church, whose rituals include peyote use. When they applied to the state for unemployment compensation, they were judged ineligible for benefits because they had been fired for work-related

---

Terry Eastland is the editor of *Forbes MediaCritic* and a fellow at the Ethics and Public Policy Center. He is the editor of *Religious Liberty in the Supreme Court: The Cases That Define the Debate Over Church and State* (Ethics and Public Policy Center, 1993).

"misconduct"—i.e., their use of a controlled substance that, by state law, it was a felony to possess. Smith and Black challenged the state's decision on the grounds that it violated the First Amendment, which forbids government to prohibit the free exercise of religion. Smith and Black won in the Oregon Supreme Court but lost 6 to 3 in the U.S. Supreme Court, with Justice Antonin Scalia writing for five of the six: "[A]n individual's religious beliefs [do not] excuse him from compliance with an otherwise valid law prohibiting conduct that the state is free to regulate."

Scalia's opinion was immediately denounced all across the political and religious spectrum. The opinion laid waste to our great tradition of religious liberty, or so it was said by critics both left and right, the unchurched and the churched, both high and low.

Scalia's specific sin was to limit severely the implications of *Sherbert* v. *Verner*, a 1963 Supreme Court decision in which the Court had, for the first time, ruled that the First Amendment's free-exercise provision requires exemption of a religious believer from a non-discriminatory secular law. Adell Sherbert, a Seventh-Day Adventist, was fired by her employer because she refused to work on Saturday, the Sabbath of her faith. Unable to find a job that didn't require working on Saturday, she filed a claim for unemployment compensation. The state turned her down; she didn't qualify for compensation, according to the state, because she could have worked on Saturdays.

Sherbert thought the state had abridged her right to the free exercise of her religion. But the South Carolina Supreme Court disagreed, and the case law seemed clearly in the state's favor. Under *Reynolds* v. *United States* (1879), it was permissible for government to regulate religiously motivated action as long as it had a rational basis for doing so. The rational-basis burden was so easy to satisfy as to foreclose the possibility that judges would carve out exemptions from otherwise valid civil law in the name of the free-exercise provision. The U.S. Supreme Court, however, came to Adell Sherbert's rescue, holding that government may burden the free exercise of religion only if it has a *compelling* interest in doing so. South Carolina, said the Court, had not met that test.

Smith raised the bar that *Sherbert* had lowered. And so it appeared to many critics of *Smith* that plaintiffs seeking exemptions from otherwise valid civil law for religiously motivated conduct would seldom if ever win. The cause of religious liberty in the United States, it was said, was in serious jeopardy (even though, by this reckoning, it would also have been in serious jeopardy from 1789 to 1963). An unusual effort to get the Supreme Court to reconsider its opinion failed, whereupon the diverse opponents of *Smith* went to Congress seeking legislation that would in effect lower the bar *Smith* had raised, thus making it much easier for plaintiffs such as the peyote-ingesting pair from Oregon to win.

RFRA Support: Unity Amid Diversity

Three years later, toward the end of 1993, Congress passed the Religious Freedom Restoration Act, which makes it easier for plaintiffs like Smith and Black to prevail in cases seeking an exemption from general law. Like the *Smith* decision, RFRA was backed by diverse groups normally on opposite sides. The legislation enjoyed the support of Concerned Women of America, home-schooling advocates, strict church-state separationists such as People for the American Way and the National Council of Churches, the National Association of Evangelicals, the U.S. Catholic bishops, and major Jewish organizations. RFRA won huge majorities in both houses, with only two senators voting against it, and President Clinton declared that it was important to him "personally."

Why did secular organizations like the ACLU and People for the American Way oppose *Smith* and support the Religious Freedom Restoration Act? In part, I think, because *Smith* represented a sharp divergence not simply from *Sherbert* but from the civil-liberties jurisprudence that such organizations have long endorsed — which is that courts exist mainly to enforce individual rights against potentially tyrannical majorities. This formulation of the task of judicial review scants the fact — as historians of the founding advise — that one of the original natural rights was the right to self-government. (Religious liberty surely was another one of these original natural rights, to my mind the first.) Through exercise of this right of self-government, majorities in localities and states historically addressed issues of moral concern, from abortion to (many, many decades ago) blasphemy. It does not take a great deal of research to establish that moral concerns are intimately related to religious beliefs, that the religious beliefs of the majority of the American people historically have been Christian in nature, and that the laws affecting moral issues that have passed in this nation have reflected the Christian beliefs of majorities. To state this differently, if any positive law is thought to reflect a kind of *unum* — the one view supported by the representatives of a majority of the people — the *unum* in these laws was shaped in substantial part by the morality based in, or at least consistent with, Christianity.

Secular groups such as People for the American Way are unlikely to regard the good society as one in which a lot of law is shaped by traditional morality. They have their own morality, sharply individualist in nature, which Gerard Bradley of Notre Dame has usefully defined as this: "[G]overnment ought to be 'neutral' among conceptions of what is good or right for individuals to do, and possesses no right to coerce or to discourage conduct unless the conduct 'harms' persons who have not consented to engage in it."[1] In operation, over the past several decades, the conduct-exemption doctrine of *Sherbert* worked in concert with other civil-liberties doctrines to advance this conception of morality at the expense of the kind supported, or likely to be supported, by majorities left alone exercising the right to self-government. As Bradley writes, the conduct exemption has proved "an efficient engine for the maintenance of the neutral, secular state." The engine threatens to "rid the polity of any trace of the authority of religion, and of the moral tradition" while making the polity into "a playpen for the autonomous self."

Interestingly, like plaintiffs in many of the historic religion-clause cases, the plaintiffs in the Smith case represented one of the "outsider" precincts. Smith and Black were not Methodists or Baptists or Presbyterians or Catholics. They represented the Native American Church — "represented" rather than belonged to it, it seems. A *New York Times* account of the case, which included interviews with the two plaintiffs and their lawyers, suggests that they were not members of the church. If not, this raises the fascinating question of whether religious-liberty plaintiffs actually need to believe in the religion they carry with them into court.

The Declining Right of Self-Government

For better or for worse, the virtually unanimous denouncement of the *Smith* decision and the passage of the Religious Freedom Restoration Act deserve to be understood as something more than a chapter in the history of religious liberty; they also constitute a chapter in the decline of the right of self-government (a long-running story), and thus of the capacity of majorities to enact laws that reflect their moral views and to change those laws as they see fit. Justice Scalia, in his opinion for the Court in *Smith,* understood perfectly well that this right of self-government was at stake in the case when he observed that the First Amendment does not require the incapacitation of "the political process," that states ought to be able to decide for themselves —as many had done prior to *Smith* and as Oregon in fact would do after it—whether to make an exception to their drug laws for sacramental peyote use.

It is not simply the traditional majority—the one informed by Christian beliefs—but also the modern or postmodern majority whose self-governing capacity is limited by RFRA. This probably explains the positions taken by religious conservatives against *Smith* and for RFRA. Michael Farris, former general counsel of Concerned Women of America (and the unsuccessful Republican candidate in 1993 for lieutenant governor of Virginia), termed *Smith* an assault on "a very fundamental religious liberty question for everyone in America." Behind this statement lies an understanding of how America has changed. The de facto Protestant establishment, and the *unum* it signified, no longer exists. A government representing a much more religiously and morally diverse people may enact or enforce rules that, though they are religiously neutral, burden the free exercise of religion by serious adherents of traditional religions. Farris understood that the conduct-exemption doctrine, or its equivalent, is a needed shelter for religious conservatives in the postmodern world. After all, the doctrine provides protection for *all,* not just for those who ingest an illegal drug as part of a religious ceremony.

The *Smith* case and its statutory fallout suggest that political and religious conservatives have conceded at least some territory to the civil libertarians. But if the kind of polity their forebears endorsed and supported is no longer possible, the good news for those who still believe in the God of Abraham and seek to transmit the moral tradition is that they will be more protected than ever before in the exercise of their beliefs.

13

Public Institutions and the Public Trust

Edwin J. Delattre

All my work on ethics and the public trust is anchored in the ancient tradition, embedded in the founding of the United States, that all who bear the public trust are obligated to live up to higher intellectual and moral standards than the public they serve. The philosophic arguments for this view have never been expressed with greater refinement than by the Scottish philosopher Francis Hutcheson in his *A Short Introduction to Moral Philosophy* (1747). Hutcheson argued that the constituting of civil government is the most important transaction in human affairs, because, in framing governments, we entrust ourselves and our dear ones to the exercise of authority by others. Accordingly, Hutcheson insisted that it was legitimate to grant pardons to informers in order to break up bands of pirates, but argued that for crimes against the public trust—crimes that attack not only lives but a way of life—no pardon is ever justified.

James Madison captured this tradition in *Federalist* No. 57: "The aim of every political constitution is or ought to be first to secure for rulers, men who have most wisdom to discern, and most virtue

---

Edwin J. Delattre is dean and professor of education at The School of Education at Boston University, and professor of philosophy in the university's College of Liberal Arts.

to pursue the common good of the society; and in the next place, to take the most effectual precautions for keeping them virtuous, whilst they continue to hold their public trust."[1] Thus, to safeguard the public trust, public institutions must consist of intellectually and morally virtuous individuals who are held accountable within those institutions.

The Founders joined to this tradition a realistic estimate of human nature—the other essential component in any adequate account of public institutions and the public trust. Madison's eloquent words on this subject are well known:

But what is government itself but the greatest of all reflections on human nature? If men were angels, no government would be necessary. If angels were to govern men, neither internal nor external controls on government would be necessary. In framing a government which is to be administered by men over men, the great difficulty lies in this: You must first enable the government to control the governed; and in the next place, oblige it to control itself.[2]

Hamilton was rather more blunt:

Why has government been instituted at all? Because the passions of men will not conform to the dictates of reason and justice, without constraint. . . .

. . . .

To judge from the history of mankind, we shall be compelled to conclude, that the fiery and destructive passions of war, reign in the human breast, with much more powerful sway, than the mild and beneficent sentiments of peace; and, that to model our political systems upon speculations of lasting tranquility, is to calculate on the weaker springs of the human character.[3]

For a variety of reasons, in recent years this tradition of higher standards has fallen on hard times. Uncritical acceptance of moral subjectivism and relativism has obliterated the idea of intellectual and moral standards as such. The reduction of human beings to victims of genetics and environment, as institutionalized in certain features of the Americans with Disabilities Act, destroys the meaning of autonomy and accountability, and obscures any realistic conception of human beings. Similarly, the substitution of membership in certain demographic groups for judgment of individual worthiness to bear the public trust has taken us even further from our tradition of high standards. The ignorance of this tradition among many public servants has led to its collapse and to the mindless advocacy within government itself of double standards. Thus, when Zoë Baird asked that her nomination as attorney general be withdrawn, President Clinton could write to her:

> You are an exceptionally gifted attorney and a person of great decency and integrity. You have responded to the call of public service with energy and a firm dedication to the mission of the Justice Department. I realize that it was your candid disclosure of the child care matter that led to the circumstances we face today. *I believe that the concerns raised about your child care situation were unique to the position of Attorney General.* [Emphasis added.]

Double standards in government, whether they arise from gender bias, other forms of prejudice, or the failure to understand fidelity to the public trust, always militate against realism and end in cynicism. Cynicism, in turn, undermines the aspiration to be worthy of public trust.

The public trust has also been undercut by a fatalism that sees public institutions as a microcosm of the larger society. This argument says that every society has, to a greater or lesser extent, all the varieties of human vice, weakness, and depravity: brutality, corruption, predation, racism, sexism, alcohol abuse, illegal drug use, cowardice, illiteracy, incompetence, disregard for the safety of others, and so on. It presumes that every institution within society will contain these faults in roughly the same proportion as the society at large. This view is factually and logically preposterous. For the most part, societies are not selective in their memberships; mere birth guarantees access. In a constitutional republic, however, no one has a birthright to a position of public trust. Traditionally, institutions that bear the public trust are expected, or even required, to be selective. If the Founders were right —as I believe—then the greater the faults in the society at large, the more careful and selective public institutions ought to be.

Restoring Chelsea

Let me tell a couple of stories that show how much turns on the way we think about public institutions and the public trust. Boston

University is the only university in the United States authorized by law to manage an inner-city school system. For six years, the Boston University–Chelsea Public Schools Partnership has carried out an experiment in restoring self-governance in a city where all public services, including schooling, had been disrupted by corruption, ruthless social engineering, and economic collapse. In the last six years, the combined efforts of state government, Chelsea's Receiver, many of Chelsea's citizens, the schools, and Boston University have brought the city back from the brink of ruin. But in 1993 our progress was dramatically imperiled.

In the fall of 1993, the Chelsea, Massachusetts, Police Department and the Boston University–Chelsea Public Schools Partnership learned that a nationally notorious gang, the Latin Kings, had targeted the city of Chelsea as a promising site for operations. This organized criminal conspiracy sought to recruit Chelsea children and youths for expansion of its criminal ventures in narcotics, weapons trafficking, extortion, and other forms of predation.

The threat to domestic tranquillity, the public good, and the safety of the community was real: since their beginnings in Chicago in 1941, the Latin Kings have demonstrated their duplicity, shrewdness, ruthless violence, and criminal dominion in urban areas and prisons. They have embodied "the fiery and destructive passions of war" in such cities as New York; Hartford, Connecticut; and Springfield, Massachusetts, pursuing illegal profits and power, without regard for "reason and justice"—without decency, constraint, or compassion for the innocent and the helpless.

Chelsea police leaders and Boston University faculty familiar with gangs and organized crime knew the gravity of the situation. Having gathered hundreds of pages of intelligence on the Latin Kings from law-enforcement and corrections personnel throughout the United States, they understood the gang's dangerous pattern of deception in gaining a foothold in a city. By convincing youths, parents, teachers, community leaders, and others that they are benign and civic-minded, the Latin Kings recruit local members, formalize their operations under a local chapter of the gang, and establish a base for their real agenda—drug and illegal-weapons trafficking, robbery, burglary, extortion, corruption of public officials, and the elimination, by whatever means necessary, of resistance and criminal competition.

Along with community leaders and youth organizations in Chelsea, the police and school officials grasped the two basic principles of dealing with gang problems: (1) Never give ground to a gang in its efforts to secure a foothold in a community. (2) Never hold ground by placing innocent people in harm's way. Accordingly, those responsible for public safety and schooling in Chelsea realized that they immediately had to mount a united front against the incursion of the Latin Kings. Furthermore, they accepted the imperative that this united front be maintained without qualification—that no youths, parents, teachers, administrators, community leaders, Boston University personnel, or volunteers be deceived about the Latin Kings and their long-term intentions. Essential to preventing the gang from becoming a violent and predatory criminal power in Chelsea were concerted resistance to recruitment, prevention of gang paraphernalia and dress in schools, public exposure of the Latin Kings for what they are, education and training of the young in resistance to gangs, proactive steps to engage the young in salutary activities, and vigilance by the community and its public and private organizations.

Education of the public began. Students, parents, and teachers were told that the Latin Kings (also known as the Almighty Latin King Nation or Almighty Latin Charter Nation) and the Latin Queens have already recruited over 20,000 members nationwide. Information was circulated identifying gang leaders; the contents of gang chartering, documents, and recruiting methods; patterns of dress, jewelry, graffiti, hand signs, and criminal enterprises. The Latin Kings—who profess dedication to education, good citizenship, ethnic pride, and the self-esteem of the young—have a covert agenda to enlist 100,000 members by the year 2000 in order to control large markets in illegal drugs and weapons. This agenda was made known to schools, youth organizations, government, health-care and drug-treatment leaders, businesses, and the media. Police and the Boston University–Chelsea Public School Partnership closely cooperated with their counterparts in Boston and neighboring cities.

In Chelsea, the united front against the Latin Kings has held. Gang attempts at manipulation of the public by deception have failed. Boston University has provided funds to send Chelsea police officers to the Gang Resistance Education and Training program (GREAT), conducted by the Bureau of Alcohol, Tobacco, and Firearms. Their expertise, along with Chelsea's DARE program, will be applied in the schools. The successes in Chelsea derive from the courage of the public and the fact that many adults and youths recognize gangs for what they are: brutish youths and adults who use terror to control others and who foment violence to create the illusion that they are heroic. In Chelsea, the lies of the Latin Kings and other gangs have been exposed, despite the fact that Boston media have been less than helpful. Although one columnist wrote some accurate editorials, the work of other naive or voyeuristic reporters has played into the hands of the Latin Kings. But in Chelsea, courageous individuals and public servants have told Latin King leaders that gang ambitions in the city and its schools will never be tolerated—and school officials, police, parents, and others are living up to these words.

Moral Realism and Decency

What was needed and brought to the situation in Chelsea was seriousness about greatness and evil—a realistic grasp of human nature, its capacity for high aspiration as well as depravity and predation —along with a shared conviction that an informed citizenry can act effectively in self-defense.

At the same time, we have acted upon the vision of the Founders, as described by constitutional scholar Robert Goldwin, that while people are not angels, they are still "good enough to govern themselves"—provided, it seems to me, they learn how.[4] We have kept in mind Dorothy L. Sayers's trenchant observation in her commentary on Dante, that "humanism is always apt to underestimate, and to be baffled by the deliberate will to evil," and that "three passions . . . may lead to violence: wrath, lust, and the will to dominate."[5] The Boston University–Chelsea Public Schools Partnership has not underestimated the worst in human nature, nor the best. Neither have we supposed the "root causes" of evil reducible to "criminogenic" environments or "ideological" error.

We have rejected intellectually and morally bankrupt programs of violence prevention and conflict resolution, programs based on the claim that all positions in a dispute are equally valid and on the self-defeating declaration that in human affairs there are no facts, no evidence, but only perceptions of facts. Instead, we are trying to apply what has been known for a very long time about the formation of good habits of learning and conduct in the young. We have rejected instructional programs that promote toleration as the highest virtue, as though nothing were intolerable. Instead, we are trying to help teachers and students acquire a discriminating tolerance. We have explicitly denied the view that consensus is the highest good, along with its corollary that all disagreements of principle can be honorably compromised away. Instead, we have shown our respect for relevant evidence over consensus in matters of policy and practice. We have denied the presumption that the so-called root causes of faction have nothing to do with human nature but are environmental and can, therefore, always be erased by communication. Though we have listened patiently to all varieties of public opinion, we have put the interests of the children above considerations of mere peace and quiet. We have refused to mount programs in health and sex education that reduce sexual life to mechanics and biology. Instead we are developing curricula and upholding teaching that illuminate the nature of moral decency in all human dealings.

We have concentrated on the achievement of literacy, not on inoculation against emotional and spiritual anemia by injections of "self-esteem." We do not suppose that the future of the urban young lies more in midnight basketball than in libraries and museums; our teachers and programs take seriously the intellectual and moral formation of the young from early childhood. We have explained the shortcomings of most "sensitivity" training: individuals are treated as mere members of groups, guilt or innocence is assigned by color or gender, all human suffering is attributed to victimization by others. We do not accept the dogmas of value neutrality and the moral equivalence of "lifestyles" that pervade schools under the name "multiculturalism." We are busy forging sound curricula and good teaching in the core disciplines, along with an ethos of high expectation for our students. We hold, with Sidney Hook, that "it is pathological to feel guilt for the misdeeds of our ancestors, or virtue because we are descendants of the victims of the ancestors of others."[6] We flatly deny the claim that children can learn and benefit only from adults who share their gender or color. We treat the children and adults of Chelsea as individuals.

Our stance in Chelsea has not endeared us to local political factions. Our Partnership is far from being a darling of the media. We enjoy no support from foundations whose patterns and priorities in funding have contributed to the trivialization of the public trust. Much of what we accomplish in Chelsea will be summarily spurned by the schools and advocacy groups that could benefit most from the principles we have applied. Unhappily, school and accreditation reform movements in the United States threaten to remain merely structural, skeletal—without the vital pulse that only the intellectual power of the scholarly and scientific disciplines can sustain. The reformers focus mostly on process and nomenclature, and in so doing they betray the public trust. Our efforts in Chelsea are an affront to much of what currently passes for educational reform.

Politics and Policing

Now, contrast this story, if you will, with something of the history of policing in the United States and with the present situation of the Metropolitan Police Department in Washington, D.C. In 1931, August Vollmer, the most respected police leader of his time, wrote that in the United States "law enforcement agencies are usually held in contempt and law enforcement is one of our national jokes." Then, as now, competent and honorable police serve the public, while inept, corrupt, and brutal police betray the public and their fellow officers.

In the more than sixty years since Vollmer's commentary, many police departments in the United States have risen far above contempt and ridicule. While expanding opportunities in policing for minority groups and women, they have improved themselves by greater selectivity in officer recruitment, more refined background investigations and recruitment interviews, and better academy and field training. Experienced officers are given in-service education. The use of force has been more rigorously limited: officers have more instructive supervision, use technology more effectively, and face greater accountability. When police misconduct is alleged, internal investigations are more thorough. Communication with the public is better. Police and law-enforcement leaders understand that a police department is not supposed to be a microcosm of the society with all its flaws.

Fidelity of a police department to the rightful expectations of the public depends above all on the selection of officers who are intellectually, morally, and physically fit for positions of public trust, but also on personal and institutional accountability for their performance behind the badge. Everywhere in America—and conspicuously in Washington, D.C.—the greatest threat to honorable, professional, and trustworthy policing is the interference of politicians who understand neither the nature of police work nor the tradition of higher standards for public servants. Political meddling in police departments takes many forms, but the most dangerous to the public interest is forcing police departments to undertake massive and rapid hiring of new officers, especially where residency requirements limit the pool of eligible applicants. Everywhere that politicians force a mandate of this kind upon police, disaster follows.

In 1980, Miami, Florida, adopted such a policy. Miami mandated the immediate hiring of 200 new police, with 80 per cent to be minority residents of the city. As background investigations and the warnings of academy instructors confirmed at the time, many recruits were utterly unsuited to be police officers. Sloppy field training, inadequate supervision, and an ineffective Internal Affairs Division permitted these officers to behave with contempt for the law. By 1988, more than a third of them had been fired. Twelve members of a group known as the River Cops had been convicted of crimes ranging from drug trafficking to murder. Many of these recruits became police officers in order to profit from illegal drug activity.

The D.C. Disaster

Every mistake Miami made was repeated in Washington, D.C., ten years later—with utterly predictable and equally disastrous results. Faced with a congressional threat to withhold $430 million unless 1,800 new officers drawn from city residents were quickly hired in 1989 and 1990, the Metropolitan Police Department added 1,471 new officers. Normal application procedures were suspended in haste, and the passing grade on the entrance examination was reduced to 50 per cent (possibly to avoid embarrassment for the metropolitan public schools from which many of the applicants had graduated). Background investigations were abbreviated to the point of worthlessness, and FBI criminal-records checks were ignored. Academy and field training were dramatically shortened, personnel policies and regulations were overlooked, and some recruits were subjected to training by incompetent and dishonorable field training officers. The standards for entry were so lax that some applicants received their letters of acceptance from the police department at the same time that they received letters denying their applications for parole from prison.

By 1994, over one hundred of the police who entered the department in 1989 and 1990 had been arrested. Their crimes included drug trafficking, rape, and murder. Nearly as many officers from those recruit classes have such bad records that they cannot be used as credible trial witnesses. At least 256 others have escaped discipline or termination because the department has not initiated disciplinary action within forty-five days of the discovery of misconduct, as required by its own rules. These officers are an affront to the interests of the public, as well as to good police officers in Washington, D.C., and elsewhere.

The part that Congress and top elected officials in the city government have played in this debacle is a disgrace. But they do not bear the blame alone. Many police leaders are better educated and more attuned to respect for the public trust than elected officials, and every good police executive in the country knows that to forsake high standards of selection and accountability in policing is the surest way to return to the days when law enforcement was held in contempt and ridicule. Everywhere that police leaders bow to political pressure for rapid expansion, joined with residency requirements, they sacrifice selectivity and reduce their departments to mere microcosms of society, unworthy of the public trust. In Washington, public officials rationalize the decline of the department as a sign of the decline in society as a whole. This indefensible excuse puts the public trust at risk. Washington is not the only jurisdiction where these conditions obtain.

No large and complex human institution can be made perfect. No program of recruitment, education, accountability, and supervision can eliminate all bigotry, brutality, or corruption from a police department, or from any other selective institution. But political meddling in departmental hiring and training policies, conjoined with tacit police acquiescence in the reduction of standards, maximizes the entry of police who are unfit to wear the badge. This is the ordeal that has now been visited on the many fine police officers in Washington and on the residents of our nation's capital.

Educational Disaster

I hasten to add that disheartening and discouraging stories about public institutions and the public trust are not confined to policing, law enforcement, or legislative bodies. Schools, colleges, and universities are on the line—as is virtually every other kind of institution that bears the public trust. Let me conclude by describing a trend in education that poses an enormous threat to the public trust.

Consider schools of education in the United States and the students who enter them. Data from the College Board in May 1993 show combined SAT scores for students who desired or intended to enter the teaching profession to be depressingly low: 866 (out of a possible 1600) for bilingual education; 788 for early childhood education; 800 for the education of exceptional children; 829 for school psychology; 924 for secondary education; 836 for junior high school education; 760 for child development and nursery school education; 834 for elementary education (by far the largest group, with 25,383 students); 837 for special education. By contrast, students who aspire to teach the gifted and talented averaged a combined SAT score of 1036—but only 144 students nationwide fell into this category. The average combined SAT score for all classifications that involve education as a field of interest is 852.[7]

Critics who maintain that College Board tests discriminate against some groups of students—by ethnicity, or color, or gender, or economic background—dismiss or qualify the relevance of SAT data in assessing the quality of schooling in the United States. But even if there is some bias, it cannot outweigh the significance of such very low combined scores for so many prospective teachers. Worse, many schools of education have such low—or open—admission standards that academically poor students have no difficulties with entry. Furthermore, accreditation standards of the National Council for the Accreditation of Teacher Education (NCATE) do absolutely nothing to acknowledge or address these facts, and neither do conditions of eligibility for membership in the American Association of Colleges for Teacher Education (AACTE).

But the NCATE agenda for the education of teachers is even more dangerous. In 1992, the National Education Association passed a resolution that it would seek to include a requirement in all bargaining agreements that only graduates of NCATE-accredited schools be hired. In July 1994, the AACTE's board passed a resolution requiring NCATE accreditation as a condition of membership in AACTE, effective July 1, 2001. In the meantime, NCATE is seeking to persuade the states to make NCATE accreditation a requirement for all schools of education, which amounts to giving NCATE control over state certification; and it is also lobbying the federal government to make NCATE accreditation a necessary condition of student eligibility for federal financial aid. Should these efforts succeed, NCATE-NEA-AACTE will hold a monopoly on the preparation of teachers—at the expense of the public trust. NCATE argues that this is the way to build a profession, by analogy to law and medicine—but the analogy is empty without high entry standards. And NCATE and its allies will make no such commitment.

An NCATE-NEA-AACTE monopoly on schools of education would be intellectually disastrous. While AACTE publications advocate standards, they express dedication to the "interests of diversity" and on this account raise objections to the "standardization of standards." Doublespeak is the order of the day. NCATE elevates process—and consensus—to the highest place in consideration of standards, and thus ends up slavishly devoted to standards that are mush. Within schools of education, NCATE demands that "faculty instruction . . . provide students with systematically varied models of instruction"; that "specialty studies provide education students with mastery of the structure, skills, concepts, ideas, values, facts, and methods of inquiry that constitute their fields of specialization"; and that "the curriculum for professional studies component(s) incorporate multicultural and global perspectives." A "multicultural perspective" is defined as "a recognition of (1) the social, political, and economic realities that individuals experience in culturally diverse and complex human encounters and (2) the importance of culture, race, sex and gender, ethnicity, religion, socioeconomic status, and exceptionalities in the education process." A "global perspective" is defined as "the recognition of the interdependence of nations and the interlinking political, economic, and social problems of a transnational and global character."[8]

Now, these are not standards at all; they are not normative. In fact, NCATE's advocacy of multicultural perspectives obliterates all distinction between culture and color, while the "global perspective" is an empirical proposition that simply happens to be false. But when one criticizes these putative standards, the NCATE Board of Directors replies that "NCATE . . . standards are meant to express *a set of beliefs* about what direction schools of education should be taking" (emphasis added).[9] Real standards are not mere beliefs. They are intellectually defensible criteria for teaching and learning.

The Accreditation Canard

Accreditation means nothing if standards are too vague or imprecise —or mistaken—to be trusted. Unfortunately, the language of accreditation, as such, is taking on a certain rhetorical and persuasive power in public discourse, and this poses a risk to the public interest. Signs of this trend in the media can be comic, but they are worrisome, too. On late-night television, commercials ask whether viewers are dissatisfied with the guidance of "amateur psychics." By dialing a 900 number, callers can receive the services of "fully accredited, professional psychics." The "professional services" cost $3.95 per minute — $237 per hour. If nothing else about "accredited" psychics is "professional," their fees are. The commercials resemble advertisements for coats and stoles made of "genuine artificial mink."

As a matter of principle and for the sake of the public trust, I have withdrawn Boston University's School of Education from both NCATE and AACTE. The defense of the public trust in future schooling cannot, in my judgment, be undertaken from within these organizations.

The magnitude of this threat, and of the trends that now imperil the tradition of higher standards in all public institutions, raises anew the question whether an experiment in ordered liberty can long endure. We would do well to acquire the vigilance and resolve suggested by the words of Walter Lippmann a quarter of a century ago in his article "A Theory about Corruption":

> The American idea of government as a public trust to be carried on by disinterested men represents not the actuality but a long step ahead in the evolution of man. . . . It is a very difficult ideal to attain, and I know of no man in America even in our time who has felt able to be completely loyal to it. . . . The campaign . . . on behalf of the idea of trust is no mere repairing of something perfect that has broken down, but the implanting of a new habit of acting in the ancient consciousness of man.[10]

The tradition is not new. But the habit must ever be renewed. In a great many of our public institutions, the habit is at best insecure. And the directions of education and political fashion could destroy it altogether. Still, it has not entirely faded away—and many of the individuals and institutions that I work with show a settled disposition toward higher standards for public servants. The public trust hangs in the balance.

PART THREE

Religion and the Civic Order

14

The Christian Citizen
and Democracy

George Weigel

According to an ancient tradition that has taken numerous modern and contemporary forms, I am a dangerous man, a threat to the public order: not because my political inclinations run to anarchism or to fantasies of dictatorship, but precisely because I am an orthodox Christian.

Now I hasten to add that this alleged conflict is not how I usually experience the relationship between my Christianity and my life as a citizen of this democratic republic. The tonality of that relationship is far better, if far more variously, described by words like "energized," "frustrated," "appalled," "comforted," and "bemused."

Moreover, and in terms of behavior, the recording angel, observing the routines of my life, would not be likely to describe me as someone who is a threat to American democracy: I pay my taxes; I vote; I obey the laws (although I do confess to an incurable addiction to jaywalking and a disinclination to let the Montgomery County Department of Ecology and Recycling tell me when I may cut my lawn); I make arguments about public policy in a civil manner; I work through the

George Weigel is president of the Ethics and Public Policy Center and the author or editor of fourteen books on religion and public life. The most recent is *Idealism Without Illusions: U.S. Foreign Policy in the 1990s*.

normal political processes to help elect candidates I favor and I accept the results of elections in which candidates I prefer lose; I present myself for jury duty when I am called. As a speculative matter, I could, I suppose, become a threat to the American regime, in the sense that I would work to overthrow it—but that change in my behavior would be the result of a fundamental change in the character of the regime, not in my religious convictions.

Nevertheless, as a student of the history of Christianity, of church-state relations in America, and of the theory of democracy, I cannot help being impressed by the number of intelligent thinkers who were —and in some cases, are—firmly convinced that people like me are mortal perils *in* a democracy, and indeed *to* democracy.

The Trouble With Christians . . .

In his splendid book, *The Christians as the Romans Saw Them,*[1] Professor Robert Wilken, now of the University of Virginia, explores the nature of the threat that primitive Christianity and its truth-claims seemed to pose to the guardians of the established order of Rome. These charges are worth revisiting, if only as a striking reminder of the truth contained in the French aphorism *plus ça change, plus c'est la même chose*.

Pliny the Younger, for example, described Christianity in a letter to Trajan as a "degenerate sort of cult carried to extravagant lengths." Celsus, the late-second-century philosopher whose critique of Christianity occasioned one of the great works of Patristic apologetics, the *Contra Celsum* of Origen, thought that Christians were socially *outré* —men of limited intelligence whose faith was the religion of the stupid and, indeed, of stupidity.

Moreover, according to Celsus, Christians were sectarians who privatized religion and damaged public life by transferring religious values from the public realm to the sphere of private association. The Christian doctrine of the Incarnation, and the Christian claim that men were saved only by the name of Christ, denied the unity of the one God and undermined the authority of the one emperor. Porphyry, the biographer of Plotinus and the editor of his *Enneads,* asked, "How can men not be impious . . . who have apostasized from the customs of our fathers, through which every nation and city is sustained?"

Closer to our own times, Jean Jacques Rousseau, in the concluding chapter of his *Du Contrat Social,* which deals with the civil religion, said this about Christianity: "Far from winning the hearts of the citizens for the state, it removes them from it, as from all earthly things. I know of nothing that is more actively opposed to the social spirit." Christianity, he continues, is a purely spiritual religion, "which is occupied only with heavenly things; the native land of the Christian is not of this world." Moreover, the political defect of Christianity goes straight back to the founder of the firm (so to speak); as Rousseau put it:

> Jesus came in order to set up a spiritual kingdom on earth; thereby the theological system was separated from the political system, and this in turn meant that the state ceased to be *one* state, and that inherent tensions emerged, which have never ceased to agitate the Christian peoples.

The result is "a continuous struggle between the jurisdictions . . . which has made any reasonable civil order impossible in the Christian states." Christianity has created circumstances in which men have "two legislations, two sovereigns, two native lands," and thus are subjected to "antithetical obligations." So the Christian can never be, at one and the same time, a pious believer and a good citizen. Christianity is, in the final analysis, *"insociable"*: the true Christian cannot, by reason of his Christianity, be integrated into society.[2]

Then there is contemporary American law. Reading through the *dicta* on religion from the past fifty years of Supreme Court First Amendment decisions, one finds that the Court has not been content to render legal decisions about controverted matters; in the course of its judgments, it has painted a portrait of religious conviction similar to that of critics ancient and modern.

Indeed, American religion, in the decisions of the Supreme Court since *Everson* in 1947, appears as a profound danger to the democratic order. According to the Court, religion is divisive. Justice Blackmun went so far as to suggest, in the 1992 case *Lee v. Weisman,* that religion is potentially homicidal. Why? Because it is inherently coercive. And why is it inherently coercive? Because it is inherently irrational. Blackmun, again in *Lee v. Weisman,* sharply contrasted "rational debate" and "theological decree." On the Court's understanding of it, religion is something the democratic state can tolerate if consenting adults engage in it behind closed doors. But, as Justice Stevens suggested in *Grumet v. Board of Education of Kiryas Joel* (1993), it's probably bad for the kids.[3]

Christian citizens ought not to meet these ancient, modern, and contemporary objections—which could, of course, be easily multiplied—by softening the claims of Christian orthodoxy. To do so turns Christianity into a vaguely agreeable and unexceptionable set of behavioral injunctions, largely having to do with tolerance, which understood according to the contemporary rubric means "anything goes, so long as no one else gets hurt." H. Richard Niebuhr's lampoon of the attempt to retool the gospel to "fit" the regnant cultural assumptions of his day remains justly famous for its demolition of the vacuity of a certain modernist Christianity: "A God without wrath brought men without sin into a kingdom without judgment through the ministrations of a Christ without a Cross."

Well, brethren, no thank you. No, the only Christianity worth considering, in itself and in relationship to democracy, is the kind of Christianity that, in Henrik Ibsen's phrase, is far more deep-down-diving and mud-upbringing. A Christianity that takes itself seriously as the bearer of great truths about the human person, human community, and human destiny is a Christianity to contend with. A Christianity indistinguishable from the editorial page of the *New York Times* is hardly worth anyone's bother.

The relationship between Christianity and democracy has engaged some of the finest theological and philosophical minds of our times, including Jacques Maritain, Reinhold Niebuhr, and John Courtney Murray, whose reflections on the American Catholic experience of democracy paved the way for the Second Vatican Council's landmark "Declaration on Religious Freedom." Nor should we forget Karol Wojtyła, who once held the chair of moral theology at the Catholic University of Lublin and who now is the Bishop of Rome, John Paul II.

Although I can neither review their work in detail here, nor settle the theoretical argument about the relationship between piety and politics, and specifically between Christianity and democracy, I can describe and defend what it is that putatively dangerous folk like me bring to the ongoing task of self-governance that is American democracy. Mine is not, I hasten to add, an essentially utilitarian defense of "useful" religion. Rather, I want to draw out some of the implications of the Christian truth-claims about the human person, human community, and human destiny for the conduct of our national experiment in democracy. These claims are, I believe, true. That they have important *public* implications is also, I think, true. But their public *utility* is not the final warrant of their validity.

Resident Aliens

Preachers and essayists alike need a text. I take my text from the second-century "Letter to Diognetus," another venerable piece of Christian apologetics and one that has had a considerable influence on contemporary Roman Catholic social doctrine. We don't know who wrote the "Letter to Diognetus," nor do we know who Diognetus was. But our anonymous apologist had this to say about the Christian community he was describing, to what we may presume was an inquiring and open mind:

> . . . though they are residents at home in their own countries, their behavior there is more like that of transients; they take their full part as citizens, but they also submit to anything and everything as if they were aliens. For them, every foreign country is a homeland, and any homeland a foreign country.

Resident aliens — that sums it up rather admirably. So what do these "resident aliens" bring to public life? How does their conception of the human person, and the human project in history, bear on their conduct of themselves as citizens of a democracy? Could it be that the Christian notion of the "resident alien" not only makes Christians good democrats, but provides essential intellectual and moral buttressing for the democratic enterprise?

I would like to suggest that Christian orthodoxy and the behavior it warrants have made at least three major contributions to the American democratic project. The first of these contributions has to do with the problem of what we might call "making space for democracy."

Let us revisit for a moment the twenty-second chapter of Matthew's gospel — a text that has become so familiar to us that we may have forgotten its revolutionary import:

> Then the Pharisees went and took counsel how to entangle him in his talk. And they sent their disciples to him, along with the Herodians, saying, "Teacher, we know that you are true, and teach the way of God truthfully, and care for no man; for you do not regard the position of men. Tell us, then, what you think. Is it lawful to pay taxes to Caesar, or not?" But Jesus, aware of their malice, said, "Why do you put me to the test, you hypocrites? Show me the money for the tax." And they brought him a coin. And Jesus said

to them, "Whose likeness and inscription is this?" They said, "Caesar's." Then he said to them, "Render therefore to Caesar the things that are Caesar's, and to God the things that are God's." When they heard it, they marveled; and they left him and went away.

This is, as I say, a revolutionary text, and its public implications have been working themselves out for almost two millennia.

The Two Realms

There are two major points in this passage concerning authority and governance that I'd like to consider. First, Jesus gives Caesar his due. He does not deny Caesar's authority. Nor did the primitive Church, even though Caesar, in the person of his procurator Pontius Pilate, had executed the Church's Lord. In fact, the First Letter of Peter in the New Testament (widely regarded by biblical scholars as based on an ancient Christian baptismal sermon) enjoined the newly baptized to

> be subject for the Lord's sake to every human institution, whether it be to the emperor as supreme, or to the governors as sent by him to punish those who do wrong and to praise those who do right. (1 Peter 2.13-14)

Similarly, Paul enjoined the Romans to

> be subject to the governing authorities. For there is no authority except from God, and those that exist have been instituted by God. (Romans 13.1)

Caesar, in brief, is not to be denied what is rightly his.

But the second crucial aspect of this Matthean text—and its parallels in the gospels of Mark and Luke—is that Jesus, by juxtaposing Caesar and God, de-divinizes the emperor, and thus declares the priority of fidelity to God. As Paul later reminded his Romans, anything legitimately belonging to Caesar is Caesar's by reason, ultimately, of God's authority. But Jesus also insists that there are things that are God's, not Caesar's. Because God is God, Caesar is not God. And if Caesar attempts to occupy the ground that properly belongs to God alone, Caesar must be resisted.

This gospel pericope has shaped world-historical events down to our times. To take but one example: for five years after the accession in 1948 of the Communist government of Poland, the Polish Church, under the leadership of Cardinal Stefan Wyszyński, tried with great deftness to reach a *modus vivendi* with the regime that would preserve the fundamentals of the *libertas ecclesiae*—the freedom of the Church. But in May 1953, the regime implemented a decree that, in effect, turned the Church into a subsidiary of the Polish state: the state claimed authority to appoint and remove priests and bishops, and all clergy were required to take an oath of loyalty to the Polish People's Republic.

Cardinal Wyszyński now chose confrontation. In a historic sermon at Warsaw's St. John's Cathedral, he threw down the gauntlet:

We teach that it is proper to render unto Caesar the things that are Caesar's and to God that which is God's. But when Caesar seats himself on the altar, we respond curtly: he may not.

Later, the entire Polish episcopate issued a memorandum that concluded with the memorable words:

We are not allowed to place the things of God on the altar of Caesar. *Non possumus!*

Resistance cost Cardinal Wyszyński three years of imprisonment and internal exile under house arrest; but he eventually won his point. Moreover, the *Non possumus!* of the Polish episcopate was, I believe, a crucial marker on a long and complex road that led from the abrogation of freedom in east central Europe after World War II to the restoration of democracy in those lands in 1989. Wyszyński's successful defense of the independence of the Church made the complete imposition of totalitarianism in Poland impossible. And from that resistance Church came, in time, the overwhelming majority of the men and women who made the Solidarity revolution of 1980, and later the Revolution of 1989.[4]

Desacralizing Politics

More is involved here than rallying the troops, of course. Because Caesar is not God, the realm of the political is not a realm of ultimacy, or of totality. By de-divinizing Caesar, the Christian claim desacralizes politics—an achievement of great *public* importance. It clears the social space in which a politics of persuasion can form. It makes possible a juridical state whose primary function is to secure the basic rights of its citizens. Because Caesar is not God, we can build a civil society. Because Caesar is not God, the state is at the service of society, not the other way around. Because Caesar is not God, we can be democratic citizens of a limited, constitutional state.

Christianity thus brings to public life what Bishop Christoph Schönborn, the Dominican theologian who served as general editor of the new *Catechism of the Catholic Church,* has described as a "leavening of division."[5] The desacralization of politics that is implied in the de-divinization of Caesar is, in contemporary terms, a crucial barrier against the totalitarian temptation—and, perhaps less dramatically, against the tendency of all modern bureaucratic states to extend indefinitely the reach of their coercive power. When a pious grandmother in Queens insists that the state cannot mandate that the techniques of anal and oral sex be taught to primary school children; when Cardinal Wyszyński and the Polish episcopate issued their historic *Non possumus!;* when Gregory VII faced down the Holy Roman Emperor Henry IV in the eleventh-century investiture controversy—in each instance we hear the echoes of that confrontation between Jesus and his critics two thousand years ago.

To summarize: by establishing what we can call the "penultimacy of the political," orthodox Christianity makes a considerable contribution to the never-ending project of "making space for democracy." Indeed, if by "politics" we mean the ongoing and public deliberation of that great question, "How *ought* we to live together?" then Christianity's insistence on the penultimacy of the political helps make genuine *politics* possible.

Virtue and the Making of Democrats

The second contribution to American democracy that Christian orthodoxy and the behavior it warrants have made, and continue to make, has to do with the kind of a people we are and aspire to be: democrats.

In recent years, Americans have been powerfully reminded that there is no democracy without a sufficient number of democrats.

Without a sufficient critical mass of men and women who have internalized the habits of the heart and the mind—the *virtues,* if you will—that are essential to democracy, there can be no democratic self-governance.

Contrary to some of the expectations of the past, American democracy is not "a machine that will run of itself." The machine can, for a time, compensate for the inadequacies of the citizenry. But over the long haul, the machine needs mechanics—and mechanics of a certain cast of mind and soul—to make it serve the ends of human flourishing. The mechanics must also affirm the superiority of this kind of machine over others, precisely because of how they conceive their own moral worth and that of their neighbors.

I do not believe that Christian orthodoxy constitutes the only set of religious and moral warrants that can transform tyrants—what we all are at birth—into democrats. But I do believe that democrats—like Christians—are made, not born. And I believe that Christian personalism and a Christian understanding of the human condition can be a powerful and positive influence in shaping the attitudes toward "the other" that are essential to the democratic experiment.

C. S. Lewis—novelist, literary critic, and premier Christian apologist of the twentieth century (a man whose books continue to sell millions of copies every year)—articulated a Christian view of "the other" that has, I think, great relevance to the project of making true democrats. On June 8, 1941, Lewis, a layman with no formal theological training, preached a sermon at Oxford in the University Church of St. Mary the Virgin, the former pulpit of John Henry Newman and Edmund Pusey. His sermon, entitled "The Weight of Glory," ended like this:

> There are no *ordinary* people. You have never talked to a mere mortal. Nations, cultures, arts, civilizations—these are mortal, and their life is to ours as the life of a gnat. But it is immortals whom we joke with, work with, marry, snub, and exploit—immortal horrors or everlasting splendors. This does not mean that we are to be perpetually solemn. We must play. But our merriment must be of that kind (and it is, in fact, the merriest kind) which exists between people who have, from the outset, taken each other seriously—no flippancy, no superiority, no presumption. And our charity must be a real and costly love, with deep feeling for the sins in spite of which we love the sinner—no mere tolerance, or in-

dulgence which parodies love as flippancy parodies merriment. Next to the Blessed Sacrament itself, your neighbor is the holiest object presented to your senses.[6]

As it happens, Lewis was deeply skeptical about modernity. He never read newspapers, took no part in politics, and would probably have been more comfortable living in the thirteenth century than in the twentieth. But in "The Weight of Glory," he seems to have described rather precisely some of the core qualities we should want to see embodied in democratic citizens today: a commitment to democratic equality that is sustainable in and out of season because it is grounded in something far deeper than a consequentialist or utilitarian calculus; an ability to discriminate between serious and spurious claims of inequality; a willingness to engage the "other" seriously, across the many barriers of difference that separate us in a society of luxuriant plurality; a commitment to truth-seeking and truth-telling, regardless of the consequences ("living in the truth," as the human-rights resistance in Czechoslovakia put it in the 1980s[7]); a certain seriousness or *gravitas* about life, but without the kind of bogus solemnity characteristic of the public ceremonial of totalitarian states; a respect for the legitimately private space of others; and a charity that displaces naked ambition as the motive for public service.

Lewis challenged the congregation at St. Mary the Virgin to live their Christianity seriously for its own sake. But that basic Christian stance of reverence toward others who are never, ever "mere mortals" can also help form the kind of political community in which people "have, from the outset, taken each other seriously"—seriously enough to engage in the public discourse that is the lifeblood of democracy; seriously enough to engage a real argument around the question: "How *ought* we to live together?"

Piety, Politics, and Plurality

Put another way, and to adopt a formulation from the theologian Paul Tillich, democratic politics require a democratic political culture —and culture is formed by cult, by religion, by that which, in the root sense of the Latin *religio*, binds us together. The question is not *whether* piety has to do with politics; the question is *what kind of piety*, informing *what kind of politics*. Christian orthodoxy is, in this sense, a "piety" that engenders reverence toward my neighbor as a unique subject who is also the object of the salvific will of God. Christian piety, properly understood, helps form precisely the kind of citizens who can make a democracy work—particularly under conditions of plurality, amidst our racial, ethnic, and religious differences.

This latter point is worth considering for a moment. One of the not-so-subtle fears at work in contemporary debates about public piety in America is the fear that vibrant religious conviction, publicly expressed in the context of debates over public policy, inevitably leads to religious intolerance and, thence, to civic strife. No doubt that has happened; it continues to happen in other venues with which we are all familiar from the newspapers. But surely the more interesting datum about the American experience is that in the United States today—in this vibrantly, maddeningly, diversely, and, it appears, incorrigibly religious society—religious tolerance is *religiously* warranted.

The roots of religious tolerance in contemporary America are to be found neither in pragmatism nor in utilitarianism. Rather, those roots reach deeply into religious soil: tens of millions of Americans believe it the will of God that we not kill each other over religious differences.[8] Moreover, that conviction is strongest, I believe, among those whose Christian conviction is the most robust. Religious tolerance in America—the management, if you will, of plurality—is, in the main, a *religious* accomplishment. While that accomplishment has important inter-religious dimensions that we should honor and respect, the basic demographics of the situation reveal that the achievement of religious tolerance in America is, in the main, an achievement of Christians.

To be sure, religious tolerance is never secure. It must always be deepened and never taken for granted. Further, I would suggest that the religious accomplishment of religious tolerance will be truly secure only when it has begun to build a genuine pluralism—instead of accepting what today passes for pluralism, that which is really, and too often, a monism of indifference.

We are used to thinking of "pluralism" as a demographic fact. But the demographic fact is *plurality*. As the late John Courtney Murray taught us, *pluralism*, genuine pluralism, is never just a sociological fact. It is a great moral-cultural accomplishment. True pluralism means not the avoidance of differences, or an indifference to differences, but the thoughtful engagement of differences within the bonds of civility. Pluralism is an achievement: the achievement, Murray put it, of an orderly conversation, which is another way of saying a "civil society."

What is it that impels us to "lay down our arms . . . and . . . take up argument," as Murray put it?[9] Again, there are many ways to build the kind of character that allows one to "take up argument" and thereby become a democratic citizen. But surely one reasonable way is via the Christian claim that we are called *to* argument, and *out of* barbarism, by the grace of Christ, the Logos of God, who is himself the guarantor of the intelligibility and ultimate benignity of the created order. "Next to the Blessed Sacrament itself, your neighbor is the holiest object presented to your senses." Not a bad aphorism for a democrat amidst plurality, seeking to help turn that plurality into pluralism.[10]

Giving an Account

Christian conviction makes a third important contribution to our democratic regime in terms of its *legitimation:* which is to say that Christian religious convictions and moral norms enable Christians to *give an account* of their democratic convictions.

In the Declaration of Independence, as we all remember, Jefferson prefaced the moral case for American independence (and the bill of particulars against George III) by bowing toward a "decent respect to the opinions of mankind." Serious political action is political action undertaken after serious moral reflection and with serious moral justification. Jefferson's determination that an account be given—and that, indeed, a *moral* account be given—was not only admirable in its own time. This willingness to give an account—or as Jefferson put it, to "declare the causes" of our actions—ought to characterize the democrat making the case for democracy in any age.

At the very least, that ought to be the case for the American democracy because, as Lincoln insisted, America is, was, and (certain contemporary critics notwithstanding) always will be a "proposition country": a distinctive political community formed and sustained by certain intellectual and moral convictions. Who is the American, this new man, asked Crèvecoeur? He is, replied Lincoln at Gettysburg, the bearer of a proposition that was itself the product of moral convictions. To give an account of those convictions is in no small part the responsibility of citizenship, at least in these United States.

What is a good citizen? Richard John Neuhaus has put the matter succinctly, in these terms:

> A good citizen does more than abide by the laws. A good citizen is able to give an account, a morally compelling account, of the regime of which he is part. He is able to justify its defense against its enemies, and to convincingly recommend its virtues to the next generation so that they, in turn, can transmit the regime to citizens yet unborn. This regime of liberal democracy, of republican self-governance, is not self-evidently good and just. An account must be given. Reasons must be given. They must be reasons that draw authority from that which is higher than the self, from that which is external to the self, from that to which the self is ultimately obliged.[11]

Father Neuhaus goes on to ask, provocatively, whether an atheist could meet this test of good citizenship. Now there are many ways of being an atheist, and it is not without piquancy to recall that atheism —being a-theos, without God, or more precisely, the gods—was the charge leveled against Christians who were thereby, by definition, regarded as subversives in times of Roman persecution. Neuhaus, however, is particularly concerned about the distinctive contemporary form of being a-theos, "without God"—which he styles the "atheism of unreason": a way of being a-theos that "denies not only the possibility of truth claims about God but the possibility of claims to truth at all."[12]

In this conceptual world, if such it may be called, where there is no truth per se, but only the truth that the relevant "community of discourse" agrees to take as true, to deny God is as nonsensical as affirming God. One wonders, Neuhaus concludes, whether it is at all possible for someone who is a-theos in this fashion to be a good citizen in the fullest sense of the term. By his own self-understanding, the atheist of unreason can give no morally persuasive or compelling account of the democratic regime, or, better, no account that can reach beyond the community of selves that happens to find it true.[13]

This judgment provoked an interesting response from a more old-fashioned atheist, Paul Kurtz, former professor of philosophy at SUNY-Buffalo and the author of Humanist Manifesto II. Kurtz rumbled, in response to Neuhaus's argument, "Is this the opening salvo of a campaign to deny atheists their rights?" To which Father

Neuhaus responded, "Relax, Mr. Kurtz. Your rights are secured by my understanding of the truth, even if mine are not by yours."[14]

Truth and Freedom

In an intellectual and cultural climate in which, as Alasdair Mac-Intyre argued years ago, it is extraordinarily difficult to say "You *ought* to do this" rather than merely "I'd *prefer* that you do this," we seem to be stymied by Pontius Pilate's famous question to Jesus in the gospel of John: "Truth? What is truth?" Perhaps cynically, perhaps sincerely, Pilate believed that the question "What is truth?" was a real conversation-stopper. So do many of our contemporaries, not least our contemporaries in the academy. But for a democracy that must give an account—to itself, to its competitors and enemies, and to succeeding generations—of the truths about the human person and human community on which it was founded, Pilate's question should start the needed conversation, not stop it.[15]

In his 1993 encyclical letter *Veritatis Splendor,* "The Splendor of the Truth," Pope John Paul II discusses the relationship between truth and freedom. Contrary to the regnant media caricature of John Paul, the Polish pope in fact celebrates and champions the modern world's emphasis on political freedom. (As a man who spent the first forty years of his adulthood living under, and struggling against, Nazis and Communists, how could he not?) But John Paul also has some sharp questions to pose.

What happens, the pope asks, when freedom gets untethered from truth? Can freedom stand by itself, without decomposing into license? And if freedom becomes license, then freedom becomes its own undoing, as every aspect of personal and social life becomes—as Nietzsche understood—merely the assertion of power. Among many other things, the death of democracy results. For when truth is democratized—that is to say, when the truth is no more than the will of each one of us or a majority of us—then democracy, unable to give a compelling account of its own truth, is defenseless before its enemies.[16] Democracy, to repeat, is not a machine that will run of itself. Our political history as an independent nation began with the assertion of certain "self-evident truths"; as Americans we ought not to find the pope's reassertion of a relationship between freedom and truth strange, or foreign.

Who Defends Democracy?

For most Americans, moral truth is religiously informed and derived; but does this fact constitute some sort of threat to democracy? To answer this question, we would do well to revisit Madison's famous *Memorial and Remonstrance,* one of the key texts in forming the American constitutional tradition of religious freedom. We are so used to the notion of "rights" as trumps, sundered from any sense of duties, that we may miss Madison's understanding of religious freedom as an inalienable right that is ordered to a prior and supervening duty. But here is the *Memorial and Remonstrance:*

> It is the duty of every man to render to the Creator such homage and such only as he believes to be acceptable to him. This duty is precedent, both in order of time and in degree of obligation, to the claims of Civil Society. Before any man can be considered as a member of Civil Society, he must be considered as a subject of the Governor of the Universe: And if a member of Civil Society, who enters into any subordinate Association, must always do it with a reservation of his duty to the General Authority; much more must every man who becomes a member of any particular Civil Society, do it with a saving of his allegiance to the Universal Sovereign.[17]

I do not argue that Christians are the only people capable of giving an account of their democratic commitments. There are other accounts, and some of them have considerable public purchase; still other accounts are thin indeed, and one fears for the future of the Republic if these thin accounts were to become dominant in the populace (as they already are among too many intellectuals). But the Christian claim that we can give such an account—that is, a defense of the American proposition and experiment based on biblically warranted moral understandings—puts Christians in a position to offer, I believe, a more robust legitimation of the American democratic regime than some, and perhaps many, others. And that is a matter of no small public consequence in a country such as ours.

By way of conclusion, let me suggest that a great paradox has emerged in the past two hundred years or so of Western history, the years in which Christendom has come to an end.

I believe it *very* good for the Church that Christendom is over and done with. The end of Christendom frees the Church for its essential, constitutive tasks of evangelization, worship, and service. The end of Christendom has also got the Church out of the coercion business, one of the great blots on its record, which Pope John Paul has called Christians publicly to repent of in preparation for the turn of the millennium. That same pope, in his 1990 encyclical letter on Christian mission, flatly rejects coercion in evangelization, writing that "the Church proposes; she imposes nothing."[18] As the Holy Father and all the rest of us know, that has not always been the case. But that it is *now* the case for one billion Roman Catholics is very good news for the Church and the world, in the twenty-first century and the third millennium of the common era. The Church has no business putting the coercive power of the state behind its truth claims; nor does the Church have any business re-sacralizing politics, of any ideological hue.

But here is our paradox: I am not sure that this disentanglement that we call "the end of Christendom" has been quite such an un-differentiated blessing for those persons and institutions charged with the tasks of governance. The machine, to repeat one last time, will not and cannot run of itself. If democracy does not tend to the safe maintenance and moral health of that social space we call "civil society," a flat majoritarianism will decay into a subtle totalitarianism, and we will be unable to keep the bureaucratic state under control. Democracy needs a critical mass of democrats, and democrats are made, not born. How shall we "grow" the democrats that we need to sustain our democracy? The American democracy, in particular, must be able to render an account of itself—to offer a persuasive and compelling moral justification for this strange, sloppy, confused, mad-dening, exhilarating, tawdry, and glorious way of doing the public business. How can we "give an account," unless we have some way of affirming the truth of things?

It is good, indeed it is essential, that the democratic state not be a sacred state. But the democratic state needs the disentangled Church —the post-Christendom Church—in order to remain a democracy governed by law, in which freedom serves the ends of genuine human flourishing.

Perhaps it could be different, as a matter of abstract speculation. But we live in a real world, not an abstract world. In this real world —on whose culture and civil society the atheism of unreason and its natural child, moral relativism, have had a profound impact—

democracy is in serious trouble. When three justices of the Supreme Court of the United States can reduce the meaning of freedom to "the right to define one's own concept of existence, of meaning, of the universe, and of the mystery of human life,"[19] we are in deep trouble.

Here we have no community of democratic discourse. Here we have no civil society. Here, rather, are congeries of monads, who can hardly be considered citizens since they are related and mutually engaged only by their capacity to contest one another's "concept of existence" by lawsuit. Here stand the state and the individual. And we ought to know, from the history of this most sanguinary of centuries, where that eventually leads.[20]

Look how far we have come from the *Memorial and Remonstrance* of James Madison. The Court seems to believe that all moral judgments are, somehow, sectarian religious judgments; and since those kinds of judgments are, on the Court's understanding, inherently private and un-public, they cannot be in play in the public square. The result is not only a public square stripped of religion but also a morally denuded American *agora* in which, by definition, there can be no account given in defense of the regime.

This is clearly an impossible situation.

So I leave you, not with a resolution of the paradox, but with the thought that the far greater burden of the end of Christendom is born by the democratic state than by the Church. The Church can now give a carefully and deeply argued account of why it supports and defends the democratic project in history. But can American democracy?

15

From Religion to Spirituality

Robert Wuthnow

Three questions about religion and values present themselves. First, is there still a core of unifying values in American culture? Second, is religion a significant source of these values? Third, does this spiritual foundation seem to be slipping away? All three questions are debated with much heat by many Americans. All three are the subject of surveys by sociologists, studies by scholars, and pronouncements by the media. The fact that we contest these questions is perhaps evidence that all is not well—that we as a nation *are* engaged in a great culture war. I want to argue that all three questions can be answered unequivocally in the affirmative. Is there a core of unifying values? Yes. Is religion important to these values? Yes. Do we feel that these values are in danger? Yes.

If pundits are fond of quoting Jefferson on these matters, sociologists are fond of quoting no one. I risk little, therefore, by quoting someone unfashionable. In his long tenure at Harvard University, Talcott Parsons wrote more on the sources of social cohesion than on any other topic. This issue so dominated his work that the generation of social scientists who came of age in the 1960s considered him

---

Robert Wuthnow is the Gerhard Andlinger Professor of Sociology and director of the Center for the Study of American Religion at Princeton University. His latest book is *Rethinking Materialism: Perspectives on the Spiritual Dimension of Economic Behavior* (Eerdmans, 1995).

191

quaintly irrelevant to the political struggles of their time. Yet Parsons's work holds insights that we can scarcely continue to ignore.

Parsons was a functionalist. He believed that all societies must satisfy certain basic requirements if they are to sustain themselves over time. One of these requirements is what Parsons called "integration." In his authoritative work *The Social System* (1951), Parsons said that for a society to achieve integration, it must act negatively by "defining the limits of permissiveness for 'private' interests"; it must also act positively by the "promotion of collective goals or interests."[1] Both tasks, Parsons argued, are achieved at a number of levels, not least of which is the institutionalization of social roles. That is, most ordinary behavior—such as working, consuming, or maintaining a family—is governed by implicit, well-established norms. These norms permit the pursuit of self-interest, but within limits; they also contribute to the common good and to an implicit consensus about the nature of that good. Parsons emphasized that basic "value orientations" are essential to social integration, because implicit norms of behavior can be held in place only by an underlying authority that renders them legitimate or binding.

Parsons does not differ dramatically from any number of other sociologists in his starting point. He is unusual, however, in emphasizing institutionalized patterns of behavior and legitimating values. Institutionalized patterns of behavior are especially worthy of attention because they are so often overlooked. That airlines run mostly on schedule, that shelves are stocked in supermarkets, that millions of Americans purchase homes and raise children, and that these children are entertained with baseball, television, and trips to Disney World— these facts are a significant source of what makes America one. And for that reason we are rightly concerned that rioting, looting, homelessness, child abuse, baseball strikes, and indecency on television may be evidence of erosion in the moral fabric. But Parsons also emphasizes values, which we must consider, for our values more than our lifestyles are the foundation of our national unity.

Conflict and Common Values

Social scientists have devoted a great deal of attention to the study of values. As with all research, such studies are limited, especially when people give lip service to values they may not practice. Nevertheless, the evidence is clear that a consensus does prevail on certain values. We cherish family, social obligations, responsibility, freedom, conviction, and equality—just as we have in the past. In one study that asked about values, 96 per cent of respondents listed family as a top value, 97 per cent stressed faithfulness to friends and colleagues, 93 per cent emphasized standing up for one's beliefs, 96 per cent cited self-respect, and 85 per cent included equality of opportunity.[2] These values also recognize diversity (my family, friends, and convictions may be different from yours), but the fact that we so universally ascribe them priority is itself unifying.

Critics note, however, that some American values may be centrifugal: they encourage too much individualism and not enough concern with collective obligations. Yet our sharing of common values is also deeply rooted in a respect for individualism—something else that unifies us. We Americans have always managed great diversity by a respect for the rights and differences among individuals. Moreover, we also hold values that temper our individualism. For instance, one study showed that 78 per cent of Americans say it is "very important" to them to help make the world a better place, 74 per cent say this about helping people in need, and 64 per cent say this about giving time to help others.[3]

Of course, people differ in the emphasis they place on various values. To some, a particular value is "absolutely essential"; to others, it is "very important." Sociologists use these differences in response to discover the soft spots in a consensus—in this case, whether segments of the population hold certain values less strongly than the majority of Americans. Take the value of family. In one study, 96 per cent of working Americans said family was "very important" to them; 92 per cent of divorced people and 94 per cent of those who were separated said the same; and 86 per cent of those who had never been married also said the same.[4] The fact that most single people eventually marry and that most divorced people remarry within a few years supports the inference from such findings that family is, indeed, a consensual value. Or consider the much-maligned younger generation—Generation X—who are allegedly without socially redeeming values. One study found that 84 per cent of them believe that working to make the world a better place is "absolutely essential" or "very important," and two-thirds are currently involved in some kind of community service.[5]

We can belabor such evidence, but it is consistent with how we debate values publicly. Significantly, we don't debate *whether* we have values; instead, we disagree about their meaning. Few in the so-called family-values debate, for instance, question the importance of families. Instead, we argue about what constitutes a family and how to strengthen families. We are unified in proclaiming values, but we see their manifestations as diverse. Lifestyles, for example, are perhaps more varied than ever before, but social analysis has always recognized the importance of distinguishing lifestyles from values. This distinction is borne out in responses: another study found that only 51 per cent of the public say it is "very important" to them to be married (62 per cent say this about having children)—despite the fact that virtually everyone cherishes the love and caring that takes place in families.[6]

During his years at Harvard, Talcott Parsons trained many students, some of whom are more widely known in the current discussion of common values than their teacher. Robert Bellah and his famous discussion of civil religion is one example.[7] Clifford Geertz and his treatment of ritual as a means of resolving cultural contradictions is another.[8] Less widely known outside of professional circles is Neil Smelser's work on collective behavior. In a book perhaps too comprehensive to be readily grasped, Smelser set forth the range of conditions necessary to determine whether or not social conflict will fundamentally rupture the social order.[9] Democratic societies such as our own, he argued, possess a number of safeguards that prevent conflict from becoming fundamentally disruptive. Most conflicts are contained as struggles about the allocation of resources, or about the means by which values are to be pursued—not about values themselves. Grievance procedures, legislative mechanisms, and even competing interests increase the likelihood that conflicts can be resolved in ways that do not challenge the core assumptions of the society.

Yet Smelser also observed that core assumptions are never without inherent tensions of their own. An effective strategy for interest groups that feel ignored, therefore, is to raise the stakes, as it were, by focusing on values themselves. Especially if legislative action is desired, a debate about values may force the institution of more sweeping proposals than if norms and resources alone are at stake. Leaders of interest groups will thus commonly appeal to basic values. But our society must weigh the dissent of such appeals against public opinion and consider them in relation to the democratic structures designed to accommodate them.

A tension persists within the core of our values between the desire for individual freedom and the need for individual restraint because Americans *are* concerned about public morality and the collective good. By the 1980s, many Americans wanted to curb what they saw as an excessive freedom deriving from the 1960s and early 1970s. Over the past decade we have heard much about public morality, ethics, social responsibility, duty, honor, virtue, and personal discipline. Some people, polls show, are convinced we need more restraint, while others remain firmly committed to the value of personal freedom. But even this tension provides an instructive lesson in the nature of common values. Most Americans who firmly believe in strict moral discipline also believe in personal freedom—to the point that their behavior is a compromise between the two. What in media accounts may appear as a deep divide in cultural orientation turns out to be relatively subtle in practice.

If we pay close attention to what research shows—rather than relying too heavily on the mass media—we see that in the diverse America of today there is a virtual consensus about the importance of certain values, that these values do influence behavior, and that they also permit behavior to vary considerably in its specific expressions. Many of these values have a socially redeeming dimension: they underscore social responsibility, care for the needy, equality of opportunity, and respect for individual rights. While not distinctly American, these values are very much part of the American heritage. They permit us to take pride in our country, to feel that we are indeed part of a single society, and yet they allow us to recognize our common heritage with all of humanity.

Diverse Religions and Social Unity

Scholars divide over the role of religion in maintaining the core values of American culture. Some argue that religion is essential; others think that religion produces division, not consensus. This debate does not simply reflect personal convictions, as much as they too may be at stake. In the social sciences, the debate is rooted more in competing interpretations of the literature we have just been considering. Parsons recognized that religion, along with the family, is a source of values and a way in which values are legitimated. Yet perhaps because of his penchant for neat schemes of classification, he associated religion more with what he called "latency management" or "pattern maintenance" than with social integration.[10] Following Max Weber, Parsons argued that religion functions mainly to protect us from disillusionment. Faced with death, illness, or evidence that "the wicked prosper," citizens remain committed to their core values because religion offers them hope, comfort, and ways of coping with evil. Parsons was thus able to argue that while religious beliefs and practices were diverse, they served similar functions and reinforced common values. Indeed, Parsons was less concerned about the alleged decline of religion than many of his contemporaries because he believed religious values were widely shared—even by self-described non-religious Americans.

Other scholars have considered religion as the conveyer of the idea of transcendence or larger meanings, and thus as a source of values for the populace as a whole. In his work on civil religion, Robert Bellah focused substantively on the explicit use of God-language in American public life to communicate the notion of transcendence. He also stressed that functional alternatives, such as civic republicanism, could be part of the civil religion as long as these alternatives envisioned a conception of transcendence in relation to the people as a collectivity.[11] Peter Berger wrote of the need of individuals and societies for an overarching "sacred canopy"; but he too made it clear that organized religion was only one of the ways in which a symbolic universe of this kind might be constructed and maintained.[12]

One way to assess empirically whether or not religion contributes to common values and social unity is to examine the relationships between religious values and other widely held values of the American population. Because virtually everyone values family, we cannot say that family is a value that depends on direct reinforcement from religious concerns. Yet those who value religious commitment more deeply do say they value family more deeply.[13] The same is true of helping the needy, making the world a better place, and doing volunteer work: those who value their faith are most likely to place high value on these other activities.[14] We can reasonably conclude from such findings that some of our most deeply cherished values would not be cherished as much were religion to disappear from the national landscape.

Religion also reinforces unifying values by providing opportunities for people to put them into practice. In my research on compassion, for instance, I found that people who believe in God are likely to value helping the needy; the effect of religious belief on *actually doing volunteer work,* however, is much stronger among those who belong to a congregation (and not just because they volunteered within their congregation).[15] Research on voting and other political activities shows the same: while many people say it is important to be involved in such activities, active membership in a religious congregation translates words into action.

Is There Really a Culture War?

Many people now voice a concern that religion has become a divisive force, rather than a source of unity. Nearly a decade ago, I wrote of the tensions that were emerging between religious liberals and religious conservatives.[16] A 1984 survey showed that the two were suspicious of each other; many people reported that their contacts with the other group had been negative or mixed; and the more contact there was, the less each group liked the other. In more recent research, I have found that some of these patterns remain. People still divide themselves along a continuum from liberal to conservative, and more put themselves at the extremes of this continuum than did a decade ago. Borrowing very loosely from my research, some have argued that religion is now the basis, not of unity, but of a culture war.[17]

Yet there is little evidence of the culture war that exists in the minds of many journalists and political operatives. Rather than being in one camp or the other, most Americans are actually in the middle. And close comparisons of people in the opposing camps show that while they differ markedly in usages of language, they differ very little in charitable, familial, or economic values.

In fact, virtually all Americans—even self-styled liberals who, critics claim, do not believe in any authoritative form of transcendence—believe in God and pray regularly to that God. Almost all of those who do not believe the Bible is the *infallible* word of God nevertheless regard it as the *divinely inspired* word of God. While most of those who hold the Bible to be literally true cannot answer simple factual questions about it, they believe it is true because some portion of it has been validated by their personal experience.

None of this denies the important differences among religious persuasions nor minimizes the significance of debate among them. It is true that religious orientation is a good predictor of political orientation, of voting, of views on abortion, homosexuality, and many other issues. But to reach a nuanced understanding of the impact of religious belief on these issues requires a distancing from sweeping generalizations about cultural disunity. One recent study, for instance, painstakingly examined a number of surveys over the past two decades to determine if the differences between conservative and liberal religious groups were producing serious differences in attitudes on family values and racial and social welfare issues, including whether or not the growing division between rich and poor might be aggravating racial and class tensions. The study found that religious differences were not becoming more pronounced over these issues; and it found that on behavioral matters—such as divorce and other indications of family fealty—religious orientations made little difference at all.[18]

Another study that sought directly to examine the "culture wars" thesis found some evidence that different world-views do produce different judgments on such issues as abortion and homosexuality; it also revealed that social position and membership in interest groups more strongly correlate with different political views. In fact, the study showed that a majority of Americans combine more than one world-view and that these combinations are a unifying and not a divisive force.[19]

It seems abundantly clear that in many other ways religion is much more a source of common values and assumptions than it is a cause of deep social antagonism. To be sure, with no religious presence at all in America, we would have no church-and-state issues. But without understanding America's religious values, it is hard to imagine American humanitarianism, our admission that most of us pray, our doctrine of basic human rights, or even our nation's continuing appeal to millions of immigrants.

America: A Sacred Place?

Evidence that religion helps maintain our consensual values notwithstanding, there is much concern that religion is being displaced and that this displacement may have far-reaching effects on our capacity to preserve civic harmony. The reasons for this concern are, at one and the same time, obvious and not so obvious. Obviously, religious groups are the main antagonists in political controversies rather than agents of reconciliation. Obviously, religion is being excluded from public life in potentially sinister ways. And obviously, with each passing year, American culture and American religion itself become more diverse. Yet by many indications, religion is scarcely weaker than it was a few decades ago and, by the standards of most Western democracies, considerably stronger than in other countries, such as in Europe, where social order has certainly not broken down. Confidence in religious organizations, membership in these organizations, and attendance at religious services appear to have remained quite stable over the past quarter century.

Why religion appears to be in an increasingly precarious position is less obvious. We can only understand this by attending to "deep structure" and not just surface evidence. The deep structure of American religion consists of our longing to occupy sacred space. Despite our insistence on the transcendence of God, we have always wanted to sacralize the ground on which we walk, to create a new Jerusalem, a city on a hill, a holy place in which to dwell.

In the 1950s we came very close to realizing this ambition. At least in our imagination, we were the chosen people who had defended the world against totalitarianism and were now called to save it from Communism. At home, we built churches and synagogues in record numbers and filled these places of worship with our offspring. Protestants were less confident that the kingdom of God could be constructed in Middletown, but they believed God would dwell in their churches and families. They were still suspicious of Catholics, but took heart from the desire of Catholics to live at peace in a land dedicated to God. Jews struggled with the terrible reality of the Holocaust by denying it, by assimilating, and by creating synagogues that were quiet places of worship. African-Americans had their own churches and, to white Americans, seemed content with a "separate but equal" stake in America. "In God We Trust" provided a comforting motto for the sacred space we created for ourselves.

The 1990s look very different. Local congregations no longer occupy the center of our neighborhoods. The Norman Rockwell painting of a white middle-class couple sitting with their two children in church on Sunday morning is an image from the 1950s. Statistically, that image now represents only eight per cent of the American population. The rest are non-white, unmarried, without children, or not actively involved in a religious congregation.

Rather than enjoying the "temple religion" of the new Jerusalem, we are more apt to experience the "tabernacle religion" of the wilderness. We meet in small groups. We sense that the gentlemen's agreement among religious leaders of the 1950s no longer pertains. We are painfully aware of our diversity. We are often distrustful of the religion industry in its variously commercialized and politicized manifestations. It seems that the religious underpinnings of our collective values are slipping away. We no longer feel that we are safely dwelling in the house of the Lord.

Shopping for Spirituality

It is important, however, to recognize that spirituality has not left us—it has just become less visible. In one national poll, two-thirds of Americans said religion was playing a diminished role in public life; yet two-thirds said spirituality was playing an increased role in their own lives.[20] What this means is that the monopoly of spirituality by the religion industry has been broken. In the 1950s, virtually the only accepted way of being spiritual was to participate in a congregation, listen to what the clergy said, and read the texts clergy recommended. Membership was exclusive, and the clergy hoped it would last for generations. This no longer is the case. At some point in their lives, most people switch congregations, if not denominations or faith traditions. Their primary loyalty is more likely to attach to a small group than to a large congregation, and they are likely to spend no more than a few years with the same small group.[21] Increasingly, people *shop* for spirituality as they do for everything else. They pick up books about angels at the shopping mall, attend an Alcoholics Anonymous meeting on Thursday, visit with their Muslim co-worker over coffee, participate in a Zen class at the YMCA, receive political information from the Christian Coalition or the ACLU, and watch an inspirational program about the sacred meaning of baseball.

Living in spiritual hyperspace, it is hard not to wonder if the sacred dwellings of our ancestors can ever be regained. We try, of course. We ask our lawmakers to bring prayer and the Ten Commandments back into the classroom. We make personalized pilgrimages to Native American sweatlodges or Tibetan temples. We worry that our separate quests, even if successful, will not sanctify the whole space in which we live. The question remains, then, of how we can be unified despite the growing diversity of our spiritual orientations.

My own view is that the increased diversity in American spirituality can be accommodated within our traditions and, indeed, be a source of unity—but not in the way we came to expect during the 1950s. The religious consensus of the future will more likely be thin than thick. It will inhere in a common recognition of the sacred, of the need for an encompassing system of meaning, and of highly personalized spiritualities. Indeed, part of what will hold us together may be our common experience of loss. Some years ago, Peter Berger put it well: "Individuals keep on constructing and reconstructing refuges that they experience as 'home.' But, over and over again, the cold winds of 'homelessness' threaten these fragile constructions."[22]

Beyond Religious Monopolies

In conclusion, at least four points of a more practical sort are worth making. The first is that debate itself is not tantamount to a lack of consensus on core values. We might not go so far as some of the functionalists of Parsons's generation did in arguing that conflict itself reinforces common values. Yet competition has generally been good for American religion, and the controversies in which religious groups have been embroiled in the past decade have at least made the public —not to mention its leaders—much more aware that religion matters.

Another point—perhaps best taken as a caveat to my main argument—is that shared values should not be understood strictly in terms of propositional, rational, philosophical, or creedal formulations of truth. If work, home-ownership, and baseball are essential to our national unity, they are not so only because they keep society in business. They are essential because they are symbolic—because they supply us with deeper meanings, with stories that we can tell our friends, with experiences that link us to the past, and that we can share with our children. It may be impossible to articulate first principles about any of these activities. We know only that we care deeply about them, and that most other Americans do, too.

With respect to religion, we need to remember that it thrives best in an arena of open discussion. Perhaps it is cynical to suggest that religion sustains itself by talking. Yet we know that human behavior is scarcely human unless it is imbued with meaning, and that meaning depends on language. American religion has always found itself in the midst of the tension between being many and being one. A story such as the parable of the Good Samaritan is known and remembered by millions of Americans. It provides a way for us to understand good deeds when we see them or when we perform them. For other Americans, this parable is outside their subculture. They do not know it or desire to know it. But they have learned stories that convey a similar message from their own traditions, in their families, and even from secular books, television, and motion pictures. Both the free exercise of religion and protection against the establishment of religious monopolies are vital to keeping religion active in American culture.

Finally, we must recognize fully that organized religion no longer holds the monopoly on spirituality it once held. Religious leaders themselves do not know how to confront this new reality. Some see it as a new opportunity for marketing their wares; others are content to live with diminished expectations; still others are exploring new media and alternative ways of influencing individual spirituality. Over the next two decades, the religion industry will undergo a radical transformation in adapting to the new diversity in American life. Religion may well experience contraction in congregational membership, regular attendance at services, and receipts from charitable giving. Many fear that religion will be completely excluded from public life with a purely secular culture as a result. More likely, the exclusion of some forms of religion will result in a rebirth of spirituality in other forms.

It has always been easy to think of American religion in monolithic terms. Despite its diversity, we have grown accustomed to thinking that religion was either on the increase or in decline, and that the residual category was secularism. The more complex demand is to think about the future in terms of *qualitative* changes in spirituality. Only then can we focus on how deeply our values are actually being influenced by our quest for the sacred.

16

The Collapse of the Mainline Churches

Thomas C. Reeves

I n the course of the many centuries that church and state were united in the West, religious bodies were often at the center of national unity and identity. One thinks, for example, of nineteenth-century Prussia and the Lutherans, pre-revolutionary Russia and Orthodoxy, the Roman Catholics in Spain, and the Church of England in the Victorian era. One scholar has written of the latter, "English Protestant religion, founded on the Prayer Book and overruled by the Establishment, with its sermons and hymns added, was the very backbone of the country. . . ."[1]

Religion was a vital part of the colonial experience in America, of course, and after the separation of church and state, Protestant denominations flourished and multiplied. Throughout the nineteenth century, religion played a major role in all areas of American life. This religion was largely Protestant and evangelical—a faith that stressed individualism, morality, practicality, hard work, a denominational conception of the Church, and a generally close identification with American institutions.

Thomas C. Reeves is professor of history at the University of Wisconsin–Parkside and is the author of several books, including the bestselling *A Question of Character: A Life of John F. Kennedy* (The Free Press, 1991).

A Christian Country

Clergymen, educators, businessmen, and Americans from all walks of life attributed their freedom, their prosperity, and their happiness to the God they worshipped in their churches. This was reflected in the nation's public schools, where Protestant morality and nationalism were blended and propagated. Pioneering educator Horace Mann warned, "If we do not prepare children to become good citizens—if we do not develop their capacities, if we do not enrich their minds with knowledge, imbue their hearts with the love of truth and duty, and a reverence for all things sacred and holy, then our republic must go down to destruction, as others have done before it. . . ."[2] Popular textbooks by Noah Webster and William Holmes McGuffey were saturated with references to Christian ethics and virtues.

Most Americans assumed that they lived in a Christian country. In 1892, following a lengthy review of historical evidence, Justice David Brewer wrote in a majority opinion of the United States Supreme Court that "this is a religious people. This is historically true. From the discovery of this continent to the present hour there is a single voice making this affirmation . . . this is a Christian nation."[3]

For the first sixty-five years of the twentieth century, churches of all denominations continued to earn the respect and admiration of most Americans. Despite jolting changes associated with the Industrial Revolution, urbanism, the rise of the mass media, immigration, education, and world war, Americans linked their personal and national existence with their confidence that they were a special people chosen by God. Churches were part of this chosenness, offering respectability along with the usual spiritual benefits. The Judaeo-Christian ethic—as the natural law fulfilled by Christ was called from the 1930s on—was accepted by practically all Americans.

In 1931, the U.S. Supreme Court declared what almost all Americans considered obvious: "We are a Christian people, according to one another the equal right of religious freedom, and acknowledging with reverence the duty of obedience to the will of God."[4] Two decades later, in 1952, this sentiment was echoed by Supreme Court justice William O. Douglas: "We are a religious people whose institutions presuppose a Supreme Being."[5]

The 1950s have been called a "golden age" of American Christianity. Church membership, attendance, and financial donations reached new heights. The National Council of Churches was created. Composed of twenty-nine denominations, its combined membership included 33 million church members and 143,000 congregations. When asked by the Gallup poll if religion was "very important" in their lives, 76 per cent of Protestants and 83 per cent of Catholics responded positively.[6]

Movie, radio, and television censorship illustrated the authority of churches to shape public opinion. Stores closed on Sundays. Colleges supervised the morals of their students. Politicians, led by President Eisenhower, continued to assure Americans that they belonged to a God-fearing nation. The words "under God" were added to the pledge of allegiance. Birth rates were high, and the Christian family was glorified; a popular slogan was, "The family that prays together stays together."

Much changed, of course, in the revolutionary period of 1965-1975. A division occurred between those Americans (often younger) who absorbed the new culture of the Vietnam war years and those who did not. A pattern of life emerged that embraced drugs, rock and punk music, feminism, free sex, abortion, gay rights, racial equality, reverse discrimination, environmental awareness, nonviolence, radical changes in education, and general anti-Americanism. The "Ike Age" seemed almost prehistoric.

Modernity and the Mainline Church

American churches—especially the mainline churches, the venerable "seven sisters" of the Protestant Establishment—were profoundly affected by developments in this era. These bodies are now known as the American Baptist Churches, the Christian Church (Disciples of Christ), the Episcopal Church, the Evangelical Lutheran Church in America, the Presbyterian Church (U.S.A.), the United Church of Christ, and the United Methodist Church.

Since the Gilded Age, these denominations had largely come to terms with Enlightenment liberalism and modern science. Their seminaries endorsed varying measures of the biblical criticism that had emerged since the late eighteenth century. They warmly greeted the rise of the social sciences and backed liberal reform movements. Church historian Sydney Ahlstrom has referred to the Federal Council of Churches, founded in 1908 by thirty-three Protestant denominations, as the "praying wing of Progressivism."[7]

By the 1920s, the mainline churches had become quite amenable to modernity. In general, their clergy were well-educated, respectable, and fashionable. Many did not feel strictly bound to scriptural commands and orthodox theological understandings. Miracles were explained away as products of an earlier, less knowledgeable period. For up-to-date people, personal feelings and experiences were the primary source of Christian truth. Mainline leaders tended to believe in the benevolence of human nature and the inevitability of worldly progress. The truth of religion, it was said, was displayed not in its doctrine but in the moral impact it made on individuals and societies.

When the new culture of the sixties met the mainline denominations, the church doors swung open. Accustomed to following current trends, mainline leaders had little will or ability to defend traditional views on anything. The mainline churches seemed especially vulnerable to the demands of feminists and homosexuals, who began altering liberal theology in radical ways. (To their credit, of course, these mainline leaders also embraced the civil-rights movement, and many took seriously the evidence of environmental destruction.)

Conservative Christianity

Conservative evangelicals (both within and outside the mainline churches) and fundamentalists chose a different approach to modern culture. They defended the absolute authority of Scripture, resisted the theory of evolution and the findings of social scientists, and stressed the importance of personal salvation and missionary activity. Throughout the 1920s, liberals and conservatives fought battles within their denominations, a phenomenon that contributed to the creation of the modern mainline churches. The humiliating Scopes Monkey Trial of 1925 helped define strict fundamentalists as an "extremist" subculture. Walter Lippmann expressed the prevailing view in 1929 when he wrote that fundamentalism "no longer appeals to the best brains and the good sense of the modern community . . . the movement is recruited largely from the isolated, the inexperienced, and the uneducated."[8] More moderate evangelicals, under Billy Graham and others, prospered in the 1940s and 1950s but still lacked the respectability awarded the liberal denominations.

In large part, the evangelical and fundamentalist churches bitterly resisted the sixties. This stance was dictated by their fearless defense of the Bible, their stern personal morality, and their alliance with political conservatism. In the 1970s and 1980s, many conservatives united to oppose such left-wing innovations as abortion on demand, pornography in the media, gay rights, and the banning of prayer in the public schools. Many worked hard for the election of Ronald Reagan and other conservative Republicans.

In the 1990s, conservative churches are prospering. The 15.3-million-member Southern Baptist Church is the nation's largest Protestant body.[9] Independent conservative churches are thriving in the nation's suburbs, appealing in an extraordinary way to young people. A recent study showed that evangelical Protestants compose more than 20 per cent of the nation's population.[10] And almost all of the religion on television—Protestant and Roman Catholic—comes from the right.

Decline of the Mainline

In sharp contrast, the mainline denominations lost between 20 and 30 per cent of their membership between 1965 and 1990. While they still claim 24 per cent of the nation's population, their numbers of active members are low. In 1992, for example, the Episcopal Church had only 1.6 million members, the Presbyterian Church (U.S.A.) had 2.7 million, and the Disciples of Christ had 656,000. While the United Methodists could boast of 8.8 million members, in 1965 they had had 11 million. By comparison, in 1992, the Mormons had over 4.4 million members, 8.2 million African-Americans belonged to the National Baptist Convention U.S.A., and there were 59.2 million Roman Catholics.[11]

As a sizable literature suggests, the mainline denominations have declined in large part because they have abandoned the basic roots of the Christian faith, preferring to teach liberal biblical interpretations, theology, and ethics. These churches demand little or nothing from members and seem wholly receptive to the secular and the faddish.[12] Wheaton College historian Mark A. Noll has referred to late-twentieth-century Protestantism as "lapsing into pallid cultural captivity."[13]

Morale throughout the mainline ranks is also low.[14] Missionary zeal is almost nil.[15] Finances have taken a sharp turn for the worse.[16]

Methodist theologian Stanley Hauerwas of Duke Divinity School said in 1993, "God is killing mainline Protestantism in America, and we goddamn well deserve it."[17]

The church headquarters, conventions, organizations, and agencies of the mainline denominations seem almost inevitably to fall under the control of liberals. Thus official pronouncements and actions often disturb people in the pews, who by and large are more moderate and conservative.

For instance, more than 40 per cent of mainline church members are Republicans, while about 25 per cent are Democrats. And according to a Gallup poll, only 19 per cent of the American people identify themselves as strongly liberal.[18] Election results bear out the generally conservative orientation of church members. In 1992, 43 per cent of mainliners voted for Bush, and 34 per cent favored Clinton.[19] Yet, as two Methodist professors of religion have declared, "It seems inconceivable that an agency of any mainline, Protestant denomination should espouse some social position unlike that of the most liberal Democrats. The church is the dull exponent of conventional secular political ideas with a vaguely religious tint."[20]

A Bleak Future

The mainline churches can hardly be seen any longer as a source of national unity. They are too liberal—theologically, morally, and politically—to appeal to most Americans, and in general they lack the spiritual resources necessary to pull people out of themselves and into a larger framework of devotion.

Virtually by definition, the evangelical and fundamentalist churches have limited appeal. Their view of truth and life is opposed by every liberal institution in the country, including the schools and the mass media. The current "culture war"—which in the words of George Weigel is really about "the establishment of officially sanctioned secularism as the American democratic creed"—is as divisive as it is inevitable.[21] Despite conservative victories in the 1994 congressional elections, it seems extremely unlikely that the country can be unified behind the Christian Right. The polls tell us that Pat Robertson cannot appeal to the broad middle of the political spectrum. And let us not forget that Robertson and Reagan, despite their obvious ideological similarities, are very different people.

Neither can the Roman Catholic Church serve as a national rallying point: it stands outside the Protestant and secular camps inhabited by most Americans; it is widely perceived as obeying the commands of a foreign leader; and it is at war within itself.[22] While the Catholic Church has been the largest single Christian denomination in America since 1890, its influence on national opinion has not been substantial.[23] The sole Catholic elected to the White House made it clear, in public and in private, that his church membership was largely formal.[24]

Ironically, public-opinion polls tell us that America remains a Christian nation. In 1988, for example, Gallup pollsters reported that nine Americans in ten said they had never doubted the existence of God, that 90 per cent prayed, that 79 per cent believed in natural law ("clear guidelines about what's good and evil that apply to everyone regardless of the situation"), that 84 per cent said that Jesus was God or the Son of God, and that about 75 per cent had at some time sensed the presence of Jesus in their lives.[25] In 1990, the Graduate School of the City University of New York commissioned a poll of 113,000 people around the nation that determined that 86.5 per cent of Americans are Christians. Only 7.5 per cent of those surveyed said they had no religion.[26] A Harris poll taken in July 1994 revealed that 95 per cent of those surveyed believed in God and 90 per cent believed in heaven. Four in five Americans described themselves as Christians, and 85 per cent of the non-Christians expressed belief in the virgin birth of Jesus. Even 52 per cent of the non-Christians expressed belief in the resurrection of Jesus![27]

The polls also tell us, however, that our faith is superficial. Gallup refers to "a nation of biblical illiterates" and presents solid evidence of that illiteracy. Only four in ten Americans know that Jesus delivered the Sermon on the Mount. Fewer than half of all adults can name the four gospels of the New Testament. Only three in ten teenagers know why Easter is celebrated.[28]

Moreover, our faith often has little to do with our churches. Data show that a majority of Americans have confidence in organized religion. But in 1988, according to Gallup, 44 per cent of Americans were unchurched. These are people who said they were not members of any church or had not attended services in the previous six months other than for special religious holidays, weddings, funerals, or the like. That figure amounted to about 78 million adults. Gallup found that overwhelming majorities—churched and unchurched—agreed that people "should arrive at their religious beliefs independent of any church or synagogue" and that one can be a good Christian or Jew without attending a church or synagogue.[29]

In 1991, Gallup discovered a slight trend toward less frequent church attendance. Fifty-five per cent said they thought the influence of religion was decreasing—the highest mark since 1974 and not exactly a vote of confidence for churches. In 1992, only 54 per cent ranked the honesty and ethical standards of the clergy "very high" or "high," down from 67 per cent in 1985.[30] When asked why they attended church less often, very few of those interviewed gave reasons that reflected a deep animosity toward organized religion. Only 8 per cent said they disagreed with policies and teachings. A mere 5 per cent said they were atheists or agnostics. For many, going to church just did not seem that important. Leading the list were 34 per cent who said they were too busy.[31] An in-depth random survey of 4,001 Americans, conducted by a team of political scientists and published in 1993, concluded that only 19 per cent of citizens regularly practice their religion.[32]

In general, then, it seems highly unlikely that our churches can contribute significantly to a much needed sense of oneness among the American people. Protestant denominations on the left lack the traditional faith and morality, the zeal, and the appeal they once enjoyed.[33] Their counterparts on the right lack the necessary public respect, especially among the educated and the opinion-makers, that is essential to a unifying force.[34] Roman Catholics are badly split between left and right. Churches of all bents these days lack attractive and effective leadership.

Of course, this bleak picture might change. For many years, prophets have cried out for a religious realignment that would win the hearts and minds of most Americans—for a union of the sensitive, the intelligent, the orthodox, the pure in heart, and, above all, those who see themselves as sinners in need of forgiveness and the love of God. Such a church might well provide us with national inspiration and unity. But this would be a church of the future. For now, the Christian denominations in this country—crippled as they are, some bent on suicide—seem far from ready to summon us to new heights.

PART FOUR

Art, Culture, and the University

17

The New University and the
New History

Gertrude Himmelfarb

Historians use the word "revolution" sparingly, as they should. They pride themselves on taking the long view. And in the long view, few so-called revolutions are worthy of the name. But some genuine revolutions have occurred, and I think we are now living through one such—a revolution in the university.

Robert Nisbet had a different word for this revolution in a book he wrote a quarter of a century ago with the provocative title *The Degradation of the Academic Dogma*. At that time, Nisbet spoke about a "reformation" in the university, but his use of the word "degradation" in the title suggests his unfavorable view of that project. This reformation began soon after World War II, when the large influx of students into American universities was accompanied by an even larger influx of government funds. The transformation of the university into the multiversity drastically altered the original mission of the university, which was based upon a "dogma."

That dogma was a "faith"—again, that religious note—in reason, in knowledge, in the rational, dispassionate search for truth, and in

---

Gertrude Himmelfarb is professor emeritus of history, City University of New York. Her most recent book is *The De-moralization of Society: From Victorian Virtues to Modern Values* (Alfred A. Knopf, 1995).

the dissemination of knowledge for the sake of knowledge. A corollary of that dogma was the hierarchy of knowledge, and the hierarchy of those who bear and impart knowledge.

Even in America, this most democratic of nations, the university was not a democratic institution. Not all subjects were equal, *sub specie universitatis*. Professors might debate the relative merits of Milton and Donne, but no one thought to invite Edgar Guest or Ogden Nash into that inner sanctum of canonical poets. Moreover, those professors who explicated and interpreted Milton and Donne did not presume —as many do today—that they are the equals of Milton or Donne. Nor did students presume to be the equals of their professors, nor for that matter, junior professors of their seniors.

Nor did the university give equal status or equal time to non-Western civilizations. To be sure, there were courses on the Near and Far East, on Latin America and Africa, but these studies were peripheral to the curriculum and conducted in the method and spirit of Western scholarship. The university was frankly "ethnocentric" (another word Nisbet used in the current sense), committed to a "faith in the Western tradition: in the ideas, values, systems, and languages that belong to the tiny part of the world that is the promontory of the Eurasian continent known as Western Europe."

All that, and much more, began to change when the university— now a multiversity—adopted a new dogma known as "relevance." This doctrine committed the university to a new agenda, one that demanded that the university solve the problems of poverty, the environment, juvenile delinquency, urban unrest, and whatever else society might ask of it. The old idea—and ideal—of disinterested knowledge gave way to an eminently interested notion of knowledge, that is, to a utilitarian, practical, functional view of knowledge. The 1960s did not initiate these developments, but they vastly accelerated them.

The sixties also accelerated the transformation of the socially conscious university into the politically conscious university. Of course, professors and students have always had political views and commitments; but before the new era, they had expressed and exercised them not as professors and students but as individuals, in an extracurricular capacity, so to speak. The sixties brought those views and commitments into the university itself—into the classroom, the curriculum, the appointments process, and the *ex cathedra* pronouncements of university officials and professional associations. This was the world of the university when Robert Nisbet wrote his book in 1970.

From Reformation to Revolution

A quarter of a century later, we can speak of a second reformation that is tantamount, in my opinion, to a revolution. This second reformation has penetrated into the heart of the disciplines, and thus into the soul of the university, as the first did not. A new dogma, affirmative action, has supplemented the old dogma of relevance. Affirmative action has been pursued and enforced, not only in the admission of students and the appointment of faculty (which seems to me the least significant aspect of that policy), but in the curriculum and the disciplines themselves.

Race, class, ethnicity, and gender have become the guiding principles of scholarship and instruction. These principles, which now go under the name of multiculturalism or diversity, require that women, blacks, Hispanics, and other "underprivileged" or "marginalized" groups, as they are called, be given equal (and in some cases, more than equal) representation in each discipline and even in each course. The resulting balkanization of the university was inevitable.

E pluribus unum has been transformed into ex uno plures, "from the one, many," as Vice President Gore put it in his famous gaffe. And with balkanization has come a further politicization of the university. This has occurred not only in the obvious sense of "political correctness" in speech and behavior, or in political criteria for appointments and promotions, but in the more insidious sense of the politicization of the very substance of education: what should be taught and how it should be taught.

Knowledge itself, according to the now fashionable theory, is nothing but a reflection of the power structure. The very idea of knowledge, of the aspiration to objectivity and truth—what Nisbet called the dogma of the university—is now deemed authoritarian and oppressive. "Everything is political," a popular slogan has it.

Everything is political—and by the same token, everything is possible. Since there is no truth, there are no standards by which one subject may be said to be more worthy of study than another. Houston Baker, professor of literature at the University of Pennsylvania (and a former president of the Modern Language Association), said more colorfully what others were saying prosaically: Choosing between Pearl Buck and Virginia Woolf is "no different from choosing between a hoagie and a pizza." He himself, he went on to say, was "dedicated to the day when we have a disappearance of . . . standards."

With the appearance in the university of courses and dissertations on comic books, soap operas, popular films, and the like, some of us believe that the day of no standards has already arrived. To be sure, not all institutions exhibit these tendencies to the same degree. Some colleges and universities make serious efforts to avoid balkanization, trivialization, and politicization. And in all colleges and universities there survive oases or enclaves of resistance to the current fashions— professors who manage to teach and write as they have always done; students who manage to acquire an education in spite of all the temptations to the contrary; special divisions or programs that provide a respite from prevailing ideologies. But these are admirable exceptions to the dominant tendencies in the university.

Such is my view of the university—perhaps a jaundiced view. Let me now present a no less jaundiced view of my own discipline, history, which is in many respects a microcosm of the university at large.

History New and Old

Only a decade ago (it seems much longer), I wrote an essay on what was then called "the new history," social history, "history from below," the history of ordinary people in their ordinary lives. My criticisms were not directed against social history itself. (In fact, I was responsible for bringing that subject into the curriculum of my own university.)

What I disputed was the claim that the new social history was the most important, indeed the only proper, mode of history, and that the traditional forms of history—political, diplomatic, constitutional, intellectual, even economic—were superficial and ephemeral. I also noted some of the implications of the new mode of history: the denigration of ideas (which were regarded as elitist); of reason (as embodied in constitutions, laws, and written documents); of leaders and individuals (rather than classes and masses); and finally, the denigration of the idea of the commonality of history, of the *unum* that has traditionally defined a nation, a people, a polity, and a citizenry.

A year or two later, when asked to address the same subject, I predicted that the next stage in the evolution of the new history would be the deconstruction of history. Some of the historians in the audience ridiculed my prediction. Surely, I was told, no "real" historian (as distinct from a well-known philosopher of history) could possibly propose to deconstruct history.

Today postmodernism, in which deconstructionism plays a large part, is the newest version of the new history. I do not say that most historians are postmodernists or deconstructionists, but only that some of the basic tenets of postmodernism have so pervaded the discipline that a good many young scholars and some older ones accept them almost unconsciously. Above all, these scholars share the radical skepticism of postmodernism: a denial that there is any such thing as knowledge, truth, reason, or objectivity; a disclaimer that one can even approximate those ideals; and more significantly, a repudiation of any aspiration or desire to do so.

Skepticism and relativism are certainly not new among historians. They are as old as the writing of history itself. Historians have always been acutely aware of the limitations of their discipline: the deficiency of the historical record, the selectivity inherent in the very writing of history, the fallibility and subjectivity of the historian, and thus the imperfect, tentative, and partial (in both senses of the word) nature of every historical work.

Professional historians, however, have always made the most strenuous effort to curb and control these deficiencies. That effort is what used to be meant by the "discipline" of history. It is why the keystone of every graduate program was a required course in "methodology," in which the doctoral candidate was taught the proper use of sources, the need for substantiating evidence, and the conventions of documentation and citation. Such courses are nearly obsolete today.

In Our Own Image

Today the idea of a discipline or methodology of history is regarded as disingenuous at best and hypocritical at worst. The facade of footnotes and "facts" (the word is now always put in quotation marks) is said to conceal the "hegemonic," "privileged," "patriarchal" interests served by traditional history. All of history, like all of knowledge, is presumed to be a reflection of the power structure. In the postmodern view, there is no truth or reality in history. There are not even any events—only "texts" to be interpreted in accord with the interest and disposition of the historian.

The relationship between postmodernism and multiculturalism is obvious. It is only if history is thoroughly relativized, and purged of any such transcendent ideas as truth, objectivity, or reality, that race, class, ethnicity, and gender can maintain the dominant roles they now have. No history, in this view, can be "privileged" over any other. None is more true, more real, more significant than any other. Each group creates history in its own image, in its own interests, and from its own perspective.

It used to be said that the job of the historian was to "reconstruct" history—that is, to reconstruct the past in the best fashion he could. Now he is enjoined to "construct" history—to "invent," "imagine," "create" it. And not only does each group create its *own* history: it prides itself on creating the *totality* of history, and creating that totality in its own image. Feminists call this the "engenderment of history." For some black historians, "Afrocentric" history serves this purpose. Gays and lesbians have no comparable term, but they have the same intention. Each group wants to avoid what is called the "add-on" strategy—adding on the "marginalized" group to the rest of history. Each wants to be "mainstreamed," to have its history pervade the whole. I would like to illustrate this new mode of history by applying it to a particular historical subject, the Holocaust.

The Holocaust Deconstructed

Hard cases, it is said, make bad law. But hard cases in the sense of unusual cases do not make bad history. The Holocaust was surely an extraordinary event, but then history is full of extraordinary events—revolutions, wars, "world-historical individuals," as Hegel put it. If a particular mode of history cannot satisfactorily account for the Holocaust, how can it account for the American Revolution? Or the Civil War? Or any event in history?

It is thus fitting to ask how the various kinds of new history measure up to this test. What do they make of the Holocaust, which is perhaps the most momentous event in modern history? Social history (*Alltagsgeschichte,* as it is called in German), the history of everyday life, does not, in fact, make much of the Holocaust. Indeed, it may entirely ignore that extraordinary event, since it describes the everyday life of

Germans during the war: the way they coped with the difficulties of rations and shortages, the way they struggled to make ends meet, the way they sent their men off to war and received news of their deaths. The sources for this kind of history will almost always be mute about the slaughter of Jews in remote concentration camps. From such a history, not only would one learn nothing of the Holocaust, but one might not even know of its existence.

I am reminded of a conference several years ago, when a young American historian took pride in explaining that he was on the "cutting edge" of the new history. He and his colleagues were investigating occupations and social mobility in three New England towns in the late eighteenth century. I asked him what bearing his studies and those of his colleagues had on what I regarded as the most momentous event in that period, perhaps the most momentous event in the history of our nation—the American Revolution. "Well, actually," he replied, "we cannot get from our studies to the revolution." He hastened to assure me that this limitation was of no consequence because he was dealing with a much deeper level of reality than the revolution.

In similar fashion the German social historian cannot "get to" the Holocaust. Nor can the structural historian get to it. Structuralism sees no individuals, no ideas, no intentions, indeed, no events in history, but only impersonal, long-term structures, forces, and institutions. This mode of history minimizes the role of individuals (such as Hitler); it denies the importance of intentions and ideas (such as anti-Semitism); it belittles the importance of events (such as the war). It cannot, in short, begin to capture the moral drama or even the essential facts of the Holocaust.

Neither can post-structuralist or postmodernist history cope with the Holocaust. Postmodernism is obliged to "problematize" the Holocaust as it does all historical phenomena—render it indeterminate, contradictory, paradoxical, ironic, metaphoric. The postmodernist is not a "revisionist" in the sense of denying the fact or the magnitude of the Holocaust. The postmodernist might even like to dissociate himself from that kind of revisionism. Yet he cannot exempt this event —or this text, as he prefers to call it—from his strictures concerning all of history. To attribute truth and reality to the Holocaust would be to "privilege" it, and that would violate the basic principle of postmodernism.

I thought I was familiar with this mode of thought, but I was unprepared for the testimony of one young woman, an undergraduate in an estimable college who reviewed my recent book, *On Looking into the Abyss,* in a student newspaper. Her review opened with an account of a discussion she had had with another student, triggered by his remark that, of course, no one believes in the truth anymore, that events are nothing more than texts to be interpreted as one likes. Looking for an event that could not be reduced to a text, one whose reality she thought he could hardly deny, she cited the Holocaust. He paused for a moment before conceding, "The idea of the Holocaust has purchase for me." "Purchase?" she asked. "It has purchase for you? Did it or didn't it happen? What is this purchase business?" "I was appropriating capitalist discourse," he replied. "The idea of the Holocaust has purchase for me as compared with the currency I derive from other ideas."

There cannot be many students around, thank God, who talk about the Holocaust, or in fact anything else, in this fashion. But that there are any, and that they are among the brightest students, and that they get such ideas from their professors, gives one pause. If people can think this way about the Holocaust, how are they thinking about other subjects that are less emotionally charged? What does it mean for history, or any other discipline, for that matter, to say that, of course, no one believes in the truth anymore?

The only cause for hope I see in this situation is, paradoxically, the volatility of intellectual fashions. Deplorable as it is, that volatility may now serve us well. Boredom may yet be our salvation. Young people may become bored with this latest historical fashion—as many have already become bored with earlier versions—bored with a history that is fragmented, trivialized, politicized, and thoroughly relativized. They may then find a new sense of excitement in a history that tries to rise above the conditions of race, class, ethnicity, and gender, a history that does not believe that "everything is political," that even dares aspire to the truth, knowing full well that the truth is never fully attainable.

A recent article in the *New York Times* on the controversy over the "National Standards for United States History" concluded by quoting Oscar Wilde: "The one duty we owe to history is to rewrite it." Perhaps a new generation of historians will rediscover the old dictum, "The one duty we owe to history is to get it right."

18

Universal Human Nature Defended Again

Deal W. Hudson

At the United Nations' 1993 Vienna conference on human rights, an odd situation developed. Countries like China, Syria, Indonesia, and Iran claimed a right to development, and specifically a right to develop in their own indigenous ways. Representatives from those nations argued that Westerners, with their human-rights agendas, were merely intent on imposing their bad Western—and, specifically, bad American—habits on a world with far different ideas of what it means to be a human being.

That the Western bureaucrats and intellectuals found themselves defending the notion of universal human nature against these charges is somewhat ironic, since the Western intelligentsia has become predominantly postmodern and thus distrustful of claims about universal human nature. In addition to a generalized skepticism about knowledge, the spread of postmodernism in the developed West has been fueled by concerns over the injustices committed in the name of the *normatively* human, and over the need to protect the particularity of undeveloped, non-Western societies.

Deal W. Hudson is the editor of *Crisis* magazine, president of the American Maritain Association, and author of *Happiness and the Limits of Satisfaction* (forthcoming, Rowman & Littlefield).

When this debate over human nature is transposed to the American scene, it takes the form of the multiculturalism debate—with its controversies over Eurocentrism, Dead White Males, and the equality of traditions. In a classroom context, these issues get mixed in with fretting over self-esteem: that is, whether boys and girls of various racial and ethnic backgrounds will feel left out or get their feelings hurt when they are asked to read British literary mainstays such as Shakespeare and Milton.

But at the heart of both of these debates is the question of human nature, specifically, the link between concepts of human nature and their supposedly destructive political consequences—injustice, prejudice, and even totalitarianism. For whenever we posit a universal human nature, it implies something normative, something that measures us, that is external to us, the measuring measure, as it was traditionally said, or natural law.

At present, we are suffering from "essentia-phobia," the fear that an essentialist view of human nature will measure our behavior against something other than our own wills, and will not allow us to do what the 1992 Supreme Court decision in *Planned Parenthood* v. *Casey* encouraged us to do: become radically self-defining according to our own preferences.

The idea of a universal human nature, however, provides our best hope for a public moral consensus, and should be defended. This *can* be done on religious grounds, and in fact we seem to be hearing more about the possibility of defending some sort of common human nature on the grounds of a common creator. Yet I think— and I learned this from the Catholic intellectual heritage—that the mediating role of philosophy is crucial in this debate. It is not that philosophy's conclusions are final or complete, or that reason alone can do justice to things like sin or eternal happiness; but in its own modest way, philosophy can play the role of mediator between groups with different beliefs, different values, and different backgrounds.

Philosophy, which seems like an abstract entity to many people, can accomplish this concrete task because, properly done, it begins with reflection on our common experience of human life. It is no accident that human beings of both sexes and from different cultures can agree on the basic needs we all share. To argue that food, clothing, shelter, health, friendship, education, and virtues are the goods of human life arouses little controversy, although their concrete instantiation may occasion disagreement.

What is often overlooked in the present debate is the importance of this fundamental agreement. It points not only toward a shared point of view but also toward the presence of a shared object of knowledge—the human person—that is the same in this hemisphere and throughout the world. Human beings can be known, their needs understood, because their common human nature provides the mind with a unified concept, an *unum,* that can be grasped.

The Unity of Being

Unum, or unity, is one of the transcendental aspects of being, which are truth, goodness, unity, and beauty. What does this *unum* or unity mean? The unity of being is stated simply: whatever *is* is what it is and is not something else. In other words, a thing is identical with itself. That may appear rather abstract, but a thing's unity provides its ground of intelligibility. If we could not count on the fact that what we are thinking about *is* what it *is,* we would not be capable of knowing anything at all. Recall the scene in Jean Paul Sartre's novel *Nausea* in which a chestnut tree melts into the ground. This is a fictional representation of the kind of denial of essence and intelligibility that was once confined to existentialist thinkers. With the rise of postmodernism, this denial has become an intellectual commonplace. Attention has been fixated upon what were traditionally called the accidents of human existence—sex, gender, ethnicity, and race—to such an extent that our common nature has dropped out of sight, replaced by a set of politically generated "identities." These identities—as a female, or a Native American, or a homosexual—supposedly place permanent barriers between the values and beliefs of the people belonging to them. Men and women, heterosexuals and homosexuals, Caucasians and African-Americans—each inhabits a different moral universe, and the universes are thought to be mutually exclusive.

As a college professor for the last fifteen years, I have watched the growth of the diversity business in both Atlanta and New York. I have always been struck by the fact that there was so much concern for differences and so little appreciation for the remarkable sameness that exists among human beings of all kinds. C. S. Lewis, in *The Abolition of Man,* offers a marvelous appendix on what he calls the Tao—the common moral teaching of various cultures. It seems to me we should constantly remind our students and one another that human beings share a common nature. This need not be hubristically "hegemonic," or threatening, but simply a reaffirmation of our human-ness. Thus we have a starting point from which to understand one another as individuals, as members of groups, and as members of distinctive cultures and societies.

To claim to know human nature is not to claim an *exhaustive* knowledge. When we say we know human nature, it sounds as if we are saying a lot, and in a way we are; but at the same time we are saying very little. The knowledge of human nature provides the starting point for the knowledge of persons and societies. Without the knowledge of human nature, this further knowledge would be impossible. So I would say to those with a postmodern sensibility: You have nothing to fear from the claim to know human nature; it merely provides a broad outline of what it means to be a human being. In short, nature is our key to discernment, especially as to the moral and political good for human beings. By discernment, I mean the ability to distinguish what is good for human communities from what is not.

An External Cultural Critique?

At issue in both forms of this debate over human nature, both nationally and internationally, is whether indigenous forms of development are subject to some external critique. Is there some sort of moral discernment that transcends the particular culture involved, or do different ethnic groups have totally discreet axiologies, epistemologies, logics, and processes? *American Experiment* has reported on something called the "Nichols Model," adopted by the federal government for the sensitivity training of federal employees (Kishere Jayablan, "Uncle Sam's Diversity Sham," *American Experiment,* Fall 1994, 2-7). The model purports to show the "philosophical aspects of cultural difference." Nichols distinguishes four groups: (1) European, Euro-American, (2) African, Afro-American, Hispanic, Arab, (3) Asian, Asian-American, Polynesian, and (4) Native American. Under the Native American axiology, the model claims, the highest value is whatever puts you in connection with the Great Spirit. For the European and Euro-American, the highest value is, rather unflatteringly, the acquisition of an object—as if the distinguishing mark of all Westerners were something like the "Midas touch," which infected all their pursuits with the disease of self-interest.

According to the Nichols model, Western feminists have somehow avoided this pitfall. Many leading feminists espouse an affective epistemology, in which knowledge is communicated through symbol and rhythm, and thus belong to the Nichols category for African, Afro-American, Hispanic, and Arab cultures. I wonder why sensible people accept such typologies when these kinds of ironies and counter-examples abound, even within the Western tradition itself. Clearly, this kind of typology is very Western in the first place. Acceptance of such devices as the Nichols Model is driven more by our awareness of past crimes and failures than by any intrinsic merit or plausibility of the typologies.

In his book *The Ethics of Authenticity,* Charles Taylor discusses the logic of the claims to authenticity and concludes, "What it all comes down to is, whether or not there is a measure which measures us independently of the individual will." This is precisely what the present age is most afraid of—the possibility of an independent measure of human action and character. What makes it so very difficult for us to accept this possibility is that we have come to realize that this measure, if there is such a thing, is not known rationalistically in a moment of intuitive vision; it is known through history and human experience. That is, what we know about human nature and the human good, we know through a kind of dialogical process between our knowledge of the human essence and the ups and downs of its historical realization—or in Aristotelian terms, between the vagaries of first nature and second nature, the nature we receive and the nature we acquire through action.

Thus we see the importance of tradition, the place in which this process of understanding human nature, behavior, and values takes place. The very possibility of discernment—discernment between good and bad, between good and evil development—is made possible by our grasp of human nature. Consequently there is an unavoidable and unresolvable tension between the principles of particularity and universality. Of course, the multiculturalists collapse the two in favor of particularity, arguing that particular cultural practices are *all* we know about the human good. But with Aristotle I would argue that politics must be grounded in a knowledge of human nature, and that we cannot escape the tension between the universal and the particular, the philosophical and the historical.

The crux is whether or not there is such a thing as transcendence for human understanding, whether the human mind is able, within discrete patterns of development and traditions, to have a vision of the human good that transcends the particular historical moment. And I say yes. Even Jacques Derrida has been forced to admit recently that justice and universal rights are a kind of "undeconstructable" universal good. It seems to me that in making that claim he joins his voice with that of George Steiner, who in his book *Real Presences* says he will wager "on the real presence in our semantic markers."

Derrida, the dean of deconstructionists, may have realized that just as there is harm done by ill-conceived moral and political dogmatism, there is just as much and perhaps more harm done by dogmatic relativism disguised as multiculturalism. And there is also a quieter and more insidious undermining of everything we cherish as human.

19

Beyond Perverse Modernism

Martha Bayles

In a trendy nightclub, a controversial playwright puts on a one-man show blasting the government, spewing profanity, urinating, masturbating, even going into convulsions onstage. To one onlooker, the performance offers "inconceivable freedom," the "fearful cynical spectacle" of an artist "struggling to eliminate both himself and the last remains of a once firmly established civilization."

Outside a venerable cathedral, a crowd of worshippers are startled by a flurry of leaflets calling for the total destruction of the building. Looking up, they see a black-clad figure in the campanile, one of a cadre of artists vowing to "go out into the streets, launch assaults . . . and introduce the fisticuff into the artistic battle." When the stunt dominates the next day's headlines, the artists rejoice.

At a fashionable gallery, a wealthy collector buys a work called *Artist's Shit*, a can of feces weighing thirty grams and priced at the current cost of gold. This collector is not alone; the lucky artist sells ninety cans.

No, these vignettes are not taken from the House Republicans' blacklist of NEA horrors. Rather, they come from the history of European modernism. The first was the German expressionist Frank Wedekind, presiding at Munich's Cafe Simplicissimus in the 1890s;

Martha Bayles is a columnist for *Forbes* magazine. She is the author of *Hole in Our Soul: The Loss of Beauty and Meaning in American Popular Music* (Free Press, 1994).

the second, a follower of the Italian futurist Filippo Marinetti, denouncing St. Mark's Cathedral in 1910; and the third, the French Fluxus artist Piero Manzoni, hawking dada doodoo in 1961.

I call this strain in modern art perverse modernism. There are other forms of modernism, but before examining them let me try to clear up some of the confusion surrounding the term *culture*. The word has a double meaning that confuses people. In the traditional sense, *culture* means purposeful activity aimed at improving and perfecting its object. Derived from the Latin *cultura*, meaning cultivation, *culture* in this sense denotes evaluation. Thus it also refers to artistic and intellectual excellence. And its synonyms include words like "cultivation," "development," and "refinement."

The second meaning dates only from the nineteenth century, when Sir Edward Burnett Tylor established *culture* as the core concept of anthropology. Here, culture refers to the whole way of life of a people. Not just intellectual and artistic activity (though these are not excluded) but behavior patterns, customs, beliefs, rituals, and the material apparatus of life, from tools to textiles, totems to sacred texts.

In the early days of anthropology, one of the chief obstacles facing Europeans studying non-European societies was their own sense of cultural superiority. For the sake of scientific objectivity and accuracy, they attempted to suppress their moral and aesthetic reactions to the things they were observing. Thus the anthropological meaning of *culture* came to denote disinterested study, not evaluation.

It is easy to make an analytic distinction between these two meanings of *culture;* it's a lot harder to keep them separate in practice. Indeed, for most people, the "culture war" is less about our society's achievements than its way of life, with the focus on social problems such as the decline of family life and moral virtues. This is not the meaning of *culture* that I will be dealing with here.

Instead, my focus will be on the traditional meaning of *culture*, including the arts and humanities. And here I include popular culture, even though (or perhaps because) popular culture is woven into daily life in a way the arts and humanities rarely are. Most intellectual discourse on popular culture is from a social-science perspective. But I don't think you can make sense of popular culture without relating it to the arts and humanites. In other words, the claims that popular culture makes upon us are always in some way related to the claims of traditional culture.

MODERNISM IN THE ARTS TODAY

Art is something about which most Americans are bewitched, bothered, and bewildered. Recall how Jane Alexander, the head of the National Endowment for the Arts, dealt with the controversy over a Minneapolis performance artist who menaced his audience with towels soaked in blood that was possibly HIV-positive. Ms. Alexander is a fine actress and an intelligent woman, but like most liberal champions of the arts, she caved in, because she has no language with which to distinguish between such antics and genuine art.

But neither do conservatives. Faced with the same situation, most conservatives would revert to good old genteel American philistinism, meaning a knee-jerk denunciation of any artwork not patently aimed at "moral uplift." American philistinism has an appealing side, namely an impatience with pretentiousness, phoniness, and snobbishness; but as a weapon in the culture war, it fizzles.

For example, a few years ago, during the Robert Mapplethorpe controversy, a prominent conservative was heard to remark that the arts should be more like sports, with clear, agreed-upon standards of excellence. However sensible it sounds, the suggestion is naive. The only game art resembles today is one in which Team A is playing baseball, Team B is divided between rugby and lacrosse, the umpire is enforcing the rules of ladies' tennis, and the scorekeeper is philosophically opposed to competition. In short, we possess not one but several artistic standards, each inherited from a different phase in the history of Western art. This history is not well known to Americans of any political stripe. Although we understand that certain topics close to our hearts, such as politics and economics, have an intellectual history, we have yet to understand this about art.

Three Conceptions of Art

To simplify grossly: we in the West have inherited three main ideas about art. First is the *didactic,* in which art is seen as having a direct, unmediated effect on the thoughts and behavior of the audience. In this view, art must be censored, because any sympathetic depiction of evil is bound to foster evil in the body politic. This didactic category has a noble pedigree, going back to Plato's injunction that the poet must sing only the truth of the philosopher-king. But it also has a shameful history, as tyrants past and present have forced art into ugly official molds intended to serve philosophical, religious, and (most recently) political-ideological truths.

Second is the *latitudinarian* idea, in which art is given a realm of its own within which evil may be depicted, even sympathetically, as part of a larger whole. This latitudinarian view, which harks back to Aristotle, is more sophisticated than the didactic one, and gives art more liberty. But until the nineteenth century, this liberty was never total. On the contrary, most Western artists, including the romanticists, continued to believe that art was an imitation of nature, and that its ultimate purpose was to serve truth and virtue. There have been countless disagreements: about technique, about how audiences are affected, about what aspects of nature ought to be imitated, and about what constitutes truth and virtue. But in all that time, and indeed in all the other civilizations of the world, art was never seen as supplanting religious or philosophical truth.

Only in the West, and only in the last century, has a third, *radical* idea appeared. Derived from late romanticism and modernism, the radical idea sees art as wholly autonomous. And not only in its own realm, as in "art for art's sake": at the extreme, the radical idea grants art total liberty to generate its own truth and virtue or to deny that such entities exist for everyone else. To some extent, this is the legacy of Nietzsche. But Nietzsche clung to the romantic distinction between the genius who generates new truth out of a deep meditation, and the superficial and immoral artist who uses the notion of genius to cloak a lack of personal and artistic discipline.

The Nature of the Wasteland

Unfortunately, the combatants in the culture war rarely distinguish between these ideas. So the extremes dominate, in both the elite and the popular culture. Indeed, the hills of Hollywood and the corridors of MTV teem with would-be geniuses whose ideas of art closely resemble most people's idea of criminality. Most intellectuals will acknowledge this fact. But that's as far as they go, because the standard highbrow line is that popular culture has always been a wasteland. Indeed, there is surprising agreement on this point between the highbrow intellectuals who deplore popular culture, and the so-called postmodernist intellectuals who self-consciously embrace it. The highbrows speak of the "gutter," the postmodernists of the "street"; but both see the brutality and obscenity of contemporary culture as coming from below, as a triumph of commercialism and popular taste.

I couldn't disagree more. Popular culture is not a monolith, a wasteland set off from genuine art by commercialism and popular taste. Some of its creations, such as classic films and jazz performances, achieve the level of high art without losing popular appeal. Moreover, the nature of the wasteland has changed rather dramatically over time.

Forty years ago, commercialism and popular taste were blamed for the *wholesomeness* of popular culture: after all, it was the network TV censors who decreed that married couples must be shown sleeping in twin beds; and it was the studio moguls with one eye on the bottom line who ordered happy endings tacked onto the plots of tragic novels. Today, by contrast, commercialism and popular taste are blamed for the *decadence* of popular culture. Clearly, there is something illogical about explaining a variable (the shift from wholesomeness to decadence) by means of a constant (commercialism and popular taste). A better course would be to trace the decadence back to its real source —that is, to perverse modernism.

Perverse modernism began a century ago, with the decadent and expressionist movements. Then it began its long march through the twentieth-century avant-garde: futurism before World War I; dada, surrealism, and the Theater of Cruelty between the wars; and such post-war retreads of these movements as Fluxus, "happenings," and what is now called performance art.

Given this history, do we have any choice? Must we accept the notion that modern art means galleries full of genitalia, stages full of sadomasochism, movies full of mutilation, and bestsellers full of bestiality? Are middlebrow critics like Richard Corliss of *Time* right when they tell us that art has only two functions: to "shock," or to "ratify the prejudices of the generation in power"?

The answer is an emphatic *no*, because modernism cannot be reduced to such crude alternatives. Take another look at history. In the 1890s, when Wedekind was onstage wetting his pants, Matisse and Cézanne were painting their most glorious canvases. In 1910, when the futurists were scattering leaflets, Stravinsky was composing his great ballet, *The Firebird.* In 1961, when Manzoni was filling his stinky cans, Walker Percy was exploring cinematic fiction in *The Moviegoer.* The best modernist art seeks neither "to shock" nor "to ratify the prejudices of the generation in power," but to create a new artistic language capable of describing and evaluating modern life.

Introverted Modernism

Unfortunately, on the way to this goal, modernism went down the blind alley that I call *introverted* modernism. That is, it took the romantic ideal of art for art's sake and carried it to extremes. Introverted modernism withdraws from the world, and humanity, into a rarefied, quasi-religious obsession with its own materials and processes. The results include some of the least popular forms of modernist art, such as serial music (in which the sequence of sounds is selected according to an abstract system rather than by the human ear), non-representational painting (in which abstract shapes are simplified to the point of sterility), and non-referential poetry (in which the words mean nothing, not even to the poet).

Introverted modernism has produced some intellectually dazzling works: just think of Webern, Malevich, and Breton. But by making a religion of art while cutting art off from all but the tiniest and most exclusive audience, introverted modernism has also provoked anger, mockery, and scorn. To cite one recent example: the "post-painterly abstraction" of the late 1950s, with its blank appearance and dense critical theory, prompted the mocking, debunking retort of pop art. Next to the stark "hard-edged" canvases of Kenneth Noland, the stark red-and-white of Andy Warhol's Campbell's Soup cans amounted to a good joke. But unfortunately, the process didn't stop there. Like his many predecessors, Warhol soon slipped from mockery into perversity for its own sake.

Perverse Modernism

Historically, perverse modernism appears whenever an artist stops creating new objects and starts pointing to any old object in the world, proclaiming, "This is art because I say so." In this spirit, the dadaist Marcel Duchamp exhibited a urinal in an art gallery. In the same spirit, perverse modernism turns art into a publicity stunt. All artists seek public esteem, but the perverse modernist demands instant notoriety. That is why, when he contemplates the modern mass media, he doesn't see imagery or materials that might stimulate serious art, the way Picasso and Braque did when they incorporated newspaper clippings into their brilliant cubist collages. Instead, the perverse modernist sees the instrument of his own celebrity. Thus, Marinetti's futurist manifesto appeared as a paid ad on the front page of Europe's leading newspaper, *Le Figaro*. Instead of working the headlines into his art, as the cubists did, the perverse modernist thrusts himself into the headlines.

Thus it should come as no surprise that perverse modernism would get grafted onto popular culture. The central argument of my book *Hole in Our Soul: The Loss of Beauty and Meaning in American Popular Music* is that this occurred in the late 1960s, in the most responsive and influential part of that culture: the music.

Some people date the excesses of today's popular music back to the rock 'n' roll craze of the 1950s. I disagree, on the grounds that there is a strong continuity between Louis Armstrong, Benny Goodman, and Frank Sinatra, on the one hand, and Fats Domino, Chuck Berry, and Elvis Presley, on the other. That continuity shows up in musical elements, such as the ability to swing, and extra-musical ones, such as courtesy toward the audience. I would further argue that this continuity persisted through such mid-1960s musical strains as soul, Motown, and the early Beatles.

The real break came in the late 1960s, when the counterculture went sour, and rock began attracting people who were less interested in music than in using such a hugely popular medium for culturally radical purposes. The harbingers of this break were the Rolling Stones, who, though they relished the blues, did not hesitate to make the blues over in the image of the stale perverse modernism that some of their members (and their manager, Andrew Loog Oldham) had picked up in art college. In deliberate contrast to the "good boy" Beatles, Oldham marketed the Stones as "bad boys," shocking the press and being arrogantly rude to their audiences in ways that were totally alien to the blues.

Things got worse in the 1970s, when a bigger and more dedicated contingent of cultural radicals climbed aboard the rock bandwagon. By the end of that decade, the strain known as punk had effectively turned rock into a species of performance art. The Sex Pistols, a band created by a fashion designer named Malcolm McLaren who had attended six British art colleges but knew nothing about music, fostered a cult of deliberate ugliness that attacked and degraded music, along with everything else.

Punk has been tremendously influential. Indeed, if you want to understand the mindset of the so-called Generation X, don't look at unemployment figures; look at punk. From punk, today's white youth inherit their taste for aggressive, noise-dominated sound; for obscene, violent lyrics; and for emotional expression ranging from sadistic lust to nihilistic rage. Indeed, I call gangsta rap "blackface punk," because I see it catering to this taste. Thus, gangsta rap is the latest step in the process by which perverse modernism has displaced the musical and cultural values that used to dominate popular music. To see how far we've come, just measure the distance between Duke Ellington and Snoop Doggy Dogg.

I would say that perverse modernists do not see popular culture as capable of producing works of genuine art. The first American cubist, Stuart Davis, understood as early as the 1920s that jazz was not just popular entertainment but genuine art, and made the music of Earl Hines and Louis Armstrong the basis of his distinctively American cubism. The perverse modernist, by contrast, gravitates to what is lowest and stupidest in popular culture, then uses it as a bludgeon with which to attack the whole idea of artistic standards. This impulse originated with Rimbaud and the decadents; more recently, it was dubbed "camp"; today, it is part of postmodernism.

Extroverted Modernism

If art-worshipping introversion and anti-art perversity were the sum total of modernism, then philistinism would seem justified. But there is a third, more robust and capacious strain, embodied in figures like Matisse, Cézanne, Stravinsky, Percy, Bergman, Picasso, and Stuart Davis. This third, *extroverted* strain shares certain traits with the great art of the pre-modernist past. It respects its own tradition by trying to live up to the highest standards of the past. It addresses its own time, forging a new artistic language to speak to a broad contemporary audience. And it doesn't pretend that art is easy, or a game; it takes a craftsman's approach, understanding that no great art can exist without great skill. And finally, it doesn't turn art into an occult religion. In my opinion, jazz is modernist music in this third and favorable sense.

Not surprisingly, the extroverted strain has produced most of modernism's masterworks. And though many of these masterworks were controversial in their day, controversy was not their reason for being.

Cézanne, for example, did not enjoy getting lambasted by the critics. Indeed, he longed to be accepted by the official art world. His work may have "shocked the bourgeoisie," but Cézanne did not revel in that fact.

Here we see most clearly the problem with today's so-called cutting-edge artists. Look at the type of controversies they stir up. Steeped in modernism, most of us automatically assume that if art is controversial, the reason must be that our society is too hidebound to deal with new ideas, sensibilities, and aesthetic practices. Reflexively, we draw a parallel between the original bourgeois reaction to modernism and the outrage today. That is, we recall that bourgeois critics abused Manet for painting in a non-academic style; that bourgeois authorities censored Flaubert for depicting adultery; that bourgeois theatergoers jeered Stravinsky's *Rite of Spring*. Therefore, we conclude, the fellow waving the bloodstained towel in Minneapolis must be a serious artist —after all, he too is shocking the bourgeoisie.

But here we must ask ourselves, what is the nature of the shock? Are today's perverse modernists introducing forbidden ideas into a repressive polity? Are they creatively defying the rigid conventions of an Academy? Are they breaking a puritanical silence about sex? Are they challenging the stilted decorum of a ruling class? I don't think so. We live in a society where the vast majority accepts the right of the artist to do just about anything he or she wants.

Obscenity as Art

Does this mean that we can't be shocked? No. One thing remains shocking: obscenity. The law defines obscenity as the depiction of "sexual conduct" in a "patently offensive way," lacking "serious literary, artistic, political, or scientific value." This definition evolved out of a century-long legal battle over the portrayal of sex in serious literature, and it represents the victory of art over old-fashioned prudery. Yet precisely because this legal definition focuses exclusively on sex, while exempting material possessing "serious artistic value," it is irrelevant to our present plight.

A better definition of obscenity comes from the legal scholar Harry M. Clor. Clor wisely argues that obscenity resides not in any particular bodily functions or conditions but in the angle of vision taken toward them:

Obscenity . . . consists in a degradation of the human dimensions of life to a sub-human or merely physical level. . . . Thus, there can be an obscene view of sex; there can also be obscene views of death, of birth, of illness, and of acts such as that of eating or defecating. Obscenity makes a public exhibition of these phenomena and does so in a way such that their larger human context is lost or depreciated.

Obscenity is shocking because it violates our sense of shame. In puritanical cultures, the slightest reference to bodily functions causes undue shame. But that doesn't mean we should never feel any shame whatsoever. Shame is the natural, universal response to nakedness, eroticism, and suffering. In most human societies, these states are taboo, meaning not forbidden but sacred and awe-inspiring, connected with the mysterious beginnings and endings of life. It is only in the modern West that people have sought to eradicate these taboos.

Or to exploit them. Today's perverse modernists equate shame with repression because they are committed to obscenity as the only reliable means of getting a shocked reaction out of the public. They flatter themselves that this reaction is akin to the great scandals of the modernist past. But in fact, it comes neither from public resistance to new artistic techniques nor from a high degree of prudery in the culture. Instead, it reflects the simple fact that most people are not exhibitionists or voyeurs. Most of us feel slight embarrassment and a strong need for either ritual or privacy when eating, eliminating, making love, suffering, and dying. If that makes us unable to appreciate "art," then we can only wonder what the word has come to mean.

Obscenity-as-art is everywhere. In the 1993 Biennial Exhibition at New York's Whitney Museum, the visitor could stroll from a room containing a photographic display of male sexual organs to another room containing a row of video monitors showing so-called "transgressive" sexual practices. In an advertisement for jeans in the popular music magazine *Spin,* a young man brandishes a handgun over the caption, "Teaching kids to KILL helps them deal directly with reality." Combined with the other impulses of perverse modernism, this compulsion to shock is now our culture's dominant sensibility. So the question becomes: Is this good news or bad news?

A Plebiscite on Perversity

How could it possibly be good news? Consider the following scenario. As perverse modernism ceases to be the preoccupation of the elite and moves into the popular culture, it will face something it has never had to face before: a plebiscite. Naturally, one hesitates to place too much faith in the aesthetic judgment of the ordinary people who will cast the deciding votes. But better they than the elite, with its perennial conviction that if something is degrading and dehumanizing, it is, perforce, art. At least ordinary people are apt to weigh the claims of art against those of civility, decency, and morality.

Ultimately, the question revolves around the mechanism by which this plebiscite gets conducted. The danger, of course, is that popular revulsion will fuel backlash, censorship, even repression. I don't consider it censorship to deny NEA funding to charlatans trading in obscenity and shock. As good anarchists and nihilists, they shouldn't want government funding in the first place. But in the grip of the right demagogue, populist censoriousness could easily go further, into a realm where big government would start looking a lot like Big Brother. At their most sophisticated, the pro-censorship forces cite Plato and Rousseau to the effect that art corrupts civic virtue. Although this line of reasoning can be very cogent, we must remember that it is potentially a criticism not of *bad* art but of *all* art. In the *Letter to d'Alembert,* Rousseau cites the dangers of *good* theater, including, presumably, his favorite playwright, Molière.

I don't believe that good art corrupts civic virtue. On the contrary, mine is the latitudinarian view of art, in which the Devil gets some of the good lines, but not all of them; in which the evils afflicting us are given their due, but not to the point of tossing aside mankind's moral compass.

That is why the mechanism matters. Defending popular taste can be tricky, after a century of totalitarian regimes' crushing artistic and intellectual freedom in the name of "the people." But it's important to note that "the people" never really cottoned to the culture imposed on them by the likes of Hitler and Stalin. Given the chance, the people have always gravitated toward the American alternative: a genuinely popular culture shaped not by ideological decree but by market forces working within a pluralist society.

That is why I keep coming back to commercialism. Unlike the German or Russian public in the 1930s, the American people wield considerable power over their culture—through the market. Indeed, today's market offers hints that the plebiscite may be working: the fastest-growing type of popular music is country; mainstream black youth are rejecting gangsta rap; "family" movies are cleaning up at the box office. To libertarians, these signs are proof that the market is a benevolent force that, if left to its own devices, will restore our better nature.

Unfortunately, there are just as many negative signs. Viewers are abandoning network television for the graphic sex and violence available on cable; broadcast news is adopting the sensationalism of the tabloids; publishers are bidding up bloodthirsty novels. And mounting social-scientific evidence suggests a link between the state of our popular culture and our twin plagues of illegitimacy and violent crime.

To social conservatives, the answer is censorship; to many liberals, stricter regulation. Both see the market as a malevolent force. Here the debate stalls, because both sides overlook the fact that the market is neither malevolent nor benevolent but neutral. With increasing efficiency, the market can popularize cultural trends. But it cannot initiate them. All it can do is respond to shifts in public taste, brought about by the usual combination of things we cannot control and things we can.

Optimistically, I count among the latter the old-fashioned tools of persuasion, debate, and education. But for these to work, we need to take a more balanced, historically informed view of the real relationship between the mass media, popular culture, and artistic modernism. In some areas of our culture, there is evidence that perverse modernism is wearing out its welcome. But elsewhere it rules, partly because a lot of people think that to reject this stale lunacy is to force culture to the opposite extreme. To judge by the totalitarian example, didactic moralism is not the way to the people's heart either.

Between these extremes lies the high achievement of the best American popular culture, with its unique genius for reaching both elites and ordinary citizens without insulting anyone's intelligence or moral sensibilities. That is where I find the most hope of resolving the culture war in favor of civilization.

MULTICULTURALISM IN THE HUMANITIES

This invocation of civilization bring us to another contemporary cultural battlefield: multiculturalism. The usual complaint against the radical multiculturalists in the humanities is that, after reducing the noblest achievements of the West to a residue of racial and sexual prejudice, they replace them in the curriculum with mediocre works by members of so-called marginalized groups. In terms of the two meanings of *culture,* this is the academic equivalent of three-card monte. By urging faculty and students to suspend judgment, to give up their inherited standards of excellence, the radical multiculturalists slip the neutrality and relativism of anthropology into the realm of artistic and intellectual endeavor, where they don't belong.

They don't belong because it is one thing to suspend taste and judgment in the name of science, quite another to do so in the name of justice. The Victorian anthropologist didn't deny his inherited moral and aesthetic standards; he merely bracketed them off as a hindrance to the immediate task of gathering data. Today's radical multiculturalists would have us do more than bracket our standards: they want us to reject them, to purge them from our minds as elitist —by which they mean inherently unjust.

The obvious flaw in this strategy is that all cultural standards are elitist, non-Western as well as Western. Should they all be rejected? Of course not. Radical multiculturalists would not dream of asking *non-Westerners* to give up their own native standards of excellence. On the contrary, multiculturalists work hard at trumpeting the exacting nature of non-Western standards.

Then comes the next fast shuffle, which is to slip the valuative meaning of *culture* (in the traditional sense) into the realm of anthropology. That is, the multiculturalists attempt to raise the humblest crafts and customs of non-Western cultures to the level of high art and compendiums of philosophical wisdom. It doesn't matter how ordinary-sounding the verse is; for example:

> Yonder to all directions I looked.
> I looked toward the north,
> I looked toward the west,
> I looked toward the south,
> I looked toward the east . . .

This is part of the Zuni world renewal ceremony, so perforce, it belongs in the *Heath Anthology of American Literature*.

Actually, I had to hunt through that anthology before finding such an ordinary Native American verse. Most have a turn of phrase, a striking metaphor, that makes them pleasing, if not in the same class as the greatest American poetry. For example, consider this "Widow's Song" from the Eskimo:

> Long will be my journey
> on the earth.
> It seems as if
> I'll never get beyond
> the footprints that I make. . . .
>
> A worthless amulet
> is all my property;
> While the northern light
> dances its sparkling steps
> in the sky.

A student doesn't have to be from an Eskimo background to be attracted by the poignant sweetness of this little lament. And the songs of Native Americans are part of the American story. What's wrong with including them in the curriculum?

At this point I know I am raising hackles, and also doubts. My question may sound innocent. But too often, a kind word for some story or poem of this or that non-Western culture is the opening salvo of a radical-multiculturalist attack on the fundamentals of literary appreciation.

Imagine a contemporary college class reading this "Widow's Song." On the one hand, you have the sensitive students who find it pretty and a bit touching. They can be brought along quite nicely to appreciate other laments, from Housman's lyrical "To an Athlete Dying Young" to King Lear's broken eloquence over the body of Cordelia. Yet in the same classroom you are likely to have a few feminists all too willing to abandon their commitment to ethnic diversity when it dawns on them, slowly but surely, that this text only reinforces the patriarchal notion that a woman's life becomes worthless after her husband's death. At this point, we trade one kind of grief for another.

So we arrive at an odd pass. The Zuni, the Eskimo, and any number of other innocent parties whose ritual language (translated into English) expresses humanity and charm, have started to look mighty suspicious, especially to those of us who would defend literature as something to be appreciated for its own sake.

Yet my point is that the Eskimo and the Zuni are not the culprits. Note that I have been choosing my words carefully. "Humble" and "ordinary" are the terms I have used to suggest why every artifact produced by a non-Western artisan is not automatically great art. But note also that I am *not* using other words, like "ugly," "obscene," "sadistic," and "perverse," which very accurately describe much of the art, or rather behavior, now prized by those who attack Western standards. That's because this kind of art has nothing to do with the Zuni and the Eskimo. Indeed, most pre-literate cultures could not even conceive of such an attack. Their conception of art, when art itself can be distinguished from ritual, is entirely *didactic*. They see artifacts and rituals as having a direct, unmediated effect on the world, including people's thoughts and behavior. Pre-literate cultures do not lack an aesthetic sense; some of their artifacts deserve study alongside the art of the West. But they do not create for what we call aesthetic reasons.

It is ironic that so many people (on both sides of the ideological fence) seem intent upon ignoring the fact that the West is the only civilization in the world to have granted art the liberty to redefine truth and virtue—and indeed, to invert them if it likes. Herein, I'm convinced, lies one of the attractions of multiculturalism, both for people whose backgrounds are not Western and for those whose are. That attraction is simply that most non-Western cultures do not conceive of art as above truth and morality. Some forms of multiculturalism contain a profoundly conservative element: a groping, however misguided, toward an older, and wiser, conception of art.

Yet I call this impulse misguided. What both sides tend to overlook is that Western civilization has more to offer than a fruitless battle between subversive radicalism and censorious didacticism. It also has the latitudinarian conception of art, in which the elevation of good over evil is seen as a necessary, but not a sufficient, condition of greatness.

The radical idea of art did not cause Fascism, Communism, and two world wars. But it did foster an artistic climate in which contempt for the morality of ordinary people was seen as a mark of superiority.

The next step was a cultural climate in which vicious tyrants, both Nazi and Stalinist, hunted down great artists in the name of that same morality.

During those dark days, the latitudinarian conception of art was understood to be the only rightful one. If we don't try to preserve it today, in our approach to popular culture as well as to the arts and humanities, then we're in for a rough ride. For, as the grim history of our century shows, the worst kind of culture war is the one between artists who hate morality and moralists who hate art.

20

Rejoining Nature and Culture

Frederick Turner

Many of us have witnessed the enormous expansion of university education in the United States that occurred during the Cold War. Most of us "boomers" are probably the product of that expanded system. And while we can say that the expansion of university education has brought many benefits to our society, it has also wrought many unintended consequences. One consequence—perhaps the most obvious—was the creation of the specialist. The curriculum, streamlined to save time and educational resources, produced specialization and a new class—the narrow specialist. The specialist is an expert in one field but ignorant of all others, and thus ignorant of the unity of knowledge. In fact, the specialist is ignorant of the very existence of links between fields that might open his eyes to the possibility of this unity. And it is the unity of knowledge—with its political consequences for the university and the American *unum*—that is the most serious casualty of the expansion of the university.

Exacerbating the problem overall is the fact that many students in the "boomer" generation were the first in their families to receive university educations; they were deprived of the broad general back-

Frederick Turner is a poet and the Founders Professor of Arts and Humanities at the University of Texas at Dallas. His most recent book is *The Culture of Hope: A New Birth of the Classical Spirit* (Free Press, 1995).

243

ground available to their bourgeois or patrician predecessors. These specialists, often with a social chip on their shoulder, chose careers in education and thus perpetuated the fragmentation of knowledge in the academy. The more broadly educated scions of wealthier families, on the other hand, usually went into business or law. The departmental system of academic organization, combined with the specialists' ignorance of other fields, has unhappily pitted the disciplines against one another for faculty appointments, research funds, and graduate students. This competition has produced deep and bitter ideological hatreds among the humanities, the natural and social sciences, and the arts.

The deepest rift of all—and the one I want to address—is between those who believe in nature and those who believe in culture. It is this division, I believe, that has in large part contributed to the fracturing of the *unum*. I propose that a return to natural science can provide the grounds for healing the breach between nature and culture and for rediscovering the values that were once a wellspring for the American *unum*.

The Two Camps

Among the *believers in nature* we can find most scientists, many political conservatives, many in the environmental movement, and even some members of the radical fringe groups of feminism, animal rights, gay rights, and the right-to-life movement. Also sharing a belief in the natural biological basis of human moral and intellectual differences are white and black racists. Among *believers in culture* are most of the current leftist avant-garde among the arts, humanities, and social sciences. Their credo holds that reality is a social construct, and the world a text that can be analyzed according to power politics. Also among the culture congregation are the proponents of ethnic diversity, the apologists of the welfare state, and those feminists who believe sexual differences are taught, not inherited. Sadly, those who believe that human beings are socially malleable have been responsible for perhaps the hugest episodes of mass murder in this century—though the apostles of ethnic cleansing, who believe that nature is inflexibly determinative, come a close second.

In the current schizophrenic state of our culture, many of us believe that culture is understood as the realm of choice, consciousness, and freedom, and that nature is the realm of deterministic and unreasoning cause and effect. This distinction perhaps originates in Kant, who conceded the whole natural world *(Naturwissenschaft)* to Newtonian determinism and Humean causality; he reserved to culture *(Geistes-wissenschaft)* the spiritual goods of ethics and aesthetics.

Tragically, in postmodern avant-garde thought, the idea of power as the determinative force behind events has migrated from considerations of the natural world to our understanding of the world of culture. Once culture was split from nature, it was easy to demonstrate that human cultural values have been shaped and manipulated by economic, social, ethnic, and political pressures. In recent years, even the values of science itself—the search for truth, empirical and rational consistency, and so forth—have been subjected to the same destructive analysis, and most contemporary academic post-structuralists reject the idea of objective, scientific truth altogether.

Contrary to the prevailing view, I argue that the rift between nature and culture is a sign of ignorance and that a wiser understanding of how the disciplines are related will help bring us back together. What we suffer from is a fashion—the postmodern fashion of fragmentation, incommensurability, and diversity, and all this is a result of the Cold War failure of the educational process.

How can we begin to pull ourselves out? In particular we need to reexamine several things: the distinction between fact and value; the assumption that nature is *not* free and creative; and the principle that biological inheritance is a limitation on human liberty that must be denied or concealed if democracy is to survive. If truth be told, for anyone with a broad general grasp of what is going on across the disciplines, there has never been a period in intellectual history when the prospects were better for a truly unified vision of the cosmos and the human world. A combination of enormously rich and fertile ideas —the updated theory of evolution, the emerging neuro-cultural synthesis in cognitive science (wherein mind is a real property arising out of the interplay of heredity and nurture), the new theory of nonlinear dynamical processes (chaos theory), and contemporary cosmology— has made possible a view of the universe that is one, open, value-rich, ordered, but not reductive or rigid. This view accommodates both determined and free relations between events. And it has room for— even *demands*—the amplest possible conception of what it is to be human. Most importantly, for our immediate purposes, it makes nature available to us once more as a basis for common understanding and as a guide for public policy.

What Basis for Unity?

No one can deny that American society is profoundly fragmented, but why turn to natural science as the basis for a new unity? Many argue that our shared past, our Constitution, and our Judaeo-Christian heritage should be sufficient to hold American society together. But these sources of cohesion have been increasingly challenged. I believe they can no longer be defended as sufficient in themselves to bind us together, though if a better basis for unity can be discovered, it should be one that can also help renew the values we now contest.

On the face of things, however, the challenges seem overwhelming. In the Christian America of the last century, for instance, the principle of separation of church and state was in fact only a theoretical problem. And after the Second World War, the American moral consensus was able to incorporate Judaism comfortably. But today, America is populated with vocal religious minorities. These range from Christian fundamentalists to peyote cultists, from New Age channelers to Voodooists, from Hare Krishnas to snake-handlers, from Lubovitchers to Branch Davidians, from breakaway traditional Catholics to atheistic humanists, from Shi'ite Muslims to practitioners of Wicca. The old consensus has broken down.

Matthew Arnold, in the nineteenth century, hoped that exposure to high civilization, to "the best that has been known and said in the world," would create a population that was at once tolerant, cultured, and morally vigorous. But one of the consequences of the failure of the academy is that the canon—the accepted heritage of the best produced by Western civilization and culture—has come under attack, and the canon cannot be used to buttress a putative religious consensus. The schools and universities, in which Arnold placed so much trust, far from being the cradle of such a civilization, have become its bitterest enemy.

Is There One American Story?

Today, the very idea of a shared American past is a bitter piece of nostalgia. "What do you mean, 'we,' white man?" asks Tonto in the old Lone Ranger joke. The recent Columbus Quincentennial demonstrates the loss of the shared national story. The fact is that America is what the historian Michael Lind calls a "mestizo" nation. All the races and cultures of the world compose it, and America is a world civilization as well as a necessarily local one. Thus a narrative of history that is essentially the family saga of one ethnic group cannot serve as the American story.

The answer, however, is not the new multiculturalism. By feel-good equivocations and flattery of the oppressed, multiculturalism seeks to conceal the cruel but undeniable truth that a particular Euro-Asian community of elites discovered the rest of the world. This elite created the objective mental structures that have enabled all humans to communicate. It has unified hundreds of tribes and cultures into one super-culture. And it has given the human race a disproportionate share of its art, science, and technology. Without the influence of Native American cultures, the United States might be a bit more like Australia. Without the influence of African cultures, it might be more like Canada. But it would still be generally recognizable as what it is. Without the influence of European culture, however, it would be like Tenochtitlán, the capital of the Aztec empire, or Meroe, the ruined capital of Cush in the ancient kingdom of Ethiopia: completely unrecognizable—another world altogether. So neither the old Anglo-Saxon nor the new multicultural account will stand up.

What about the Constitution? Can it glue the country together? Alas, we have seen the result of making law the basic coinage of human intercourse. There is no theoretical limit to the litigiousness of our society. Lawyers are our new mercenary warriors. They roam the country as did the *condottieri* of old, or the more recent protection-racketeers of the 1920s. We are in a new Hobbesian war of each against all, and the courtroom is our battlefield.

As many commentators from Václav Havel to Amitai Etzioni have pointed out,[1] neither a constitution nor a government can assure a decent human community. Before the collapse of the Communist bloc, the Soviet Union had a constitution as fully enlightened as ours —indeed, it was based on ours—but this piece of paper did not protect the population from the gulag. What is needed is what Havel and Etzioni call "civil society." Civil society is the informal network of institutions that preserves what we mean by democracy. These institutions are our families, businesses, churches and synagogues, professional associations, schools and universities, social clubs, sports organizations, museums, theaters and symphonies, coffee shops, publishers, and so on—many of which are not run on democratic lines at all. And when government, and even legal interpretations of the Constitution, interfere too closely in the affairs of such bodies, they tend to corrupt them.

Economics and Political Culture

The conception of the human as primarily an economic being is deeply embedded in our political culture. Of the three promises of the Declaration of Independence—life, liberty, and the pursuit of happiness—the first is a noble sentiment more honored in the breach than in the observance. We still make war, execute criminals, and abort fetuses (all of which, incidentally, I regard as necessary evils). The second promise, liberty, requires definition. The third, the pursuit of happiness, is really a disguised definition of the second. The original phraseology for the pursuit of happiness was "the pursuit of property." Again, the pursuit of property is consistent with Locke's rooting of social organization in the protection of the property rights of the individual. Perhaps the greatest achievement of constitutional government was the creation of the capitalist free-market system. While the free market is the indispensable engine of human progress for the foreseeable future, the reduction of all to the market, and the tendency of untrammeled liquidity to destroy all values in its path, are still indefensible against the core criticism of Karl Marx.

The Constitution, moreover, embraces a very narrow conception of the human, and though this document may be the greatest political achievement of the human race, it is surely not the final one. The Constitution is based on the idea that man is naturally solitary, and that native liberty essentially means being free from custom and the authority of others. (I use the old masculinist terminology for the sake of historical flavor.) These notions largely derive from the thought of the English philosopher John Locke. Locke's *Second Treatise of Government* centers upon an account of a solitary—a "wild Indian" wandering alone through a forest and feeding himself with the fruits of its trees; on this thought-experiment the rights of man are based. The *Second Treatise* laid the theoretical groundwork for the Framers; it was preceded by a *First Treatise,* which is a relentless and bitter attack on patriarchy, both as the rule of fathers, in particular, and as the leading candidate for a politics based on natural sociality in general.

Why did not Aristotle's definition of man as a political animal—a being social by nature—carry as much weight in the Constitution as it plainly did in the public-service ethics of the Framers themselves? Perhaps because Aristotle's conception could easily be shown to work for the city-state, but did not seem applicable to the continental federation that was the Framers' mandate. The cognitive dissonance between city-state ideals of public service and collective loyalty and national ideals of individual rights and private self-actualization returned to haunt the Union in the Civil War.

The concept of the naturally solitary and independent human individual—accoutered with the freedoms that solitude and independence bring—today exists as a destructive bias affecting our most fundamental social arrangements. Family responsibilities are put second to individual desires. The authority structures and collective welfare of social organizations are swept aside by individual rights. The star is the social rebel, whether society is at fault or not. The artist's idiosyncratic originality is elevated above the quality and value of the artwork itself. Without ethics we lapse into hedonism. And we are becoming a lonelier and more fragmented society. The splendid notion of the *free* human being is one of the great achievements of our history; but it needs to be paired with the idea of the *responsible* human being. In short, the Constitution needs to be supplemented by the notion of the human being as naturally social, a proposition we can agree upon by appeal to shared evidence—that is, science.

Wrong Solutions: Left and Right

Our social unity has suffered huge breaches, and our society is damaged by the biases of our system. Various attempts have been made to repair both, and the biggest actors in these endeavors have been the Religious Right and the Liberal Left. In both their analyses of our afflictions and their proposed solutions, we see writ large the separation of nature and culture, fact and value.

First, the religious right has largely seen the problem as a failure of moral education, and it holds that moral education is essentially founded upon revealed religion. Its members have sought to disguise or secularize religious teaching so as to evade the legal separation of church and state, and thus to impose on the schools by democratic vote their version of moral education. They also have dismissed the idea of human evolution, seeing it as reducing humans to the moral automatism of beasts (again, the separation of nature and culture, fact and value). Environmentalist, neuroscientific, and comparative anthropological perspectives on the place of humanity in nature are denied and denounced as nature-worship, materialism, or relativism. Not only have the ACLU and the courts seen through the secular disguise of the ethics program of the religious right, but increasingly so do the kids—with their exquisitely fine-tuned detectors of hypocrisy. (How ironic that the religious right, which in the sincerest and noblest way wants to save society, must disguise its cure as a bureaucratic state education requirement!) But it will not do, I believe, to sacrifice our cognitive honesty, our pursuit of the truth, to an expedient social end, however laudable.

The other main attempt at a solution has been undertaken by the liberal left. This movement, essentially, has not just permitted radical selfishness and hedonism but has enshrined them as liberty. It has tried to repair the spreading damage to society by government intervention— paid for by taxation and justified on the grounds of compassion. The result of the left's equally well-meaning program—which, unlike that of the right, has actually been implemented—has been catastrophic.

The liberal program has created the underclass, the new caste of the homeless, the decline in family income as families fragment into matriarchies and predatory male gangs. It has created the wave of violent crime in the cities as boys, abandoned by their liberated fathers, seek authority unsuccessfully in one another and in themselves. It has crippled the economic growth of the nation—which otherwise could have produced the surpluses to fuel such grand and unifying collective enterprises as the space program and a renewal of the arts. It has produced a generation of people whose faces are incapable of dignity: because they have been seduced by bland collective acceptance of irresponsible personal behavior; because they have never been given the necessary encouragement to self-discipline; and because their society will not permit them to feel shame and repentance—the portal to a changed and empowered life. The key words of the liberal left about personal moral failures are: "There's nothing to be ashamed of." But without the capacity for shame, we are indeed nothing, and we should indeed be ashamed if we knew how.

Significantly, the left and the right deny the connection between human beings and the rest of nature. The social-constructionist left —probably the majority—regards as sexist and racist *any* suggestion that anatomy might be at least a part of destiny, and that we inherit a human nature from our human and animal ancestors. Both the religious right and the social-constructionist left implicitly accept the idea that nature is deterministic: to the extent that we have a nature, we are unfree. The environmentalist left, on the other hand, denies the relation between humans and nature for a different reason: if the core ideological story of humans despoiling nature is to make sense, nature must be good and humans must be bad. If humans are nature's own creation—the dominant species anointed by nature to take its place at the top of the food chain—the case breaks down.

To maintain the shreds of social cohesion, both the liberal left and the religious right, then, are forced to conceal the truth. We are drawn again to the separation of culture and nature. Let us try a different tack: Can the new synthesis in science, to which I have adverted, provide a basis on which to broaden the *natural* base of human values? Can this enlarged commons of potential sympathy supply us with a renewed sense of human siblinghood? And, finally, can the idealism of the American project be renewed on this basis?

Toward a Unity of Knowledge

While I cannot go into details, I believe that the new science rejoins fact and value, nature and culture, and thus makes possible a unity of knowledge that would support the following propositions:

■ *Mechanism or Freedom:* The old idea holds that nature is deterministic, mechanical, and unfree, and that human culture is the only arena of creativity and freedom. This dichotomy between a deterministic nature and a free human culture is untrue. Nature contains free, creative, and unpredictable elements as well as deterministic and predictable ones—and so do we. We are an elaborated, accelerated, and more reflexive part of nature, not another thing altogether. Thus facts —the given—and values—the realm of free moral and aesthetic choice—co-exist in both human and non-human nature.

Earlier notions that the physical universe is a senseless and meaningless process, given meaning only by god or man, seem to be contradicted by the best new knowledge. It now appears that the universe has a history of its own; this history is majestic, beautiful, potentially intelligible, and satisfyingly meaningful. Our former complacent and comfortable pessimism has no foundation. The facts *are* valuable.

■ *Evolution and Hierarchy:* The history of the universe is evolutionary in that the many, the complex, and the diverse emerge out of the one, the simple, and the homogeneous. It is hierarchical in that higher values emerge out of, and depend on, lower values; at the same time the higher values validate and control the lower values. Like space, time itself has become a more complicated medium of events as the complexity, ability to communicate, and self-reflectiveness of time-sensitive organisms—from complex chemical systems, through primitive and advanced forms of life, to human beings—has increased. This being the case, humanity has a collective responsibility to assist, or at least not to hinder, the universe in its further development; and since we are part of the universe, we owe it to the rest of nature to put our own house in order. "The best that has been known and said in the world" is essentially the fruits of our efforts to assist the universe in its evolution, and it forms the basis of any future progress in that project.

■ *Nature or Nurture?* Contrary to the social constructionist, human beings are not born as blank slates to be inscribed by culture. While the species-world of human beings has the ability through imagination and science to comprehend the vast variety of other points of view in the universe, human nature does indeed exist. It has elaborate and distinguishing features, distinct characteristics of its own. This nature is wired into a specific body, brain, and nervous system, and it is shared by all human beings everywhere. We inherit a large part of our emotional, mental, and physical makeup from our genetic heredity, and diverse individuality is an essential part of what we are.

The human race is a continuum, in which everyone is related by blood to everyone else at greater or lesser remove. So-called races are a relatively arbitrary way of dividing up that continuum in terms of recognizable features, but should be of further interest to no one except physical anthropologists and the scientifically curious; race is certainly not the concern of the government. Xenophobia, the fear and hatred of the other, is a universal, adaptively useful, and innate human characteristic—which does not need racial differences to flourish. It is not taught and cannot be cured by social measures. It can only be transcended by the cultivation in individuals of greater intelligence, love, and knowledge. Pervasive and significant sexual variations between human males and females also exist and are biologically based. But in men and women whose development is complete, those variances are but slightly different paths to a humanity that includes, as well as transcends, sexuality.

▪ *Social, Not Solitary:* Human nature is essentially social. Without the presence of certain specific social institutions such as the family —including mothers and fathers, and preferably other relatives, or at least excellent substitutes for them—human nature will not develop properly. Our nature is designed to function in a context of certain specific, culturally taught skills, such as language and the arts. The universality of human nature is attested to by the massive parallels among independent civilizations at equivalent stages of their history —such as the interrelated development of irrigation, the city, the pyramid, the priesthood and sacrifice, and the divine monarchy in Mesopotamia, Mexico, Egypt, and elsewhere. The achievements of law, art, religion, technology, science, and the like are thus the creations not of particular cultures but of the species as a whole.

Nature and nurture, given adequate health in both, are but the ingredients that a person uses to construct a life and a work. The self-organizing and autonomous system of a sane and healthy person can create its own social and physical environment and seek out the ingredients it needs to meet its own criteria for life success; but it needs a specific set of moral, intellectual, and aesthetic elements in its early background to achieve this state. Thus the care and education of children is the first priority of any truly human society.

▪ *Religion and Development:* Some form of religious belief, language, morality, devotion, commitment, and ritual seems to be essential for human beings to develop and live in the most effective and fulfilling way. The elimination of religious language from human communication creates a huge gap in our potential knowledge, understanding, and aspiration. That gap or void is sometimes filled by the promotion of goals, ideas, and fetishes not meant to carry religious weight. Sometimes the lack of religion festers into ideological fanaticism or the meaningless pursuit of possessions. Sometimes it results in an emotional or intellectual stunting or distortion of the individual. And sometimes it remains as a yawning misery in people's lives. One does not have to find religious centering solely in the supernatural. The universe itself—if we could see it with fresh eyes—is miraculous, beautiful, meaningful, and creative. But the language of the supernatural nicely expresses the capacity of nature and human beings to transcend themselves and produce radical surprises, just as chaos theory says they do.

■ *The Cybernetic Economy:* Economic wealth is essential for any further progress and is achievable only at present through the mechanisms of market capitalism. Human beings are indeed rationally selfish economic individuals, although this is not the only, or even the most basic, or important, aspect of our nature. Perhaps "capitalism with a human face" will emerge from the new cybernetic memory technology. A computer credit system that can remember effortlessly all exchanges of goods and services, calculate risk and opportunity cost, and adjust the books so as to let its clients know their economic obligations and prerogatives, will in theory render money obsolete. Perhaps the ancient human system of gift exchange, with its deeply communitarian and empathetic aspects, will again be feasible on a new technological basis.

■ *Society and Child-Rearing:* The highest priority for any society is child care, since the survival of the species depends upon it. If child care is the highest priority, then child neglect is worse than murder, and if we regard murder as a capital crime, we should view child neglect the same way. If our primary concern is to raise children, then by implication a ban on polygamy makes no sense. Sociobiologists point out that the worst environment for raising children is that created by serial marriage—that is, divorce and remarriage—since children are abandoned by at least one of their caregivers.

How might society adjust its marital conventions to assure stable environments for the care and raising of children? First, we should note that monogamy is not the natural tendency of the human species. It is a biological fact that human males tend to lose their initial sexual attraction to a female after her early child-bearing years; and unless the deeper attraction of friendship is formed between the partners— an attraction not guaranteed by the initial falling in love—a human male will begin to look elsewhere for places to sow his wild oats. It is also normal for the female to stray from one partner in order to acquire greater economic resources from one male while optimizing the genetic contribution to her offspring from others. Polygyny and polyandry, which largely circumvent these problems, should be permitted where economically feasible.

Another approach, which also recognizes the priority of child care, would require that the state subsidize complete families; or that there should be a socially binding economic test for the right to bear children.

Sexuality that assists child-rearing, such as heterosexual marriage, should be encouraged by society. Sexuality that hinders child-rearing, such as adultery and heterosexual promiscuity, should be discouraged. (Sexuality that neither assists nor hinders child-rearing, such as homosexuality, should be ignored by society, which has no interests in it either way, unless for epidemiological or other such reasons.)

The New Value Base

The new value base, founded on the points I have enumerated above, might add to the existing rights of the American citizen such rights as early family care by (at least) two parents; full exposure to a religious tradition; apprenticeship within some guild of work or service; the chance and training to participate in some grand project of human art or science; and full information about one's economic debts and privileges. And it might add new duties such as care of the environment, both natural and man-made, and economic and civic support of child-raisers.

Some of the new rights could not be achieved in all cases and would often conflict with the old rights; but perhaps this would all be to the good. Why is it the duty of the state, for instance, to secure all the rights of its citizens? When the state attempts to secure rights that as an institution it is unfit to deal with at all, it ends up damaging those rights themselves. The recognition of the state's incapacity in this area would be a healthy dose of realism. We, as a nation, suffer from the huge misapprehension that all rights can actually be secured; that the world is set up so that perfect fairness and justice can—with enough good will—be accomplished. This is an illusion—and a dangerous one—that implies the presence of ill will and encourages paranoia.

But in fact, if we adopt the new understanding of the universe as essentially nonlinear, reflexive, and irreversible in its operations, we can see that absolute fairness is impossible. By abandoning complete fairness and justice as a goal, we will thereby cease to make "the best" or "perfection" the enemy of the good that we can reasonably attain. Instead we will receive the grace, mercy, gifts, and other surprises that come when a richly communicating, open system is allowed to work itself out, and its most productive and beneficial systems of cooperation receive the natural reward of survival.

Within this new and enlarged consensus, the old American unifying values might find a more secure and honorable place. The Judaeo-

Christian tradition would be perceived not just as one religious ide-
ology among many, but as the main religious representative in our
history (and a major one in the world's history) of a grand human
aspiration and an essential human need. We would again share America's past—neither as heroic but biased, as in the traditional account,
nor as valueless and disenchanted, as in the postmodern revisionist
account, but simultaneously as tragic, heroic, and profoundly hopeful.
For the American achievement is that it is humankind's greatest attempt—riddled indeed with failure, but still undefeated—to take up
the responsibilities that nature seems to have fitted us for. And the
Constitution then appears as the necessary condition and defense of
the individual enterprise that will supply the economic fuel for this
grand attempt.

The first step that we can take toward a political culture in which
the new unity and consensus can be restored would involve the reform
of the university. A new liberal arts curriculum needs to be established,
while the current post-structuralist humanities establishment should
be gently bypassed, or offered the chance of renewal by a thorough
education in the natural and human sciences.

The new curriculum should teach a view of the world in which
the traditional disciplinary distinctions are recognized only as convenient administrative units and interesting fossils of academic history.
The new curriculum will look in some ways like the great unified
world-views of the Taoist sages, the Athenian Academy, the medieval
Thomist university, and the humanist Renaissance. It will dissolve the
huge barrier between *Geisteswissenschaft* and *Naturwissenschaft*. It will
become a vital source of inspiration for technology and art. And it will
begin to forge the fragmented subcultures of our nation into a vital
new civilization.

PART FIVE

Immigration

21

The New Politics of Immigration

Peter Skerry

My approach to immigration is from the perspective of a political scientist preoccupied with the state of our political institutions. While what I say will draw specifically upon what I have learned about Mexican-Americans, I will generalize from those findings. My argument might be entitled something like "Thoughts Tending Toward a Restrictionist Immigration Policy," or perhaps "Reservations About Currently High Levels of Immigration." But ultimately I want to examine some of the broader questions raised by and about immigration, given the present state of American political institutions.

Here's a quick picture of the immigration situation today: In fiscal year 1992, about 974,000 immigrants were granted legal permanent-resident status in the United States. (Today the immigrant flow into the United States is about 45 per cent Asian, 40 per cent Hispanic, and the rest a rather diverse mix.) From 1983 to 1992, 8.9 million were granted permanent-resident status. Compare this with the decade beginning in 1905, when immigration, at its historical peak, totaled something like 10.1 million. If we count the 200,000-300,000 illegal immigrants who settle here each year in addition to the total legal influx, then, in absolute terms, the past decade has seen a record

---

Peter Skerry is a fellow at the Woodrow Wilson International Center for Scholars. He is the author of *Mexican Americans: The Ambivalent Minority* (Harvard University Press, 1995).

259

number of immigrants. But today's numbers are much lower in proportion to total population than those at the beginning of the century. The average annual rate from 1983 to 1992 was something like 3.7 immigrants per thousand U.S. residents, while the annual rate from 1905 to 1914 was around 11.1 immigrants per thousand—about three times higher.

In addition to the numbers, however, other factors have affected our ability to absorb newcomers. Our social, economic, and especially political institutions are far different from those at the turn of the century. This fact, though widely ignored, has enormous implications for how our society responds to immigrants.

The Values Question

Something that gets a lot of attention these days, especially from conservatives and neoconservatives, is the "values question." In the debate over immigration, one argument holds that the newcomers bring unwelcome, alien, or dysfunctional values—as we have heard from Pat Buchanan or, in a somewhat less rabid form, from Peter Brimelow. This perspective shows little awareness of how immigrants' values themselves change in the United States, and change very rapidly. For instance, when I mention Mexican-Americans to most people, whether well-educated elites or the man on the street, they conjure up crowded barrios where no one speaks English or wants to learn it. I understand the concern. But the preponderance of the quantitative as well as the anecdotal evidence shows quite rapid linguistic and cultural assimilation.

The pro-immigrant version of the American values discussion is that immigrants bring important habits, such as the work ethic and firm family values, and that somehow, once planted among us, these habits will infuse our flagging American culture with new life. Francis Fukuyama's "Immigrants and Family Values," in the May 1993 *Commentary*, is the best example of this argument. But this perspective divorces values from any institutional context. It winds up sounding like mushy-headed sociology, the likes of which William F. Buckley and other conservatives denounced in the 1950s for its abstraction from social or economic reality. By assuming that values are static and immune to countervailing influences, analysts like Fukuyama fail to recognize that the values of immigrants may change quickly, and perhaps not in directions we like. Indeed, immigrants may become like the rest of us, showing signs of decadence, sloth, or whatever other vices we believe afflict America today.

Yet the values debate exhibits no sense of ambiguity about how values can play out in deceptive and not always functional ways. Take, for example, family values, which are important for both social order and group and individual mobility. I argue that they are a necessary but not sufficient condition for positive social and individual outcomes. Yet strong family values can also stand in the way of desired outcomes, especially for Mexican-Americans. Systematic evidence of this is hard to come by, in part because social scientists do not want to look too closely at this phenomenon. Nonetheless, I would argue that just as strong families and family values tended to inhibit the individual mobility of Italian-Americans earlier this century, so those same strong family values can inhibit the individual mobility of Mexican-American children today.

I learned this lesson a long time ago from Edward Banfield's *The Moral Basis of a Backward Society*. I was reminded of it in San Antonio, Texas, where I talked with public officials charged with enforcing truancy laws. They laid the problem out quite clearly: Working-class Mexican families, particularly those recently arrived, mistrust the institutions of the broader society, even if those institutions are run by Mexican-Americans. Such families do not readily send their teenage daughters to school, given the broader cultural currents in American society today. And if there are young children who need babysitting, the parents are all the more inclined to let their older daughters stay home and care for those children. As for Mexican-American working-class males, many are not particularly drawn to school. Like the working-class youth of many other groups, they want to go out, earn money, and prove their manhood. Hard-pressed families might well let them stay away from school in order to work and contribute to the family finances.

Mexican-Americans take pride in their strong family values. But press them and they are likely to acknowledge that those strong families can pose problems for ambitious or aspiring individuals. This is one of the problems I have with the neoconservative embrace of immigrant family values.

Bridges From Private to Public

Let me turn now to my primary concern: institutions. What Peter Berger and Richard Neuhaus refer to as "mediating institutions"— churches, unions, community organizations—are much weaker than they were during earlier periods of immigration. Certainly neighborhood and community institutions are declining, if not dead. At the same time, political institutions likewise are much less effective than their counterparts earlier this century. For instance, the political role of unions is weaker, as are political parties generally, especially at the local level.

At the turn of the century, local party organizations (the much reviled and unappreciated political machines) mediated: they brought newcomers into politics by connecting individual and familial economic concerns with developments in the broader public arena. Immigrants need such mechanisms to move them beyond the private sphere of primary-group relationships—that is, relationships with friends and neighbors, the full-blooded, face-to-face relations of daily life. Immigrants from peasant societies earlier this century came from closely knit communities, as do many Mexican immigrants today. And here in the United States, working-class culture tends to reinforce such primary-group relations. But these, especially among immigrants, need to be expanded and developed into the public realm, into sets of more instrumental relationships, whereby immigrants learn to engage in politics and other public activities with persons outside their own group. But this process of moving from private, primary-group relations to the more instrumental and secondary relationships of the public realm is not necessarily automatic.

Certainly the political machines helped broaden public contacts. Insightful sociologists like Morris Janowitz have talked about these and similar institutions as providing bridges from the private to the public realm in an earlier era. Yet immigrants did not then, and do not now, come here primarily to become American citizens, in the sense of voting and participating in the polity. In large part they come here to better themselves economically, and the machines connected the economic aspirations of immigrants with the broader world of politics. They made that connection vivid—sometimes too vivid, in ways that were offensive to established American values. "You vote for me and I will get you a job": that was part of the corruption of the machines. But instead of looking only at the corruption, we should also note that the machines taught newcomers the importance of participation in the political system, which was an invaluable albeit flawed civics lesson.

Upside-Down Politics

The machines are long gone, but what has replaced them? In their stead are what I call post–civil-rights institutions, especially the institutions that have grown out of the 1975 Voting Rights Act and other such affirmative-action efforts. In addition to the changes wrought by the media, politics and government have become much more centralized at both the state and national levels. The net outcome is that local political institutions are much weaker or non-existent. The new world of post–civil-rights institutions does not help newcomers negotiate the gulf between the public and the private the way the machines did. Because there are few, if any, alternatives to them, today's institutions encourage newcomers and their leaders to define themselves as discriminated-against racial minorities, in terms very much like those of black Americans, for whom those institutions were set up in the 1960s.

One of the binds we are in today as a society is that as a result of this big shift in our political institutions, we have only one way of talking about disadvantage: that is, by defining a group as a racial minority similar to blacks. This creates problems on all sides. It forces conservatives into denying disadvantages that in fact exist. Yet there is much evidence to support conservatives who do not acknowledge that groups like Mexican-Americans fall into the racial-minority category. Indeed, the use of such categories encourages those who are in fact disadvantaged to make claims of racial discrimination that are not only inaccurate and unreasonable but divisive.

As my book *Mexican Americans: The Ambivalent Minority* shows, Mexican-Americans do not fit neatly into the post–civil-rights array of institutions. In fact, our affirmative-action, racial-minority regime has turned immigration politics among Mexican-Americans totally on its head. Up to the mid-1960s, Mexican-American leaders held, albeit begrudgingly, a rather restrictionist position on immigration. In 1966, at the dawn of the civil-rights era, George Sanchez, an educator and political activist at the University of Texas and a leading spokesman for Mexican-Americans, argued, "Time and time again, just as we

have been on the verge of cutting our bicultural problems to manage-
able proportions, uncontrolled mass migrations from Mexico have
erased the gains and accentuated cultural indigestion." That was the
usual position of the leadership in those days.

Now our affirmative-action regime rewards Mexican-American
leaders for increasing their numbers as much as possible. Today's
leaders have little motivation or concern to organize the rank and file
for any political purpose. In the past, leaders like Sanchez came out
of a union-oriented movement for which, as for other political organizations, newcomers posed problems because they undercut the
established membership; hence the tendency to be restrictionist. But
in today's much less organization-based politics, we have a system that
rewards numbers—in many cases numbers alone. Hence the politicization—and novel importance—of the U.S. census.

The Numbers Game

The United States has recently sustained levels of immigration that
mask ongoing assimilation but benefit Mexican-American leaders,
who point to the teeming, troubled barrios and argue that Mexican
immigrants, and Mexican-Americans generally, need extraordinary
help. In response, nativists get very upset. The reality is that assimilation—the movement up and out of the barrios—is very powerful
and, in fact, is undercutting the power base of Mexican-American
leaders. Yet as long as the barrio is replenished by high levels of
immigration, it serves those leaders well.

And as I mentioned, sheer numbers get rewarded: "If we are 40
per cent of Los Angeles County, we deserve 40 per cent of public-
sector jobs"—as well as 40 per cent of the county's delegation to the
state legislature, to Congress, and so on. These numbers are independent of voting and citizenship status, because all individuals, legal or
illegal, voters or non-voters, are counted in the census. What drives
the process is the competition for sheer numbers.

This is not necessarily a conscious decision on the part of Mexican-
American leaders, nor is it part of a grand Machiavellian scheme. But
the way things are structured now, those leaders have few incentives
to look more carefully at the impact of immigration, negative or
positive, on their communities. Although this may be changing as the
magnitude of immigration strains our politics, most of what I have

seen to date demonstrates that all the political incentives are in the direction of maximizing the numbers.

An important consequence of this numbers game is the potential and actual conflict it sets up, specifically between Mexican-Americans and black Americans. It is not hard to see that the proportionate claim of black Americans to representation and jobs diminishes as the number of Mexican-Americans increases. This is a touchy subject, one I have been criticized for raising, as though I am pitting one group against the other. Unfortunately, it is the numbers game itself that is pitting Mexican-Americans and blacks against each other.

Hispanics v. Black Americans

This raises another question that I think warrants our attention: the impact of immigration, in general, on black Americans. No one wants to talk about this, because, I think, the impact is not positive. There is little published research in this area, other than a raft of labor-market studies by economists showing that immigrants have either no or, at most, a marginal negative labor-market impact on blacks. A sigh of relief follows, the topic is changed, and research monies go elsewhere. But such studies hardly resolve the matter. Black Americans certainly feel threatened by immigration, and I, for one, am not convinced that their view is irrational. The field has been left to economists, usually of liberal persuasion, who are all too happy to find no effect. Then, having found little or no labor-market impact, we ignore other arenas where conflict and competition between immigrants and blacks—in politics, public services, or housing—is evident.

Conservatives and neoconservatives, to the extent that they have attended to this problem, seem to think that immigrants will teach black Americans a needed lesson about how to make it in this society. But I am not at all sure that this is what is being learned. And I fear the consequences when black leaders, who have avoided this issue as much as anyone else, finally get around to accusing the rest of us of preferring immigrants over black Americans. There will be hell to pay. And however opportunistic such declarations will seem, there will be considerable truth in them.

To return to the role of Mexican-American leaders in our contemporary affirmative-action regime: my book has been interpreted as criticizing these leaders personally and individually, which was neither my intention nor the result. Indeed, were I in their shoes, given the political institutions within which they must operate, I would probably pursue the same racial-minority path. But as an outside observer I am constrained to tell it like it is. My argument has also been interpreted to mean that Mexican-American leaders are the source of the problems I identify; that if they somehow disappeared, the right-thinking rank and file would pursue a more traditional immigrant ethnic politics. No, I do not think that would happen. The reasons, and especially the institutional changes, lie much, much deeper than any group of leaders.

In the same vein, I strongly disagree with observers such as Francis Fukuyama and Linda Chavez, who argue that a small number of Mexican-American leaders are trying to prevent members of their group from assimilating. The scores of leaders I have talked to know better. They understand that assimilation is ongoing, powerful, and unstoppable. That is one reason for their pro-immigration, virtually open-borders stance: new immigrants replenish barrios that would otherwise gradually empty out.

Now, the history of Mexican-Americans does lend itself to a racial-minority interpretation, for in a lot of places in the Southwest, particularly south Texas, they were treated like a racial caste. That history cannot be ignored. And while the institutional framework within which Mexican-Americans now operate encourages preoccupation with that history, the people themselves do not need that framework to be reminded of it. It is passed down from generation to generation. Many Mexican-Americans I know have grandmothers who experienced conditions in places like south Texas that one would be hard pressed to defend or explain away. My point is simply that all available evidence underscores that Mexican-Americans today are in a very different environment, and that the memories of the past are inaccurate guides to the present and future.

Recognition and Deracination

More fundamentally, we are confronted with deep-seated aspirations for recognition that are not easily or wisely ignored. Nor are they new. Other groups in our history have felt deprived, discriminated against, or otherwise marginalized, and have sought recognition and redress from America's mainstream institutions. This is a familiar story. Much less obvious are other sources of such aspirations, which, I argue, actually result from assimilation. For example, a substantial segment of Mexican-Americans in California today assimilates so rapidly and completely that many feel deep loss and a kind of deracination. They see themselves as cut off from their past and their culture.

Many young second- and third-generation Mexican-Americans, for example, speak little or no Spanish. If they go to college, they begin to confront the costs of assimilation—that they may not, for instance, be able to communicate with Spanish-speaking relatives. Soon they are referring to themselves as "Chicanos" and demanding Chicano-studies courses and the like. Conducting interviews for my book, I was repeatedly told such personal histories, and other research confirms what I heard. I am convinced that this dynamic among many Mexican-Americans in California is a reaction against a particularly assimilative and absorptive culture. I suspect that this happens with other groups in California also, and that the same dynamic arises elsewhere in the United States today. My hunch is that our pervasive popular culture and the mass media have much to do with this phenomenon. Indeed, contrary to what is frequently argued, the media may make assimilation much more rapid today than ever before.

Does this mean that I approve of Chicano-studies programs and affirmative action for Hispanics? Not at all. But one may reject such efforts as self-interested power plays (which they frequently are), or simply as ill advised, while still acknowledging that they reflect a deep-seated and even admirable striving for self-understanding.

Of course, assimilation is not necessarily benign and peaceful. Certainly the most astute analysts of the phenomenon—sociologists like Robert Park at the University of Chicago earlier this century—saw assimilation as necessarily and inherently conflictual, though not fatally so. If we depict assimilation otherwise, disappointment is inevitable. Like Park, social reformer Jane Addams saw assimilation as one of the forces that undermined immigrant families at the turn of the century. Certainly parental authority was undermined when children felt that their immigrant parents could not teach them what they needed to know in order to succeed in America.

In this vein, how do today's tensions and conflicts compare with those of the past? Many of us tend to bowdlerize the past or at least to forget the conflicts caused by earlier immigrants. We forget Father

Coughlin, who played an important role among Catholics; or Al Smith, who was rather a provocateur during Prohibition; or James Michael Curley, a hero to the Boston Irish, who twice elected him to public office from jail. This is part of our political culture and history. The tensions of assimilation are exacerbated today by our political institutions, but it is important to bear in mind that the process of assimilating immigrants has always been fraught with perils and problems. We would be best advised to attend to all aspects of immigration and assimilation, rather than the extremes that either demonize or romanticize them.

Here is another way to put it: Assimilation is a multi-dimensional process. We often assume that social and economic assimilation necessarily leads to political assimilation. What I am saying is that social and economic assimilation, under today's institutions, may lead to a kind of *incomplete* political assimilation that is extremely troublesome, divisive, and problematic. This is the core of my argument. We ask over and over again, "Will these newcomers assimilate?" My answer is, "Of course they will assimilate." But the important question is, How? To what standards and institutions?

The answer lies largely with the mainstream political culture. And given the post–civil-rights, affirmative-action institutions in which we live, the mainstream is teaching new immigrants some lessons that bode ill for the American *unum*.

22

Race and Immigration

Juan Williams

What have been the major vehicles of social transformation in the United States during this century? Immigration has certainly been one. So was World War II: having stood up against Fascism and Nazism, black soldiers came home with higher expectations of what it meant to be an American citizen. They saw themselves in a way that went beyond the simple matrix of black and white in this country, and this led to increased expectations of change. In the 1950s, the idea of social transformation was embodied in a movement—actually in many ways in one man, Thurgood Marshall—to break down legal segregation in American society. Then in the sixties came Martin Luther King and the idea of mass protest. People who felt the society was not open to them became willing to challenge authority in a more confrontational way. The seventies brought a sort of sadness and even depression in the aftermath of riots, and the Vietnam War, and Watergate. Things were not going as well as we had intended. The Civil Rights Act and the Voting Rights Act had been passed, but great difficulties remained, surfacing in arguments over affirmative action and busing. In the 1980s Ronald Reagan talked about his desire for a colorblind society. The counterargument was, "Can we honestly think that in America

---

Juan Williams is a journalist with the *Washington Post*. He is working on a biography of Thurgood Marshall.

we can ever be colorblind, having lived through this tremendous history of racial division?"

Now, in the nineties, what shape do the arguments over race in American society take? The bellwether of this period is immigration, which affects the very concept of civil rights. When we think about reinventing the American people, about *e pluribus unum,* we must think more and more about the tremendous surge in immigration we are experiencing. It reminds me of a joke Milton Berle told about the Irish immigrant who comes to the United States and is lucky enough to get a job pretty quickly. When someone asks him about his job he says, "Well, I'm just a laborer, but isn't this a great country—I've gotten a job tearing down a Protestant church!" Even as people reinvent themselves as Americans by coming here and jumping into blue jeans, drinking Cokes, and eating at McDonald's, they feel free to retain their ethnic identity, adding their own ingredients to the flavor and texture of life in America. We are no more the melting pot; we are now what the demographers call the salad bowl, where the lettuce and the tomato and the cucumber all keep their identity even as they become part of a common product.

With record levels of immigration, of course, we get moments of sharp discord. California's Proposition 187, though it focused on illegal immigrants, exemplified the growing insistence on immigration restrictions, not just in Florida, California, and Texas but, increasingly, all over the country. And who are the most negative when it comes to new immigrants? Union members, black people, and older Americans. The union members obviously see immigrants as competitors for blue-collar jobs. Blacks see immigrants as another group pushing ahead on the ladder of upward mobility. Older Americans see immigration more according to the Pat Buchanan view: the American identity itself is under threat because these newcomers are not like the people who came in the past.

A Society in Transition

In 1940, 70 per cent of our immigrants were from Europe. Today only 15 per cent are from Europe, while 37 per cent are from Asia, and 44 per cent are from Latin America and the Caribbean. These immigrants are more insistent on outwardly retaining their native culture. In what is a record high, 13 per cent of Americans don't speak

English at home. Previously, people were embarrassed by parents and older relatives who either did not learn English or spoke it with a strong accent. The largest non-English-speaking group entering society is, of course, Spanish-speaking people. In 1976, there were about sixty-five Spanish-language radio stations in this country; today there are 311, plus three TV networks and 350 newspapers. In New York, Los Angeles, and Chicago, and also the Washington, D.C., suburbs, more than 100 languages are spoken in the school systems. The push to declare English America's official language is certainly understandable.

What we have in the United States at this midpoint of the 1990s is a society in rapid transition. Over the last twenty years, the births of children of racially or ethnically mixed marriages have increased almost 30 per cent. And, of course, marriage is the main assimilator, second only to child-rearing. There are many more Latinos—so many more that by the end of the decade there will be more Hispanic youths than black youths in the country. We are fast approaching a century where, the experts predict, by 2050 only half of the population, not the current two-thirds, will be Anglo. A population that today is 12 per cent black, 9 per cent Latino, and 3 per cent Asian, will in fifty-some years be 22 per cent Latino, 16 per cent black, and 10 per cent Asian.

These rapid changes, combined with the economic forces that are now creating internal migration in the United States—migration away from the Rust Belt areas—are changing the shape of our nation and the political power of geographic areas. Today, 70 per cent of the immigrants go to California, Florida, New York, New Jersey, and Illinois. By 2010, 60 per cent of Americans will live in the Southwest. Texas has become the second largest state in the country, surpassing New York. Demographic power is political power. These demographic changes create changes in the way that we advertise, in the kinds of food we eat, in the music we listen to. They also create changes in attitudes, particularly about such matters as abortion, the place of women, and the ideals of marriage and family.

Redefining Civil Rights

What particularly interests me in this blender running at high speed is the redefinition of the idea of civil rights, particularly in regard to

black America. The old black-white argument that we are accustomed
to is quickly becoming anachronistic. In Washington, D.C., for instance, we have seen Latinos riot against the black city government,
saying that they are not getting their fair share and that the police
department is insensitive to them. They are rioting against blacks, not
against whites. This is a black-brown dialogue. In other places there
is conflict between Korean store-owners and blacks—a black-Asian
dialogue. The question is no longer solely between blacks and whites;
now Asians and Hispanics are involved in a dialogue with blacks that
is quite different. In the vote on Proposition 187 in California, blacks
and Asians were actually split on this issue, while Hispanics were
three-quarters in opposition.

These are new games. There are far more angles than before, and
they require new strategies. They require a new language for talking
about race and about what constitutes social progress in America.
Social progress will no longer necessarily be just a matter of blacks
gaining equality with whites. Today's more open situation involves
browns and Asians and others.

In my experience as an American, color has long been the divide:
you are either white or you are non-white. Part of the immigrant
experience of coming to America is learning how the underclass is
defined in this society—and a large part of what that has meant is
being non-white. To some extent, the current waves of immigrants
confuse but don't erase those old lines of black and white. During the
Los Angeles riots after the Rodney King case, the instinct on the part
of people in my profession, the press, was to say that this was a
black-white situation; later we found out that most of the people who
had been arrested were, in fact, Hispanics. And most of the people on
top of buildings protecting their stores were Asians. Again, this
changes the way we view race.

What is most notable here is that today's immigrants view the racial
dynamic very differently than those of us who are accustomed to that
dynamic as it played out from the 1940s to the 1980s. And this is
because immigrants still come to America with the idea that this is
the land of opportunity. They don't come here with the slave experience in mind, or with any thought of experiencing legal segregation
and government oppression on the basis of race. What they see is
opportunity.

Where do the American people find common ground today? How

do we understand the new way in which Americans are mixing? What is most important is access to education and the related benefit of mobility, so that people are economically able to move to areas such as the Southwest and Southeast where the economy is booming. Civil rights in the nineties is not so much about being pushed to the back of the bus as about getting that bus to take you out of the old neighborhood—out of those old and decrepit schools that seemingly cannot be improved, out of the old low-paying jobs—and into an America where race can be downplayed, and where you can conduct yourself as a new person seeking out new ways of sustaining yourself and your family.

This is the radical agenda of change today. It is an agenda that the old civil-rights activists are struggling to understand. As they insist on larger and larger shares, on set-asides and other traditional programs, they are taking themselves away from the mainstream dialogue in the American body politic and culture.

This, in my view, is where we are today with the conversation about race in America.

23

Reinventing the American People?

John O'Sullivan

In the 1972 film *Lady Caroline Lamb,* the young Melbourne makes his first speech in the House of Commons, attacking the death penalty for sheep-stealing on the grounds that it persuades juries to acquit even the guiltiest defendants. To his surprise, the young Whig politician is congratulated by the leader of the Tory opposition, George Canning.

"It was a Whig speech, Sir," Melbourne responds nervously.

"Yes," replies Canning. "A Whig speech—but Tory arguments."

My sentiments exactly about many of the theses advanced by pro-immigration conservatives like Linda Chavez. I agree with almost everything they have to say—except their conclusions. But then, immigration is an issue on which I find myself on the opposite side to many of my closest friends and political allies.

William Bennett, for instance, has advanced the view that there is no immigration crisis. His argument is that since immigration is not at present directly linked to social collapse or riot, perhaps we should concern ourselves with more pressing questions—reforming the Social Security system, for instance.

To be sure, there is no immigration crisis in the usual sense of the word *crisis*—namely, an acute problem of massive proportions

John O'Sullivan is the editor of *National Review.* He himself is an immigrant from the United Kingdom.

requiring immediate attention, without which some catastrophic event will occur. (In a few states, like California or Florida, of course, the locals seem to think that uncontrolled illegal immigration fits that description.) In that sense, however, there is also no budgetary crisis, no Social Security crisis, no education crisis. All these are simply serious problems that are getting worse and, left unattended, will produce a crisis in due course. Social Security will at some point go bust, requiring either major surgery or a massive infusion of tax dollars. Is it sensible to suggest that we should forget about Social Security until that happens? That we should issue no warnings, propose no reforms? I don't think so. Similarly, immigration at its current levels is producing long-term serious problems for America—economic problems, problems of cultural cohesion, political and demographic problems—and it behooves us to propose solutions to these problems.

Bill Bennett's point was based upon William Kristol's well-known formulation during the Clinton health-care-reform controversy that there is no health crisis. This shrewd skepticism helped to sink the president's health-reform proposals. It's worth pointing out, however, that Kristol's phrase was coined in reply to the president's assertion that there *was* a health-care crisis. Kristol conceded that there were specific *problems* in health care requiring specific reforms. And the same holds true for immigration.

This is perversely illustrated by a proposal by Bill Bennett and Jack Kemp to deal with immigrant-driven problems in California and Florida by increasing federal aid to these states. (It is mildly ironic that this proposal comes from people who assert that the real problem is not immigration but the existence of the welfare state.) This proposal encounters the following objections: (1) it will increase the pressure on the budget, tax cuts or no tax cuts; (2) it will increase and extend federal power over the states; (3) it will mean that people in Iowa and Minnesota are required to subsidize services in California on the extraordinary grounds that those services are likely to be used by illegal immigrants; (4) it will tend to persuade opinion-informers in the government and the media that the problem has now been solved; and (5) it will therefore reduce the pressure to do anything about the underlying problems. Let me now turn to those underlying problems, first in the economy, and then in the culture.

IMMIGRATION AND THE ECONOMY

The economic problems of immigration are a matter of serious and prolonged dispute among experts. I cover some of them at length in my *National Review* article, "America's Identity Crisis" (November 21, 1994). The evidence suggests that the economic benefits of immigration to native-born Americans are extremely modest—on the order of one-tenth of 1 per cent of GDP annually, according to Professor George Borjas, himself a Cuban immigrant and professor of economics at the University of California, San Diego. Its perverse side effects —notably, redistributing income from poorer to richer Americans— are much larger, on the order of *2 per cent* of GDP annually.

That's the overall impact. More specifically, the pro-immigration side of the argument has to explain certain inconvenient economic facts. To begin with, if immigration has the dynamic economic impact usually claimed, why did the growth rate of the American economy actually stagnate once the great immigration surge following the liberalization of immigration rules in 1965 got under way (i.e., in the late sixties)? Then again, if immigration is necessary to growth, why has Japan's rate of growth spectacularly outperformed America's in the post-war world, despite almost no immigration at all? Pro-immigration advocates have yet to devise a satisfactory answer to this question.

Japan also comes to my aid in regard to another pro-immigration contention: that if it weren't for immigrants, all the services and businesses founded or operated by immigrant labor would not exist, and the U.S. economy would be understaffed and inefficient. Let's test this against one of Charles Murray's thought-experiments. Imagine that for the past forty years Japan had admitted immigrants on the American scale. Had that been done, today innumerable businesses and service industries would exist in that country on the basis of immigrant labor, and anyone who proposed halting immigration would be told that Japan simply could not be run without it. An immigration restrictionist would have no ready reply to these arguments, because they would seem to be confirmed by the evidence of his senses. But our experience in the real world, where there actually was *no* immigration to Japan, tells us he would be right to contend that the Japanese economy would prosper without immigrant workers.

So, if immigration is not an economic necessity, is of only the most marginal benefit to native-born Americans, and has perverse redistributive side effects, why is it a good thing economically? The fallback pro-immigration position seems to be that immigrants don't cost much. That is a very modest claim, but as it happens, it is also dubious. Immigrants are on the average more likely to go on welfare than native-born Americans. Those studies that claim the reverse turn out to have excluded certain immigrant groups such as refugees, now entering America at a rate of more than 100,000 a year. By excluding disfavored groups from the immigrant total while keeping all native Americans in a single block (when, of course, we know that different groups of Americans have different rates of welfare participation), this method of comparison obscures something quite important: namely, that America at present is increasing the number of groups who rely disproportionately on welfare for their livelihood.

Almost no one denies that some immigrants go directly into the underclass. The latest research suggests that, once in the underclass, immigrant groups and their descendants may remain there for as long as four generations. Together with the evidence that immigration serves to reduce job opportunities for lower-paid Americans, notably minorities, this suggests that even in narrow economic terms immigration is a divisive force in American life. It is exacerbating trends toward welfare dependence and income inequality.

IMMIGRATION AND THE CULTURE

The impact of immigration on cultural cohesion is even more important than its economic effects. A multicultural society is a contradiction in terms and cannot survive indefinitely. It either becomes monocultural or runs into trouble. There *are* multicultural societies, but they tend to be pre-modern, undemocratic in their political organization, and ridden by ethnic conflict when the ethnic groups are not geographically separated. Contrary to frequent assertion, America has never been a multicultural society, although it has had cultural ghettos. But it has been a *multiethnic* society in which new arrivals assimilated to something that already existed: namely, an American culture and national identity whose British foundations had been enriched by the contributions of other cultures over time.

One result was that America enjoyed linguistic and cultural unity, which helps to explain its success. As my colleague Peter Brimelow argues, modernization puts a premium on linguistic unity. Open societies are held together by information flows, so that anything that impedes those information flows renders the society less efficient. That is why the nation-state where everyone understands everyone else is an efficient way of organizing human beings. This will be perversely confirmed by people who have ridden in a New York taxi whose driver doesn't know enough English to ask someone else the way.

Reinforcing Ethnic Cultures

There are three good reasons to suspect that a high and continuing immigration rate undermines America's common culture and identity. First, it *strengthens and reinforces ethnic cultures in American society.* The arrival of more and more people speaking a language other than English means that those already here who speak that other language will have more opportunity to do so, and therefore less incentive to learn English. Cultural ghettos—which would otherwise be absorbed into the surrounding American culture—survive and even expand; they get more recruits and fewer defections. Hence, Miami is now a largely Spanish-speaking city, known as the capital of Latin America.

Moreover, immigration is not a neutral factor in maintaining the welfare state and multicultural and bilingual programs. It fosters and expands constituencies of people who favor those programs, which makes it harder to get rid of them.

A second reason why immigration has a negative effect on the common culture and national identity is that the arrival of more people from different cultures *tends to sharpen the sense of ethnic difference among native-born Americans.* Historically, high levels of immigration have stimulated the rise of movements and ideologies that emphasize ethnic differences. Some of these ideologies are separatist, such as Afrocentrism and black nationalism. Some stress diversity, and the equality of cultures—for example, multiculturalism. Both types tend to be hostile to the notion of a wider American identity that encompasses all existing ethnicities.

The same point can be seen in miniature from the census. Although everyone is invited to give an ethnic identity, a minority of respondents reject this and identify themselves simply as Americans. Peter Brimelow points out in his book *Alien Nation* that this tendency to self-identity as American diminishes sharply wherever immigration introduces or strengthens ethnic diversity. For instance, self-reported "Americans" make up a high proportion of the homogeneous English-origin counties of Maine but a smaller proportion in those counties that have settlements of French-Canadian immigrants.

In periods of little or no immigration, common national identity tends to assert itself; in periods of high immigration it seems to retreat.

Derogating American Culture

The third effect is that high immigration, by juxtaposing American culture to immigrant cultures, *makes American culture seem arbitrary, irrational, and even oppressive.* After all, much of culture consists of rules, conventions, habits, and practices that are taken for granted. They are, quite literally, the common sense of the community. When immigrants arrive in large numbers with cultures that stress different rules and even disregard those embodied in American culture, this reduces the status of American culture from *what is* to one of several *what-may-be*s. It becomes merely the Anglo culture, one whose rules, standards, and conventions are thought to be alien to non-Anglo citizens and hence cannot be imposed upon them.

Because tolerance is such a strong component of Anglo-American culture, Americans are much more vulnerable to this cultural sapping than, say, the French. In his *Atlantic Monthly* article (April 1994) on the effects of immigration on the small town of Wausau, Wisconsin, Roy Beck gives a startling example of this. Immigrant Hmongs in Wausau schools have a high rate of under-age pregnancy, which is a sure sign that the laws on statutory rape are widely disregarded in that community. But the authorities have taken no action, because they feel that early parenthood is part of Hmong culture. It scarcely matters whether or not this is so; the story illustrates the weakness and nervousness of American culture when faced with what it believes to be immigrant-created cultural diversity. Even on so painful a question as sex with minors, it hesitates to assert its own standards confidently. Those standards will therefore decline: because self-identified Americans cannot enforce them on immigrants, they will tend to enforce them less upon themselves.

Increasingly we will find ourselves picking our way through a legal minefield. For instance, over a dozen states have now passed laws—which are probably unconstitutional—allowing the religious use of the drug peyote by those Americans who can demonstrate that they are at least partly of Native American ancestry. The greater the diversity of cultures, the fewer the laws based on American culture we feel entitled to insist are valid for all citizens. We will gradually drift toward a polity in which only a few abstract legal rules unite a variety of peoples who, culturally speaking, live in different worlds. America then is reduced to that "idea" that some proponents of immigration think is the very definition of American identity. Alas, it is not a very bright idea.

The evidence of our senses is that areas of high immigration tend to be areas of ethnic conflict: Los Angeles, Miami, the Adams-Morgan area of Washington, D.C., Crown Heights in Brooklyn. I am *not* saying that immigrants are responsible for such violence; very often they are the victims of it. The point it that immigration fosters conditions in which subordinate ethnic cultures thrive, the sense of national identity and solidarity is weakened, and the rules and conventions that order our lives when the police are not around (the common culture) fall into disuse.

Multiethnic but Monocultural

This does not mean that a multiethnic society is doomed to conflict and disintegration—though doubtless it will have more inclination in this direction than an ethnically homogeneous nation. My point is that a multiethnic society can succeed only if it is also a monocultural society. Indeed, "multicultural society" is a contradiction in terms, for a society without a common culture is not a society. And a society with a *high* and *continuing* level of immigration will gradually cease to enjoy a common culture.

But let me stress the two adjectives. I believe that continuing *modest* infusions of immigration can be lived with; the arrivals can then be assimilated. Equally, I think a *high* level of immigration followed by a pause (which is what happened in the past) can also be successfully accommodated. But I don't believe that a high and continuing rate of immigration can be sustained. The strains it creates will be intolerable.

This important distinction between a multiethnic society and a multicultural society is rarely stressed. A multiethnic society has to become monocultural—*not* multicultural—to survive. Otherwise the differences, disputes, and simple inconveniences likely to arise between ethnic groups will be frozen into permanence by cultural distance—just as the really quite similar tribes in Northern Ireland have had their national passion sustained by religious separatism.

Because it minimizes conflict, a monocultural society has a natural tendency to produce a new ethnicity over time, given intermarriage and shared experience. We are accustomed in today's debates to thinking of ethnic division as between whites and minorities. We forget how recently the monolithic white majority was a squabbling group of English, Welsh, Germans, Scots, Irish, Italians, Poles, and so on. That national consolidation was brought about by, among other things, a forty-year pause in immigration following the Immigration Act of 1924. And, tragically, it was at the very point when black America was being drawn into this national majority—the great American middle class—that mass immigration resumed and undermined the status of poorer black Americans in the labor market.

The "Transforming" of America

Immigration on our present scale is said, by INS Commissioner Doris Meissner, to be "transforming" America. But should government be in the business of transforming—or reinventing—a people? No. I am reminded of Bertolt Brecht's remark when the East German Communist government crushed the 1953 workers' strike: "The people have lost the confidence of the government, so the government has decided to dissolve the people and elect a new one." In much of the rhetoric of the liberal establishment, one hears echoes of Brecht —in its constant refrain that the American majority is a racist, sexist, homophobic one against which minorities need to be permanently protected; in its almost obsessive social engineering that decrees exactly how many people of each ethnic group should be placed in what positions; in its promotion of an immigration policy that is demographically transforming America into a different people and a multicultural community; above all, in its repeated proclamations that the present American majority, largely white, will be a minority by 2050, and that this reinvention is a welcome development.

To object to this is held to be evidence of racism, of a fear or dislike of black or brown Americans. Well, if it is racist to warn of the changing ethnic composition of the American people, then it must also be racist to welcome that change, since that would suggest fear or dislike of white Americans.

And in what sense would the "people of color" who would constitute this new multicultural majority in 2050 be American? Some would obviously be American in the most straightforward sense of the term. They would have been born in America and educated in American schools; they would have watched American television programs, played American sports, perhaps fought in American wars. If such black or brown Americans were to become the majority in 2050, we could all view this with complete indifference. A changing ethnic balance in society resulting from different ethnic birth rates among people of the same nationality—people profoundly committed to one another in a wider American ethnicity and sharing a common destiny —should not make white Americans feel culturally dispossessed.

But that is not what is being hinted at in the demographic forecasts. The prediction that today's largely white majority will be a minority in America by 2050 depends entirely on current and forecast immigration levels. And the immigrants and their children may not in any real sense be as American as apple pie. Some may become so. Others, living in a welfare state with multicultural programs, may remain alien —retaining languages and cultures separate from those of the American nation. In effect, instead of experiencing ethnic changes *within* the American nation, which ought to be acceptable as the outcome of spontaneous action by American families, the American nation will have been overwhelmed by people from cultures whose putative spokesmen are already demanding a wholly different definition of American nationality on the grounds that they constitute a forthcoming new American majority. INS Commissioner Doris Meissner said approvingly, "We are being transformed." If so, that has been accomplished by public policy without public discussion. It is not racist to object to that; it is simply democratic.

Immigration and the multiculturalism it feeds are threatening the bonds of common nationhood and the underlying sense of a common national destiny, bringing forward the danger of a balkanized America. This process is being carried forward by public policy even though the economic benefits to native-born Americans are trifling. According to every poll taken in the last forty years, the American people realize these dangers. Only politicians and intellectuals—including conservative intellectuals—are oblivious to the dangers or persist in explaining them away.

Some of my friendly opponents in this argument, like Jack Kemp and Bill Bennett, are not so much explaining these things away as making a vigorous and principled case on the other side of the argument. So let me make one concession: I will sympathize with them if they feel resentment at hearing my arguments expressed with an English accent. But then, as Jack Kemp himself often says, "it's left to immigrants to do the dirty work in this society."

Notes

INTRODUCTION
"Restoring Self-Governing Community"
ROBERT ROYAL

1. Robert D. Putnam, "Bowling Alone: America's Declining Social Capital," *Journal of Democracy* 6, no. 1 (January 1995): 65-78.

2. For a study of the new forms of association, see Robert Wuthnow, *Sharing the Journey: Support Groups and the Quest for a New Community* (New York: Free Press, 1994).

3. Christopher Lasch, *The Revolt of the Elites and the Betrayal of Democracy* (New York: Norton, 1995). See in particular chapter 6, "Conversation and the Civic Arts," 117-28.

4. For a lively examination of this subject, see Ray Oldenburg, *The Great Good Place: Cafés, Coffee Shops, Community Centers, Beauty Parlors, General Stores, Bars, Hangouts and How They Get You Through the Day* (New York: Paragon House, 1989).

5. See Richard W. White, Jr., *What the Homeless Crisis Tells Us* (San Francisco: ICS Press, 1992).

6. Gertrude Himmelfarb, *The De-moralization of Society: From Victorian Virtues to Modern Values* (New York: Knopf, 1995).

7. See Allen Greenberg, "Architecture and the American Unum," address at the Ethics and Public Policy Center, March 17, 1995 (unpublished), and Vincent Scully's Jefferson Lecture, "The Architecture of Community," May 15, 1995.

8. The use of the word "paranoia" about government is clearly excessive. For most people, "healthy suspicion" is probably a better description. It is worth noting that "anger" toward government is not nearly so widespread, amounting to only 9 per cent or so of Americans. See Richard Harwood, "The Anger Isn't Out There," *Washington Post,* May 30, 1995, A13. The "angry white male" paradigm, too, seems unsupported by social-survey data.

9. Putnam, "Bowling Alone," 67-68.

10. Arthur Schlesinger, Jr., "In Defense of Government," *Wall Street Journal,* June 7, 1995, A14.

11. "The Hidden History of Mestizo America" (unpublished typescript, 1995), p. 27: "Historians know how Anglo-chauvinists invented a racial typology and racial categorization to exclude and exploit many of America's peoples. . . ."

12. On this and related issues see my *1492 and All That: Political Manipulations of History* (Washington: Ethics and Public Policy Center, 1992).

13. G. K. Chesterton, *What I Saw in America,* in *Collected Works,* vol. 21, ed. Robert Royal (San Francisco: Ignatius Press, 1990), 52.

14. Few people know that in 1974 Congress passed the Ethnic Heritage Studies Program Act after pressure from various ethnic leaders. A strict constitutional scholar might question the legal foundation and purpose of such an act, but more worrisome is that as school programs on ethnic groups have ballooned, time devoted to standard American history has decreased, with predictable effects on students' knowledge of the most basic principles of the American past.

15. Arthur M. Schlesinger, Jr., *The Disuniting of America* (New York: Norton, 1992), 17.

16. Ibid., 13.

CHAPTER 1

"Whose America Is It?"

MICHAEL BARONE

1. Robert Wiebe, *Segmented Society: An Introduction to the Meaning of America* (New York: Oxford University Press, 1975).

2. Henry Adams, *History of the United States of America During the Administrations of Jefferson and Madison.*

3. David Hackett Fischer, *Albion's Seed: Four British Folkways in America* (New York: Oxford University Press, 1989).

CHAPTER 2

"Individualism Before Multiculturalism"

GLENN C. LOURY

1. Ralph Ellison, *The Invisible Man* (New York: Signet Books, n.d.), 307-8.

2. Charles Griswold, "Empathy, Separateness, and Community: Adam Smith on the Moral Imagination" (unpublished draft, Department of Philosophy, Boston University, November 1994), 22.

3. Ibid., 24.

4. Paul Sniderman and Thomas Piazza, *The Scar of Race* (Cambridge: Harvard University Press, 1994), 103.

5. See Richard Herrnstein and Charles Murray, *The Bell Curve* (New York: Free Press, 1994).

6. I Cor. 10:13, NIV.

7. See, for example, Thomas Sowell, *The Economics and Politics of Race: An International Perspective* (New York: William Morrow, 1983). Sowell chronicles numerous instances around the world in which group differences in economic status do not correspond to the presence or absence of oppression.

8. Michael Walzer and E. Kantowicz, *The Politics of Ethnicity* (Cambridge: Harvard University Press, 1982).

9. Martin Luther King, Jr., "I Have a Dream," reprinted in F. Broderick and A. Meier, *Negro Protest Thought in the Twentieth Century* (Indianapolis: Bobbs-Merrill, 1965).

10. In a revealing misappropriation of King's legacy, civil rights advocate Mary Francis Berry claimed, on the eve of the first observance of Martin Luther King Day, that the then disputed Executive Order 11246, which authorizes federal affirmative action programs, was "a kind of affirmative action that Martin Luther King firmly believed in." (Interview on ABC's "This Week with David Brinkley," Sunday, January 19, 1986.) The fact is that Dr. King died years before these regulations came into existence.

11. Lest this appear an exaggeration, consider the following: In her book *A New American Dilemma: Liberal Democracy and School Desegregation* (New Haven: Yale University Press, 1984), political scientist Jennifer Hochschild argues that the unwillingness of American courts and legislatures to override popular, democratically expressed opposition to massive, cross-district busing for school desegregation exposes our nation's limited commitment to the ideal of equal opportunity. In his 1993 bestseller *Race Matters* (Boston: Beacon Press), noted black scholar Cornel West asserts that "visible Jewish resistance to affirmative action and government spending on social programs" amounts to "assaults on black livelihood." In a similar spirit, black Congressman Charles Rangel (D-NY) made headlines during the 1994 campaign when he alleged that the Republicans' advocacy of tax cuts was racist in motivation.

12. Orlando Patterson, *Slavery and Social Death: A Comparative Study* (Cambridge: Harvard University Press, 1982).

13. Nathan Huggins, "Ethnic Americans," *The Yale Review*, Autumn 1982, 87.

14. Booker T. Washington, *The Story of the Negro: The Rise of the Race from Slavery* (London, 1909), 2:47-48.

CHAPTER 7

"The Crisis of Constitutionalism"

RICHARD E. MORGAN

1. Herbert Storing, *What the Anti-Federalists Were For* (Chicago: University of Chicago Press, 1981), 13.

2. Martin Diamond, "The Declaration and the Constitution: Liberty, Democracy, and the Founders," in Nathan Glazer and Irving Kristol, eds., *The American Commonwealth, 1976* (New York: Basic Books, 1976), 47.

3. Rogers M. Smith, *Liberalism and American Constitutional Law* (Cambridge: Harvard University Press, 1985), 14-15 (emphasis added).

4. W. B. Allen, ed., *Works of Fischer Ames* (Indianapolis: Liberty Classics, 1983) 1:642.

5. Diamond, "The Declaration and the Constitution," 49.

6. Quoted in Clinton Rossiter, *The First American Revolution* (New York: Harvest Books, 1950), 9.

7. Philip B. Kurland, "Federalism and the Federal Courts," *Benchmarks* 2 (January 1986): 17.

CHAPTER 10
"Don Vito Corleone, Friendship, and America"
PAUL A. RAHE

1. See Mario Puzo, *The Godfather* (New York, 1969).

2. See Paul A. Rahe, *Republics Ancient and Modern: Classical Republicanism and the American Revolution* (Chapel Hill: University of North Carolina Press, 1992).

3. *Amicitia* and patron-client relations figure prominently in the recent literature on ancient Rome. See Ronald Syme, *The Roman Revolution* (Oxford, 1939); Ernst Badian, *Foreign Clientelae (264-70 B.C.)* (Oxford, 1958); Erich S. Gruen, *Roman Politics and the Criminal Courts, 149-78 B.C.* (Berkeley, 1974); and Matthias Gelzer, *The Roman Nobility* (Oxford, 1975). See also *Patronage in Ancient Society,* ed. Andrew Wallace-Hadrill (London, 1989), and Donald C. Earl, *The Moral and Political Tradition of Rome* (Ithaca, 1967).

4. The classic study of this phenomenon is by Marcel Mauss, *The Gift,* trans. Ian Cunnison (New York, 1967).

5. Livy 1.57-60 and 3.44-54.

6. Livy 2.3-5.

7. Aristotle, *Politics* 1252b27-1253a39. See 1278b15-30, 1280a25-1281a10, 1283b42-1284a3; *Nicomachean Ethics* 1097a15-1098b9, 1169b16-18.

8. Aristotle, *Politics* 1260b36-1264b25.

9. Plato, *Republic* 1.331d-332b.

10. See Mary Whitlock Blundell, *Helping Friends and Harming Enemies: A Study in Sophocles and Greek Ethics* (Cambridge, 1989).

11. Herodotus 6.23; Thucydides 1.20.2, 6.53.3-59.4; Aristotle, *Constitution of Athens,* 18-19.

12. It is not clear whether Antileon hailed from Heracleia in Lucania (Parthenius, *Narrationum Amatoriarum libellus* 7) or from the better-known Metapontum (Plutarch, *Moralia* 760c). For Melanippus and Chariton, see Plutarch, *Moralia* 760b-c; Athenaeus 13.602a-c; Aelian, *Varia Historia* 2.4.

13. Aristotle, *Politics* 1313a37-b5; Athenaeus 13.602d.

14. Xenophon, *Hiero* 1.32-38.

15. I trust that no one will argue that G. E. Moore should be placed in the first rank.

16. Michel de Montaigne, *The Essays of Michel de Montaigne*, trans. and ed., M. A. Screech (New York, 1991), 205-19.

17. See Albert O. Hirschman, *The Passions and the Interests: Political Arguments for Capitalism Before Its Triumph* (Princeton, 1977).

18. Consider Francis Bacon, "Of Friendship," and "Of Followers and Friends," *Essays or Counsels Civil and Moral*, 27 and 48, in *The Works of Francis Bacon*, ed. James Spedding, Robert Leslie Ellis, and Douglas Denon Heath (London, 1857-1874), VI:437-43, 494-95, in light of Aristotle, *Nicomachean Ethics*, 1158b29-1159a13.

19. Cf. *Of the Advancement of Learning*, II.xxi.9, in *The Works of Francis Bacon*, III:430, with Machiavelli, *Il principe* 15, in Niccolo Machiavelli, *Tutte le opere*, ed. Mario Martelli (Florence, 1971), 280; and see Spinoza, *Tractatus politicus*, 1.1-7, in Benedict de Spinoza, *Spinoza opera*, ed. Carl Gebhardt (Heidelberg, 1925), III:273-76.

20. Machiavelli, *Il principe* 15, in *Tutte le opere*, 280. Cf. *Istorie fiorentine* 8.29, in Machiavelli, *Tutte le opere*, 837-38, with the much less radical critique of the ancient utopians advanced by Livy: 26.22.

21. Machiavelli, *Discorsi sopra la prima deca di Tito Livio* 1.6, 37, 2 Proemio, in Machiavelli, *Tutte le opere*, 86-87, 119, 145.

22. Machiavelli, *Discorsi sopra la Prima deca di Tito Livio* 1.3, in *Tutte le opere*, 81-82.

23. Cf. Machiavelli, *Il principe* 18, in *Tutte le opere*, 283-84 (which should be read in light of 15, in *Tutte le opere*, 280), with Cicero, *De officiis* 1.11.34-35, 13.41.

24. Bacon, *De dignitate et augmentis scientiarum* 8.2, in *The Works of Francis Bacon*, I:789 (translated at V:75-76).

25. Consider Machiavelli, *Il principe* 3, 5-9, 15, 17, 19-21, 24-25 (in *Tutte le opere*, 258-72, 280-96) with an eye to 22-23 (in *Tutte le opere*, 293-94).

26. See Machiavelli, *Discorsi sopra la prima deca di Tito Livio* Ep. Ded., in *Tutte le opere*, 75.

27. Machiavelli, *Discorsi sopra la prima deca di Tito Livio* 1.45, in *Tutte le opere*, 82-84. In this this connection, see Quentin Skinner, *The Foundations of Modern Political Thought* (Cambridge, 1978) I: *The Renaissance*, 180-86, and *Machiavelli* (New York, 1981), 48-77. For the ancient commitment to political and social harmony, see Rahe, *Republics Ancient and Modern*, 55-229.

28. Machiavelli, *Istorie fiorentine*, 7.1, in Machiavelli, *Tutte le opere*, 792-93.

29. See Harvey C. Mansfield, Jr., "On the Impersonality of the Modern State: A Comment on Machiavelli's Use of *Stato*," *American Political Science Review* 77 (1983): 849-57.

30. Letter to Mercy Otis Warren on 16 April 1776, in *Papers of John Adams*, ed. Robert J. Taylor (Cambridge, Mass., 1977-), IV:124-25.

31. Benjamin Rush, "Of the Mode of Education Proper in a Republic," *Essays, Literary, Moral & Philosophical* (Philadelphia, 1798), 6-20 (esp. 10-12, 14-15).

32. Thomas Jefferson, *Notes on the State of Virginia*, ed. William Peden (New York, 1972), 164-65.

33. Letter to Edward Carrington on 16 January 1787, in *The Papers of Thomas Jefferson*, ed. Julian P. Boyd (Princeton, 1950-), XI:48-49.

34. Letter to Roger C. Weightman on 24 June 1826, in *The Writings of Thomas Jefferson*, ed. Paul Leicester Ford (New York, 1892-99), X:390-92.

35. Letters to Edward Carrington on 16 January 1787 and to Abigail Adams on 22 February 1787, in *The Papers of Thomas Jefferson*, XI:48-50, 174-75.

36. Draft of the Kentucky Resolutions, [October] 1798, in *The Writings of Thomas Jefferson* (ed. Ford), VII:304.

37. Jean Bethke Elshtain, *Democracy on Trial* (New York, 1995), xii-xiv.

CHAPTER 11
"The Post-Constitutional Era"
Gerard V. Bradley

1. Michael Kammen, *A Machine That Would Go of Itself* (New York: Knopf, 1986), 162.

2. Ibid.

3. U.S. Constitution, Article VII.

4. A copy of the Confederate Constitution may be found in M. DeRosa, *The Confederate Constitution of 1861: An Inquiry into American Constitutionalism* (Columbia, MO: University of Missouri Press, 1991), 135-57.

5. I realize that what I am saying asserts without evidence a highly controversial proposition in constitutional law. I am working on a book that, in significant part, is intended to vindicate this assertion.

6. I do not doubt that judicial review in some form was originally expected, though its scope, finality, and method — as originally understood — hardly correspond to our experience of it in the last generation or so.

7. W. Nelson, "Changing Conceptions of Judicial Review: The Evolution of Constitutional Theory in the States — 1790-1860," 120 *University of Pennsylvania Law Review* (1972): 1166, 1177, 1172.

8. Kammen, *A Machine*, 8.

9. Ibid., 10.

10. *Planned Parenthod* v. *Casey*, 112 Sup. Ct. 2791, 2816 (1992).

11. John Rawls, *Political Liberalism* (New York: Columbia University Press, 1993), 237.

12. Ronald Dworkin, *Life's Dominion* (New York: Knopf, 1993), 145.

13. Ibid.

14. Ibid.

15. 112 Sup. Ct. at 2807.

16. 330 U.S. 1 (1947).

17. *Lee* v. *Weisman*, 112 Sup. Ct. 2649 (1992).

18. 112 Sup. Ct. at 2677.

19. Ibid.

20. Charles Taylor, "Religion in a Free Society," in M. Peterson and R. Vaughan, eds., *The Virginia Statute for Religious Freedom* (New York: Cambridge University Press, 1988), 109-10.

21. Ibid., 323.

22. *The Federalist Papers* (Mentor edition, 1961), 79.

23. Ibid., 78.

24. Ibid.

25. Ibid., 324.

CHAPTER 12

"Religious Liberty in a Diverse Society"

TERRY EASTLAND

1. Gerard V. Bradley, "Beguiled: Free Exercise Exemptions and the Siren Song of Liberalism," *Hofstra Law Review* 20 (1991): 308.

CHAPTER 13

"Public Institutions and the Public Trust"

EDWIN J. DELATTRE

1. Jacob E. Cooke, ed., *The Federalist* (Middletown, CT: Wesleyan University Press, 1961), 384.

2. Ibid., 249.

3. Ibid., 96, 212.

4. Robert Goldwin, "Of Men and Angels: A Search for Morality in the Constitution," in *The Moral Foundations of the American Republic*, ed. Robert H. Horowitz (Charlottesville: University of Virginia Press, 1979), 11.

5. Dante, *The Divine Comedy, I: Hell*, trans. and intro. by Dorothy L. Sayers (Baltimore: Penguin Books, 1949), 68, 120, 147.

6. Sidney Hook, *Out of Step: An Unquiet Life in the 20th Century* (New York: Harper and Row, 1987), 604.

7. Unpublished data from Student Descriptive Form 1993-94, provided by the College Board Summary Reporting Service.

8. National Council for Accreditation of Teacher Education, *Standards, Procedures, and Policies for the Accreditation of Professional Education* Units (Washington, D.C.: NCATE, February 1992), 48-50, 64, 65.

9. "NCATE Board Reaffirms Importance of Innovation" and "UAB Standards Committee Takes Action on Cultural Diversity Issue," in *NCATE Reporter* 1, no.1 (November 1992): 4, 5.

10. Walter Lippman, "A Theory about Corruption," in *Political Corruption: Readings in Comparative Analysis,* ed. Arnold J. Heidenheimer (New York: Holt, Rinehart and Winston, 1970), 296-97.

CHAPTER 14

"The Christian Citizen and Democracy"

GEORGE WEIGEL

1. Robert L. Wilken, *The Christians as the Romans Saw Them* (New Haven: Yale University Press, 1984).

2. Cited in Cristoph Schönborn, "The Hope of Heaven, the Hope of Earth," *First Things* 52 (April 1995): 32-38.

3. See Russell Hittinger, "The Supreme Court v. Religion," *Crisis,* May 1993, 22-30, and Nathan Lewin, "The Church-State Game: A Symposium on *Kiryas Joel,*" *First Things* 47 (November 1994): 39-40.

4. See my study, *The Final Revolution: The Resistance Church and the Collapse of Communism* (New York: Oxford University Press, 1992).

5. See Schönborn, "The Hope of Heaven," 34.

6. C. S. Lewis, "The Weight of Glory," in *The Weight of Glory and Other Addresses* (New York: Macmillan, 1980), 19.

7. See chapter two of *The Final Revolution.*

8. See Richard John Neuhaus, "What the Fundamentalists Want," *Commentary,* May 1985, 43.

9. See John Courtney Murray, *We Hold These Truths: Catholic Reflections on the Democratic Proposition* (New York: Doubleday Image Books, 1964), 34.

10. See my essay, "Achieving Disagreement: From Indifference to Pluralism," *This World* 24 (Winter 1989): 54-63.

11. Richard John Neuhaus, "Can Atheists Be Good Citizens?" *First Things* 15 (August-September 1991): 21.

12. Ibid., 20.

13. Ibid.

14. Richard John Neuhaus, "The Public Square," *First Things* 42 (April 1994): 67.

15. On this point, see Richard John Neuhaus, "The Truth About Freedom," *Wall Street Journal,* October 8, 1993.

16. Ibid.

17. Cited in Neuhaus, "Can Atheists Be Good Citizens?" 21.

18. *Redemptoris Missio,* 39.

19. Justices Kennedy, O'Connor, and Souter, in *Planned Parenthood of Southeastern Pennsylvania v. Casey,* 112 Sup. Ct. 2791, 2815 (1992), at 2807.

20. On this point, see the editorial "Abortion and a Nation at War," *First Things* 26 (October 1992): 9-13.

CHAPTER 15

"From Religion to Spirituality"

ROBERT WUTHNOW

1. Talcott Parsons, *The Social System* (New York: Free Press, 1951), 132, 135.

2. These results are from a survey conducted by the Family Research Council in New York in September 1993.

3. Robert Wuthnow, *Acts of Compassion: Caring for Others and Helping Ourselves* (Princeton: Princeton University Press, 1991).

4. Results are from my analysis of the Economic Values Survey conducted for my book *God and Mammon in America* (New York: Free Press, 1994).

5. My analysis of a national survey of American teenagers conducted in 1992 for Independent Sector, Inc.

6. General Social Survey, 1993; my analysis.

7. Robert N. Bellah, *Beyond Belief* (New York: Harper & Row, 1970), and *The Broken Covenant* (Boston: Seabury, 1975).

8. Clifford Geertz, *The Interpretation of Cultures* (New York: Basic Books, 1973).

9. Neil J. Smelser, *Theory of Collective Behavior* (New York: Free Press, 1962).

10. Talcott Parsons, *The System of Modern Societies* (Englewood Cliffs, NJ: Prentice-Hall, 1971), 4-6.

11. Bellah, *Broken Covenant.*

12. Peter L. Berger, *The Sacred Canopy* (New York: Doubleday, 1967).

13. From my own analysis of data from several national surveys.

14. Wuthnow, *Acts of Compassion,* chapter 5.

15. Ibid.

16. Robert Wuthnow, *The Restructuring of American Religion* (Princeton: Princeton University Press, 1988).

17. James Davison Hunter, *Culture Wars* (New York: Free Press, 1991).

18. Timothy T. Clydesdale, "Money and Faith in America: Exploring the Effects of Religious Restructuring and Income Inequality on Social Attitudes and Family Behavior" (Ph.D. diss., Princeton University, 1994).

19. John Evans, "Culture Wars or Status Group Conflict? Ontological Wars or Ideological Conflict? An Empirical Test of the Culture Wars Thesis" (Department of Sociology, Princeton University, 1994).

20. "Religion in America," a survey conducted for *U.S. News & World Report* by the Tarrance Group, March 1994. Thanks to Jeff Sheler for making these data available.

21. Robert Wuthnow, *Sharing the Journey: Support Groups and America's New Quest for Community* (New York: Free Press, 1994).

22. Peter Berger, Brigitte Berger, and Hansfried Kellner, *The Homeless Mind: Modernization and Consciousness* (New York: Vintage, 1973), 188.

CHAPTER 16

"The Collapse of the Mainline Churches"

THOMAS C. REEVES

1. John R. H. Moorman, *The Anglican Spiritual Tradition* (Springfield, IL: Templeton, 1983), 180.

2. Quoted in Alice Felt Tyler, *Freedom's Ferment: Phases of American Social History From the Colonial Period to the Outbreak of the Civil War* (New York: Torch, Harper-Collins, 1962), 239.

3. *Church of the Holy Trinity* v. *United States,* 143 U.S. 457, 465, 471 (1892).

4. *United States* v. *Macintosh,* 283 U.S. 605, 633-634 (1931).

5. *Zorach* v. *Clauson,* 343 U.S. 306, 312 (1952).

6. George Gallup, Jr., and Jim Castelli, *The People's Religion: American Faith in the 90's* (New York: Macmillan, 1989), 36.

7. Sydney E. Ahlstrom, *A Religious History of the American People* (New Haven, CT: Yale University Press, 1972).

8. Quoted in George M. Marsden, *Fundamentalism and American Culture: The Shaping of Twentieth-Century Evangelicalism, 1870-1925* (New York: Oxford University Press, 1982), 191.

9. Kenneth B. Bedell, ed., *Yearbook of American and Canadian Churches 1994* (Nashville, TN: Abingdon Press, 1994), 253-59.

10. Barry A. Kosmin and Seymour P. Lachman, *One Nation Under God: Religion in Contemporary American Society* (San Francisco, CA: Harper, 1988), 197. The growth of evangelical churches may be tapering off, however. The Lutheran Church-Missouri Synod grew less than 0.1 per cent from 1991 to 1992, while the Southern Baptists increased a mere 0.83 per cent. One compelling explanation is that evangelicals are beginning to imitate their mainline cousins. See David F. Wells, *No Place For Truth, Or Whatever Happened to Evangelical Theology?* (Grand Rapids, MI: Eerdmans, 1993).

11. See Bedell, ed., *Yearbook of American and Canadian Churches 1994,* 253-59. Compare the estimates gleaned from the survey conducted by sociologists Kosmin and Lachman in *One Nation Under God,* 15. The United Church of Christ, they thought, had only some 161,000 members, and the Disciples of Christ about 144,000. The Roman Catholics numbered about 46 million, and the Mormons had only about half of their reported numerical strength.

12. See, for example, Benton Johnson, Dean R. Hoge, and Donald A. Luidens, "Mainline Churches: The Real Reason for Decline," *First Things* 31 (March 1993): 13-18; Princeton Religion Research Center, *The Unchurched American . . . 10 Years Later* (Princeton, 1988), 3-4; Richard John Neuhaus, *The Naked Public Square: Religion and Democracy in America* (2d ed., Grand Rapids, MI: Eerdmans, 1986), 234-46; Leonard R. Klein, "Lutherans in Sexual Commotion," *First Things* 43 (May 1994): 31-38; Wade Clark Roof and William McKinney, *American Mainline Religion: Its Changing Shape and Future* (New Brunswick, NJ: Rutgers University Press, 1987), 170, 177-88, 227, 241-42.

13. Mark A. Noll, "The Lutheran Difference," *First Things* 20 (February 1992): 59.

14. See Roof and McKinney, *American Mainline Religion,* 150-51.

15. E.g., Gallup and Castelli, *The People's Religion,* 141; Roger Finke and Rodney Stark, *The Churching of America, 1776-1990: Winners and Losers in Our Religious Economy* (New Brunswick, NJ: Rutgers University Press, 1992), 167.

16. See John and Sylvia Ronsvalle, "The State of Church Giving Through 1991," in Bedell, ed., *Yearbook of American and Canadian Churches 1994,* 12-15; "Bottom Lines," *In Trust,* Summer 1993, 25, and Spring 1994, 21-22. Perhaps the best single modern source on donations to religious organizations is Robert Wuthnow, *God and Mammon in America* (New York: Free Press, 1994), especially 226-54.

17. Quoted in Kenneth L. Woodward, "Dead End for the Mainline?" *Newsweek,* August 9, 1993, 47.

18. Gallup and Castelli, *The People's Religion,* 224.

19. John C. Green, James L. Guth, Lyman A. Kellstedt, and Corwin E. Smidt, "Murphy Brown Revisited: The Social Issues in the 1992 Election," in Michael Cromartie, ed., *Disciples and Democracy: Religious Conservatives and the Future of American Politics* (Washington, D.C.: Ethics and Public Policy Center, 1994), 51.

20. Stanley Hauerwas and William H. Willimon, *Resident Aliens . . .* (Nashville, TN: Abingdon, 1989), 38.

21. George Weigel, "Talking the Talk: Christian Conviction and Democratic Etiquette," in Cromartie, ed., *Disciples and Democracy,* 92.

22. For good examples of the enormous literature on this topic, see James Hitchcock, *Catholicism and Modernity: Confrontation or Capitulation?* (New York, 1979); Anne Roche Muggeridge, *The Desolate City: Revolution in the Catholic Church* (San Francisco: Harper, 1990); Donna Steichen, *Ungodly Rage: The Hidden Face of Catholic Feminism* (San Francisco: Ignatius Press, 1991); and James W. Demers, *The Last Roman Catholic?* (Ontario, 1991). See also any issue of the *National Catholic Reporter* (on the left) or the *National Catholic Register* (on the right).

23. The standard date of 1850 has been corrected in Finke and Stark, *The Churching of America,* 110-13.

24. See Thomas C. Reeves, *A Question of Character: A Life of John F. Kennedy* (New York: Free Press, 1991), passim.

25. See Gallup and Castelli, *The People's Religion,* 4, 17, 45, 63-64, 66, 73, 90, 102, 140.

26. Kosmin and Lachman, *One Nation Under God,* 2-5.

27. *Milwaukee Journal,* September 17, 1994.

28. See Gallup and Castelli, *The People's Religion,* 8, 18, 60.

29. Ibid., 132-39; Princeton Religious Research Center, *The Unchurched American,* 2, 7.

30. Robert Bezilla, ed., *Religion in America: 1992-1993* (Princeton Religious Research Center, 1993), 44, 57, 62.

31. Ibid., 45. In 1992, Gallup found that 45 per cent of Protestants and 51 per cent of Catholics went to church regularly. Those numbers had remained reasonably consistent for over a decade. In 1993, a much publicized and controversial study concluded that only 19.6 per cent of Protestants and 28 per cent of Catholics were in church in any given week. See C. Kirk Hadaway, Penny Long Marler, and Mark Chaves, "What the Polls Don't Show: A Closer Look at U.S. Church Attendance," *American Sociological Review,* December 1993, 741-52.

32. Kenneth L. Woodward, "The Rites of Americans," *Newsweek,* November 29, 1993, 81-82.

33. See Os Guinness, *The American Hour: A Time of Reckoning and the Once and Future Role of Faith* (New York: Free Press, 1993), 376-84.

34. See James Davison Hunter, *Culture Wars: The Struggle to Define America* (New York: Basic Books, 1991), 311.

CHAPTER 20
"Rejoining Nature and Culture"
FREDERICK TURNER

1. Amitai Etzioni, *The Spirit of Community: Rights, Responsibilities, and the Communitarian Agenda* (New York: Crown Publishers, 1993). See also Václav Havel, *The Power of the Powerless: Citizens Against the State in Central-Eastern Europe* (Armonk, NY: M. E. Sharpe, 1985); *Open Letters: Selected Writings, 1964-1990* (New York: Knopf, 1991).

Index of Names